Machine Learning and Cognition in Enterprises

Business Intelligence Transformed

Rohit Kumar

Apress®

Machine Learning and Cognition in Enterprises

Rohit Kumar
Pune, Maharashtra, India

ISBN-13 (pbk): 978-1-4842-3068-8   ISBN-13 (electronic): 978-1-4842-3069-5
https://doi.org/10.1007/978-1-4842-3069-5

Library of Congress Control Number: 2017959563

Cover image by Freepik (`www.freepik.com`)

Managing Director: Welmoed Spahr
Editorial Director: Todd Green
Acquisitions Editor: Celestin Suresh John
Development Editor: Matthew Moodie
Technical Reviewer: Jojo John Moolayil
Coordinating Editor: Sanchita Mandal
Copy Editor: Brendan Frost
Compositor: SPi Global
Indexer: SPi Global
Artist: SPi Global

I dedicate this to my parents (Namita & Ramesh K. Sinha)
&
Vagi, Sim, Gayatri, & Adi
for supporting me

Contents at a Glance

Contents

About the Author

Rohit Kumar has a masters in computer science including artificial intelligence, bioinformatics, and business intelligence.

He has been working as a senior enterprise architect and project manager in business intelligence, business process automation, reporting, and big data analytics.

He has worked with organizations like IBM, Cognizant, Patni (now Capgemini), and PriceWaterhouse Coopers.

He also has experience/interests in Omnichannel marketing solutions, BlockChain, Data Lake, cognitive computing, and cloud technologies.

He has consulted for 30+ clients across the globe in multiple industry verticals toward IT transformation. He has experience with customers in various industries (e.g., Fast Moving Consumer Goods (FMCG), retail, pharmaceutical, telecommunications, electronics, education, manufacturing, healthcare, logistics, utilities, banking, real estate, e-commerce, and publishing).

Rohit also serves as guest lecturer for faculty development and PhD scholars for various universities while creating extensive learning programs in SAP and analytics for various organizations. He already has numerous online publications on SAP SDN and LinkedIn. He also has contributed many offline contents for various organizations. Rohit has also conducted multiple training programs for many top IT organizations and headed training departments in the areas of business intelligence, e-commerce, analytics, big data, data security, and encryption.

LinkedIn: `https://www.linkedin.com/in/rohitkrit/`

About the Technical Reviewer

Jojo Moolayil is a data scientist and the author of the book *Smarter Decisions: The Intersection of Internet of Things and Decision Science* (Packt, 2016). With over five years of industrial experience in data science, decision science, and IoT, he has worked with industry leaders on high-impact and critical projects across multiple verticals. He is currently associated with General Electric, the pioneer and leader in data science for industrial IoT, and lives in Bengaluru, the Silicon Valley of India.

He was born and raised in Pune, India and graduated from the University of Pune with a major in information technology engineering. He started his career with Mu Sigma Inc., the world's largest pure play analytics provider, and has worked with the leaders of many Fortune 50 clients. One of the early enthusiasts to venture into IoT analytics, he converged his learnings from decision science to bring the problem-solving frameworks and his learnings from data and decision science to IoT analytics.

To cement his foundations in data science for industrial IoT and scale the impact of the problem-solving experiments, he joined a fast-growing IoT analytics startup called Flutura based in Bangalore and headquartered in the valley. After a short stint with Flutura, Jojo moved on to work with the leaders of industrial IoT, including General Electric, in Bangalore, where he focused on solving decision science problems for industrial IoT use cases. As a part of his role at GE, Jojo also focuses on developing data science and decision science products and platforms for industrial IoT.

Apart from authoring books on decision science and IoT, Jojo has also been the technical reviewer for various books on machine learning, deep learning, and business analytics from Apress. He is an active data science tutor and maintains a blog at http://www.jojomoolayil.com/web/blog/.

Profile

http://www.jojomoolayil.com/
https://www.linkedin.com/in/jojo62000

I would like to thank my family, friends, and mentors.

Acknowledgments

I acknowledge Vagisha and Smriti for helping in refining project process definition areas. And for all the late-night coffees. Without their support it would have been very difficult to manage my work and writing. They helped me to keep free from everything else and focus.

Gaurav Kumar (IBM) for allowing the use of his picture and also doing modeling for one picture in the book.

Preeti Singh (IBM) for providing feedback as a reader for refining the content for the sake of better understandability.

Introduction

In my experiences in technology and consulting for my various clients, I have seen that there is always a new technology around the corner which is fascinating and promises lots of new stuff in terms of usability and functionalities. The good thing is that these technologies are progressively more potent and vivid in functionality and business use cases, but they can be confusing too.

The reasons are interesting. The technology follows business needs and progresses along with it. But not all businesses are very much into the latest technology adoption based on their exact needs and various other reasons. Even so, there is always a bigger chunk of business that actually tries to follow what is needed progressively for them in terms of technology adoption. This is where the confusion starts. When an organization wakes up to look for a change, the technology might be generations ahead from what they are into currently. That is where good consulting capabilities come into the picture. Also, awareness on the part of the CXO and other decision makers is absolutely important. But there might be gaps here as well: technology notoriously progresses in leaps and bounds, and attempting to understand it in terms of how it was earlier won't help at all.

This book is centered around this problem. This is designed first to provide all the basic knowledge toward understanding machine learning and cognitive computing and the other topics covered. But it also presents a new framework called PEIB (a brand-new framework I have defined in this book), which is designed to help decision makers understand where to start with adopting and adapting these technologies for their specific organizational needs and structures and how to achieve success in this process. This is seen in the core chapter of this book: Chapter 10, Transformation Roadmap.

Readers are advised to go progressively through the chapters and build the prerequisite understanding in the right order.

I have tried to keep the details and descriptions of even the technical areas as much possible in business-understandable language and with plenty of examples.

Wherever needed, I have provided real and hypothetical business use cases or case studies to ensure that the concepts are well absorbed.

Let me first describe here the details covered through the chapters, and then I will present a general idea of the book.

Details Through the Chapters

The book starts with the journey of business intelligence (BI), where we discuss the historical perspective and the shifting paradigm of business intelligence. There is a discussion about how it looked when BI started and how it progressed over the years. We discuss a scenario with both older and newer perspectives of business intelligence to understand the difference.

In Chapter 2, we briefly discuss the need to go for cognitive and machine learning. For the sake of understanding there, we have a small discussion about the difference between artificial intelligence and machine learning. The reason we have this here, though we have these topics handled individually in further chapters, is just to set the right context of the discussion within the scope of this chapter. We conclude this chapter with a quick discussion about why cognitive computing is necessary. This chapter is the springboard for the discussion about each of the individual topics further, while just giving a quick idea about why these were required.

Chapter 3 is centered around basics of AI. The basics of AI are needed to be able to have prerequisite understanding of further concepts, like machine learning and cognitive computing. The scope of this book is not technical and so in-depth technical descriptions and details are not included. I have taken only those basics which help us to harness needed knowledge to be able to adopt and adapt these technologies. Supervised learning, unsupervised learning, and reinforced learning are also explained with examples and figures. The need for AI is again discussed here but in further depth. Approaches toward AI are also discussed here.

Chapter 4 talks about machine learning basics. It includes some detailed examples about training models and tasks. The very interesting technological concept of deep learning is also discussed with an example for easy understanding. Some good examples are mentioned throughout this chapter as well, and a very interesting business use case of Netflix is presented at the end.

Throughout the book you will notice various graphs and pictures drawn with great effort to help visualize things better.

From here we move to the interesting topic of natural language processing (NLP) in Chapter 5. NLP is a very wide area of study. For the scope of our book, we have kept it to just the minimum needed. The topic is described briefly with examples and clear steps to explain how it works.

Predictive analytics is another topic discussed in some detail in this book in Chapter 6. The discussion starts with an overview of predictive analytics and also talks about the properties of the data which has to be taken care of to have a proper Predictive analytics. In some detail, the process of predictive analytics is then discussed together with a clear figure to visualize it. Also, different types of analytics are discussed. Some important products are also mentioned in this chapter. The chapter ends with some interesting use case examples for a better understanding.

Chapters 7 and 8 are dedicated to build up knowledge toward cognitive computing. Cognitive computing is an area which is deeply influenced by human or animal cognition studies and properties. So, Chapter 7 starts with a discussion of cognition. The concepts of cognitive computing follow after that. The cognitive architecture and, in some more detail now, the question of "Why cognitive?" are mentioned in this chapter. Some interesting use cases are presented too. The chapters also include within them the design principles of cognitively designed systems. This is a very important discussion. Details are explained by a simple day-to-day example. The complexity of decisions possible using the cognitive solution is also discussed here. Various examples are presented to understand the underlying concepts. A detail on the relationship of cognitive to AI and ML is also presented in this chapter.

Chapter 9 talks about the parallel evolving IT-BI system (PEIB), a term I use for the first time. I have given this term to the new generation of the IT landscape and business intelligence, which evolve together in response to need. We understand the intricacies of how the IT and business relationship works today. Gaps and limitations are examined in this chapter. Then we discuss the changing paradigm in this relationship and the need for the same. I have defined this new term PEIB then in this chapter and also how it is placed. Some very interesting figures are added to supplement understanding. Then, the properties of such a system are described further and it's examined why this is a game changer for business. Chapter 8 ends with a case study to understand all inputs from Chapters 7 and 8.

Chapter 10 is the core chapter. I have defined a new framework, the PEIB framework, in this chapter. So, this is the actual chapter which helps in answering the question that may be asked: "Yes, the technology is good, but how should I go about these changes and where should I start?" This has a detailed description and definition of this framework. Since this is the core chapter, it's also the longest. I can't describe much further about this chapter, as something which hasn't existed heretofore is detailed there. So, the only way to better understand that is to reach there and learn.

Chapter 11 talks about the road blockers, hurdles, risks, and mitigations that could get in the way of such a transformation as discussed in Chapter 10.

Chapter 12 talks about the parallel evolving cognitive business. This is also a term I have created, and now with all the knowledge accumulated through all previous chapters, is used to define and describe a real cognitive system.

The concluding chapter, Chapter 13, talks about the path ahead for organizations implementing such solutions or planning to go through such transformations, including a detailed discussion for IT service providers and IT consultants.

General Idea of Book

The book focuses on the problem of helping organizations adopt and adapt ML and cognitive computing toward transforming into data-driven and cognitive organizations.

So, there are four areas of this book. The basics of technical concepts needed as prerequisites are detailed in the first area. Here, the basics of AI, ML, NLP, predictive analytics, and cognitive computing are discussed. Since the book is not intended to be technical, these are explained in simple language and with plenty of examples. The concepts of cognitive computing are explained in comparison to human cognition.

Once the basic knowledge has been built and a clear understanding of its need has been obtained, the next and core part now is around the problem area of how to adopt and adapt. It mentions in great detail the intricacies of how it should be done, via a new framework defined and presented through this book and named the PEIB framework.

The third part is about the possible blockers, risks, and mitigations that need to be considered to ensure that everything mentioned in the previous parts can be done very successfully.

The fourth and final part then describes the concept of the cognitively driven business to give a glimpse into the results; it concludes with a deep thought about the path ahead.

I hope this book helps my readers come up with a sound understanding about the adoption and adaptation of such technology and the way of business transformation, along with all the necessary basic technical awareness needed.

I hope organizations can come up out of various difficulties and inefficiencies of the past and conquer the future with the right approach and means adopted today. May everyone associated be happy!

I finish this introduction with a quote by Bil Keane:
Yesterday's the past, tomorrow's the future, but today is a gift. That's why it's called the present.

Rohit Kumar
1st August, 2017
Pune

CHAPTER 1

■ ■ ■

Journey of Business Intelligence

The scope of this chapter is to build up an initial understanding of business intelligence (BI) with definitions. This chapter is also aimed at building a basic understanding of how it started and what the initial use cases for it were. I will also cover the paradigm shift into the industry business usability use case for business intelligence.

■ **Note** This chapter stresses building up readers' initial understanding of the core subject area. So, even if you are familiar with business intelligence terms, it is still advisable to go through this chapter in order to connect with the thought process initiated via this chapter; this will help in the presentation of more advanced topics in later chapters.

Business Intelligence

Business intelligence is not an alien word for the IT and business departments within almost all corporations, whether small or big. There are already many players with business intelligence products on the market. The following are some of the popular players in the market (in order of price, from high to low):

- SAP

- IBM Cognos

- SAS

- Pentaho

- Alteryx

- MS SQL – BI Edition

- Tagetik

© Rohit Kumar 2017
R. Kumar, *Machine Learning and Cognition in Enterprises*,
https://doi.org/10.1007/978-1-4842-3069-5_1

- GoodData

- Board

- BI360 Suite

- iDashboard

- Mits Distributor Analytics

- Dundas BI

It is of the utmost importance for a business to have at least some business intelligence solutions so that it can act and manage operations intelligently. This required data as information to be right in front of their eyes. It could be as simple as Microsoft Excel-based pivot tables and charts.

Here is my definition: "business intelligence is a set of technologies and means to acquire data in various formats from various inbound data sources and to churn out meaningful reports, or visualizations, or alerts from it, which in turn supports the business in its various aspects and in turn business as a whole."

So, the definition itself puts forward the importance and vast applicability of these technologies, that is, churning out content about what and how you are doing from all data sources you have been working with. With today's technologies, it is even possible to use structured as well as unstructured data equally for business intelligence–based interpretation of data.

Until recently, a data warehouse was the primary or even sole source of business intelligence. However, with changing technologies and high-speed memory–based databases (e.g., HANA), it is even possible to do entirely without a data warehouse. A transactional system could be directly utilized for reporting. The division between separate OLTP (online transaction processing) and OLAP (online analytical processing) systems is going away. OLTP systems used to have primary responsibility for supporting day-to-day business transactions, with OLAP systems running modeling and reporting exercises on subsets of data extracted into them from OLTP. This is data warehousing capabilities and business intelligence.

Technology now has made it possible to bring in advances to provide the best possible analytical business intelligence, and on the other hand it is also helping it become more agile, simpler to achieve, and more scalable; it has also made it possible to have more rapid deployments and achieve more return on investment (ROI) with less investment overall. In other words, the diminishing line between OLTP and OLAP has made it possible to avoid having two separate systems and has resulted in further cost reductions.

It could be said that more agility in business warehouses has been created by the decoupling happening within data warehouse–based data marts. So, it's no longer required for the long, complex sequence of data marts to be coupled together into one data warehouse flow. Instead, it becomes a single-layered virtual architecture and more oriented toward a functional perspective, in contrast to the architecture's earlier technical reporting perspective, and this increased functional perspective in the design makes it free to accommodate changes that may arise with future needs. This makes it more agile and easy to scale up in the future. The agility and flexibility to scale up are very much sought-after criteria for selecting a suitable business intelligence product. In simple terms, it means less redevelopment in deploying solutions with new additions that stem from the changing needs of the business.

Analytics is a subset of business intelligence which is primarily related to running statistical algorithms (generic for business process or customized for organizations) in the back end before more complex results are displayed using reports and dashboards. Various kinds of analytics are part of the off-the-shelf packages of almost all business intelligence products.

The most basic business intelligence reporting is limited to simple reporting based on key performance indicators (KPIs) aggregated to display performance summaries of business processes and areas for business decision improvement; this is also called a decision support system (DSS). At times, it serves to report organizational summaries to top management; thus, it may also be known as a management information system (MIS). In the preceding scenarios, the reporting could be technically just an aggregation of various levels with a multidimensional organization of data for a more flexible display of information.

■ **Note**   With the advancement in database technologies and landscape simplification, it is possible to achieve more real-time information via business intelligence.

The various usability use cases of business intelligence are as follows:

- Measurement of performance matrix & KPIs

- Providing a collaborative platform for data integration & exchange

- Visualization of department data

- Knowledge management

- Regulation compliance management

- Planning operation support

- Predictions

Current statistics show that total business intelligence market revenues stand at $13.3 billion worldwide. Also, as a prediction, almost 75% of people in businesses will be using one or another business intelligence tool by 2020.[1]

Increasing the scope of cloud-based software-as-a-service (SaaS) and infrastructure-as-a-service (IaaS) is helping business intelligence products find their way to customers of all sizes, as they need to pay-as-per-use according to their requirements.

Due to lower maintenance costs and higher security commitment, even some bigger players have dropped inhibitions and have moved to cloud solutions. Some customers worth mentioning are Coca Cola, HTC, Best Buy, and PricewaterhouseCoopers (PwC).

---

[1]https://cisonline.bu.edu/news-resources/why-business-intelligence-is-key-for-competitive-advantage/

This book will take you on a journey through the world of business intelligence, including its association with cognitive science and its theories. It will then help you through a framework to achieve the expertise you desire.

Let us first peek into the past and observe just how business intelligence started in some detail.

Why & How It Started

The intelligence driven by business intelligence is supported by multiple types of multisource and single-source data. Just like we demonstrate our intelligence by mixing up multiple sources of present and past data and experiences, business intelligence does the same. This is not possible to do with just a single source of information. Until now, the concept of learning from experience—"thinking"—was the missing link, but now this can be achieved using cognitive computing and analytics. Cognitive computing and analytics concepts are discussed from Chapter 2 onward.

The very first to mention the term "business intelligence" was Richard Millar Devens in his work *Cyclopedia of Commercial and Business Anecdotes*[2] in 1865.

From the book: "Henry Furnese figures largely among the bygone bankers who gave renown to the financiers of that period. Throughout Holland, Flanders, France, and Germany, he maintained a complete and perfect train of **Business Intelligence.**"

This example of a banker using relevant information to win business use cases as early as the 1860s speaks to the critical importance of business intelligence. Unfortunately, he used this knowledge harvesting and interpretation technique to win business by fraudulent means, and so the first use of business intelligence was in a negative direction. Whether for good or for ill, however, business intelligence was limited at that time to being a tool to make relatively simple decisions; multiple-use cases evolved only with time.

Other important names in this regard are Hans Peter Luhn (IBM) in 1958 and Howard Dresner (Gartner) in 1989.

Devens first mentioned the label "business intelligence," and Dresner coined its modern definition; but due to the actual first thorough work in this subject, Luhn is considered to be the father of business intelligence.

In October 1958, Luhn published an article in *IBM Journal* on the topic.[3] He mentioned that "an automatic system is being developed to disseminate information to the various sections of any industrial, scientific or government organization. This intelligence system will utilize data-processing machines for auto-abstracting and auto-encoding of documents and for creating interest profiles for each of the 'action points' in an organization. Both incoming and internally generated documents are automatically abstracted, characterized by a word pattern, and sent automatically to appropriate action points."

---

[2]https://archive.org/stream/cyclopaediacomm00devegoog#page/n262/mode/2up/search/business+intelligence
[3]http://altaplana.com/ibmrd0204H.pdf

He ended his article saying that "the auto-abstracting and auto-encoding systems are in their early stage of development and a great deal of research has yet to be done to perfect them. Perhaps the techniques which ultimately find greatest use will bear little resemblance to those now visualized, but some form of automation will ultimately provide an effective answer to business intelligence problems."

Luhn described business intelligence solutions to the problem of apprehending the interrelationships of presented facts in such a way as to guide action toward a desired goal.

Going Ahead

With the onset of the 20th century, the technology to hold larger volumes of data and to manipulate it electronically became available. This technological maturity also fed upon itself, in a sense, to propel even more data management capability. After World War II, the world was going through a postwar economic boom. This period, called a golden age of capitalism by some, was seen as a rapid second industrial revolution. These factors all led to research like Luhn's on business intelligence to help businesses to adapt, prosper, and better manage their resources.

Many things described in his paper are still considered to be important: ad hoc or individual queries as differentiated from regular standard queries, security and data ownership (who should know what), auditing of data, performance optimization, and learning systems based on individual use patterns.

Significantly, he also mentions that advanced machines and technologies would be required to achieve all of that.

So, it would be wrong to think that self-learning machines, delivering business intelligence based on artificial or cognitive intelligence, are a new concept. Luhn, the father of business intelligence, even conceived of social features. Only the onset of demand in business with growing global competition was necessary for their achievement through advancements in technology.

Luhn presented a research paper called "The Automatic Creation of Literature Abstracts" to demonstrate technical research in this area.[4]

At its core, he described business intelligence systems as the ones which understand, create abstracts, and churn out reports from large volumes of data to establish interrelations that provide insights to help in making decisions.

Luhn provided a broad vision at a very early time which is still valid; moreover, he provided initial ideas to connect it with various use cases to help in making smart decisions.

By the 1980s

Despite all the theoretical descriptions, demand from business, and advances in technical capabilities, it was not until the 1980s when businesses started to use computers. Before this, data was supposed to be converted from punched paper records to microfilms and tapes to manipulate. This was technically feasible, but for businesses, using this at larger scales and at higher frequencies was a big pain.

---

[4]http://courses.ischool.berkeley.edu/i256/f06/papers/luhn58.pdf

Then, one by one came a series of products as DBMS systems to hold large volumes of data. After hierarchical DBMS by IBM and network DBMS by Honeywell in the 60s, finally the legendary "relational DBMS" was born at IBM in the late 70s. This provided the possibility of highly organized and huge DBMS to store everything possible using computers instead of paper or punch cards. So, technology integrated transaction systems directly as sources of data. This data was huge and organized with a complete presence in electronic format; no more need to convert format or preprocess. So, businesses were generating data which could be used in situ for business intelligence. This was a good change, because it provided a platform where business intelligence and its usability could be focused on more precisely, instead of merely thinking about possibilities.

Businesses started to see the advent of new departments called information centers, which sat in between IT and business. IT was focused on maintenance of all IT systems—hardware, software, and network—while information centers were data-centric. They knew which kind of data sits in which format and where. They were responsible for helping business to get hold of right data and for identifying and using the correct tools for it. Some of the initially available tools were Crystal Reports, MicroStrategy, and Business Objects. All this started to happen around the 80s.

The 80s saw the emergence of the concept of data warehouses as dedicated systems to help in business intelligence reporting. This was developed first by Barry and Paul (IBM). It emphasized distinct OLTP and OLAP systems. It said that for maximum effect in letting the data warehouse run business smartly, OLTP systems and decision support business intelligence systems should be used in conjunction. This concept of warehouse systems brought about the concept of ETL (extraction, transformation, and loading). It provided concepts, best practices, and data flow methods to extract relevant data to these warehouses from OLTP systems.

Data from disparate OLTP systems started to flow in a common format into these data warehouses using various ETL methods and tools.

These data warehouses would extract data into respective business areas and then, based on reporting requirements, would compress it into smaller data marts for performance. These systems, also called OLAP systems, were good at providing responses to complex analytical queries of these stored data.

This growth of business intelligence was parallel to ERP (enterprise resource planning). So, businesses could establish synergy between multiple departments and, without bothering with data entry, use it to get critical answers for their questions.

In 1989, Howard Dresner from Gartner Group coined the term "business intelligence" as an umbrella term for all related concepts such as DSS, executive information systems (EIS), data warehouse–based data storage, extraction and analysis, OLAP, and ETL. By this time, the birth of business intelligence 1.0 was done.

Business intelligence 1.0, termed BI 1.0 for short, was a full-fledged ETL-based system. It was good in terms of performance and usability, but the key demerits were as follows:

- It took too much time to see data, and there were delays in seeing data after its generation in OLTP system

- It was very complex and cumbersome to get the solution in hand

- It was too dependent on experts to use the tools

- Training required tools that were too complex

So, on one hand, a successful first generation of fully functional business intelligence had been born. On the other hand, after the initial honeymoon period, it was becoming apparent that good results were too time consuming to achieve due to the complexity of use. So, it was a little like a razor which before each shave must have its blades replaced by designated experts only, or at the very least under their training (and this training takes a long time).

Another issue was high maintenance costs of application, solutions, and hardware. This also had a limiting effect on its use in industries.

So, BI 1.0 had two facets: data and reporting. One end handled the entry of data up to data marts, and the other pulled reports out of it.

On Entering the 2000s

Technological advances in the late 2000s started to overcome these primary difficulties and drawbacks. More real-time data access possibility and self-service options brought in the era of business intelligence 2.0, or BI 2.0 for short.

The most important differentiating factor between BI 1.0 and 2.0 was that while 1.0 focused on ETL and reporting using tools, 2.0 focused on better access, easier access, and expanding the databases. It could include wider databases by utilizing more of the Internet.

BI 2.5, which was the next in the series around 2005, added even more huge data computation capabilities onto what was already a huge data scope by then; it did this by using the Internet. Zettabytes of data were capable of being processed in little time to process information in dimensions previously unthought of. Data democratization also came as another important change. Cloud capabilities are further added advantages in this era.

Now with the addition of cognitive capabilities, business intelligence is entering the new era of BI 3.0. The scope of this book's subsequent chapters is to describe this new BI 3.0 and cover how to implement it in and adapt it to your organization.

So, as a conclusion to "why and how," we can say that it started with the emerging needs of expanding markets and its increasing operating complexities. Although the very first thought process by Luhn, the father of business intelligence, covered all aspects of a complete business intelligence system, it has yet to be implemented successfully in his full definition. BI 3.0 probably will complete this long-awaited implementation. On one hand, its origin and growth are need based, and on the other hand, technology had been a limiting factor. In his article "A Business Intelligence System," Luhn described how these systems would cover social aspects; this was more or less accomplished by the time we reached up to BI 2.5. But he also described an "adaptive system to the need of the user," and that seems to be happening in BI 3.0 via cognitive capabilities.

Initial Use Cases

The initial use cases for business intelligence could be broadly divided into two time frames: in the 1960s and in the 1980s up to the late 90s.

In the 60s, even before the birth of the first generation of ERP (known as MRP; material requirements planning), business intelligence was oriented more toward organizing and automating recordkeeping. There was no real business intelligence in the sense we know it now. The initial databases in the form of files and cabinets were big overhead and full of redundant data. Spread across hardcopy files and folders, the data was hard to reconcile or audit. The initial idea was to just automate this record-keeping in a way that would sort out all the shortcomings mentioned earlier. The technology was not that all supportive; it still needed the hybrid action of using paper or punch records and then transferring them manually to microfilms and tapes. But all this taking of pains was still worthwhile to get a neat electronic record as a result. Meanwhile, somewhere in IBM's lab, Edgar Codd was inventing a new way of database management: the relational database management we use even now.

By the 70s, Codd's (IBM) version of the database was in place, which was good enough to store data in new tabular forms; however, data was quite fragmented. The data was missing the relationship functionalities necessary to generate good business intelligence–supported visualizations. The technology was a limiter in this case; if it would have been feasible technically, businesses would certainly have cherished that. But with the kind of technology available then, all they could achieve was electronic records which could be retrieved on demand; of course, this alone was much better than bulky and unmanageable paper cabinets and folders. So, this era did not have actual use cases where some data mash-up and visualization were provided or even possible; what happened instead was bringing data entry to files and then to fragmented tables as electronic records. Other use cases were in the form of MRP in production management and control.

The start of the 80s brought along with some new technology leaps in the form of relational databases and data warehousing concepts. This age brought in technologies to seek and get more in terms of actual business intelligence solutions and products. The very first breed of efficient and cutting-edge tools came in this period, and with this it was possible to run use cases like DSS, EIS, and MIS on consolidated data utilizing central data warehouses. Practicing ETL required bringing data to so-called OLAP systems to run complex business queries. Businesses started to see new IT-business hybrid departments known as information centers. These people would know where the data is and would use tools to extract desired information for business users and analysts. This was the time for real IT-owned developments happening on large scales. Businesses would plan to their satisfaction a summary of queries they would like to see from various departments or combinations. IT would figure them out, develop them, and hand them over. They could see combinations of data from multiple departments; for example, production people could see sales pipeline data, and finance could easily keep an eye on day-to-day expenses incurred by marketing. As personal computers were already in place and even first-generation ERPs were already there, no data entry manual effort was required. Automated ETL activity would take care of this. There were rich visualization tools available, like business objects, to allow fine visualization on top of data. Use cases would run, as every department even in big enterprises had the central warehouse get data harmonized and stored in one place, to be automatically displayed via reports developed by IT.

So, as a summary initial use case, between the 60s and the 80s, business intelligence went from the very beginnings of data entry automation all the way to advanced database-supported data warehouse marts and the ability to support rich combined data with great visualizations on top of it.

In the 60s, early adopters for initial use cases were the military, finance, and banking industries. Even retail markets were primary adopters. AT&T and Bell Atlantic in telecommunications and Wal-Mart in the retail industry were pioneers and were known as initial use case holders for business intelligence.

AT&T invested millions of dollars to have a huge legacy-based data warehouse to churn data from services and customers. Although initially it was used for so few users that it was possible to count them on your fingers, it nevertheless later helped to establish a system which had all the data and business intelligence tools to be able to segment prospective customers. This took a lot of time, effort, and money, but it paid off in the form of the gain of millions of accounts just because of that. With time, AT&T upgraded its warehouses and business intelligence solutions, and so its grip on market and customers increased. The initial business intelligence, by setting up a legacy-based warehouse, brought down its customer acquisition cost to lower than ever before. Investment for the cause was bringing more value for the money. At that time in history, however, data warehouse and business intelligence were so new that no one bothered to think in the direction of establishing a concept of return on investment (ROI) for these investments. Developments were cumbersome, complicated, and time consuming. But with the distinct rise in profits because of this, ROI benefits were visible and were flaunted by business intelligence– and data warehouse–selling companies.

The early 90s saw government agencies like the US Naval Warfare Center coming to use these solutions. A data warehousing and business intelligence project was launched to combine data from 30 different disparate systems to bring together 12GB of data (a big project in 1991) equivalent to about 12 billion characters of information. This served 700 users across Virginia, Maryland, and Florida, simplifying the naval information management system. The efforts to get accurate and timely details on any planned or executed project would flow in harmony to the desired user on demand, instead of tapping in into 30 systems with unharmonized data. This came up as one of the early adoptions of these technologies by any government. Later government adopters were healthcare and financial organizations.

One of the prominent and successful early use cases of business intelligence was that of insurance agencies. Aetna Life Insurance and Travelers Insurance were leaders in the 90s. They were getting mountains of data from individual motorist insurance and claim data. This gave them an opportunity to visualize the cost separation between underinsured and uninsured motorists, but it was nearly impossible to take advantage of this opportunity without these technologies. This helped them to negotiate insurance rates with government, issue competitive pricing when new competitors entered the market, and analyze sales in multiple product areas. Some even claimed to gain 1000% more ROI due to this.

One of the most famous and successful use cases remains that of Wal-Mart. They were acclaimed as masters in supply chain management. Being the world's largest retailer and having a customer base of about 100 million supported by over 25,000 suppliers, supply chain management was quite a challenge. Understanding what goes to which shop floor, and how much and when, is the key to successful supply chain management. Behind the scenes, business intelligence on top of the central warehouse had its hidden wheels rolling. With this magic, Wal-Mart could obtain deep insights into this huge customer base and their shopping patterns. It was a 1-terabyte data warehouse in 1992. This was one of the largest databases of that time. Any transaction data was available to managers in about seven minutes. This was near-real-time insight into data in those years. All in all, it was a very successful solution for the time, as illustrated by the example in which one store suddenly displayed a huge spike in the sale of computers in one region. Practically immediately, the same offer was replicated in all stores in that region, and the sales spike was also replicated for all these stores.

Later Use Cases

The later use cases for business intelligence could be divided broadly into two time frames: the early 2000s and the later 2000s before 2015.

By the start of the 2000s, businesses were having a myriad of business intelligence products running on top of data warehouses. They could by now in reality see ROI benefits brought forward by these solutions. That was all fine and dandy, but something had also changed by this time. Businesses were using this for over a decade and slowly almost everyone came to be using the same. This brought the ROI and any other benefit graph to a plateau. The businesses, depending on the type of industry vertical and the subarea of interest, were mostly using standard scenarios. Industry standard contents were not very well established, and due to coming from a generation of data entry automation into the first generation of data warehousing, the businesses were implementing identical IT solutions in their respective areas. The solutions were more strategic in nature to achieve only tactical objectives at the end: a big machinery of IT and business churning out a big catalogue of reporting after a long and complex process. As you may imagine, there were fewer chances for agility or scalability of solutions. To differentiate themselves from competitors, these businesses required a more direct tactical solution, one more responsive to individual business change plans and one that could be adopted more rapidly. More user-friendly tools serving users with little or no IT background were also desired. It was previously the IT specialist's domain, but now the concept of more potent power users was desired.

Unfortunately, this was not yet the time when completely user-friendly solutions had arrived on the market. Lighter products with less time to production were available by now, but IT teams were still required to develop every bit of them.

With the onset of additional products, it was even possible to have ad hoc querying possibilities and vastly faster calculations on ultrafast new-generation databases like the in-memory–based SAP HANA database.

By now, highly agile developments incorporated the latest visualization possibilities, including mobile-based reporting solutions. Ultrapowerful databases had lightning-fast reporting capabilities, at times even without actual ETL. On top of that, social integration and the use of unstructured data at par with structured data filled a good number of the gaps. Cloud was another enabler for further reducing cost and increasing availability. It brought along solutions with SaaS (software-as-a-service), IaaS (infrastructure-as-a-service), and PaaS (platform-as-a-service) kinds of options. So, business intelligence along with the latest and most modern data warehousing capabilities was looked upon as the most possible mature solution. A report connected virtually with multiple OLTP sources would do a million calculations in a few seconds and display, in real time, data sheets or visualizations on a user's screen. Several high-end analytic capabilities also came up (e.g., predictive analytics, descriptive analytics, diagnostic analytics). Prescriptive analytics has still not been achieved to its fullest. But this is not the last stop. We will discuss this in the next section, "Shifting Paradigm."

Continuing with the discussion about the types of analytics, they are depicted with a complexity-versus-value perspective in Figure 1-1.

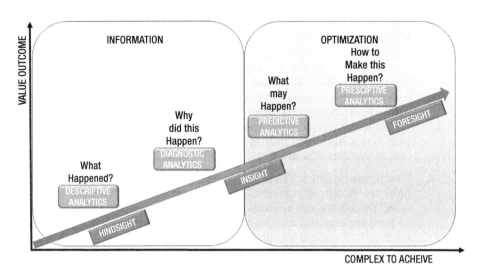

Figure 1-1. *Types of analytics*

The following are brief descriptions of all four types of analytics:

1. Descriptive Analytics: This is about what has happened. The result set throws details on "what happened" during the timeline in question (e.g., a company considering a certain cost case to analyze where the flab is and how to get rid of that). About 35% of organizations do it frequently. This is coming out of the historical data and thus is considered hindsight. It is the least complex to achieve, as this is mostly data drilled up or down. The value is considered to be the least, as it just helps in finding out "what happened" and nothing beyond.

2. Diagnostic Analytics: This is about "why this happened"; it's mostly to solve a specific problem. This is assisted by techniques like data drill down, data mining, and analysis of correlations. Approximately 10% of organizations use these techniques, and only half of them do so frequently. Diagnostic analytics is also done mostly using historical data, but it goes beyond the previous in terms of data mining and correlating pattern analysis. It takes the historical data beyond just looking at it as it is and converts it into data points to understand "why this must have happened." In short, this is insight from the historical data.

3. Predictive Analytics: This type of analysis shows "what may happen." It combines contextual data with behavioral data and determines probable future outcomes (e.g., modern CRM and marketing solutions for understanding customer patterns in order to decide which campaign should be addressed to which customer segment). Currently, very few organizations use it frequently, as it is far more complex; on the other hand, it provides great value. It needs some complex mathematical models to predict using an array of data mixed with the operational data of business.

4. Prescriptive Analytics: This goes one step further and proposes "better paths of actions to avoid less good or bad ones." This is not easily available in mature form now but it is on the verge of getting into that bracket. It includes the use of machine learning and cognition. It's the most complex of the four and goes beyond to add further technologies to be able to prescribe solutions by thinking about the problem. We will be covering thinking machines in Chapters 7 and 8.

Shifting Paradigm

From the latter half of 2014, business intelligence saw a shifting paradigm; the use case went more toward predictive and prescriptive analytics. Also, the use case of IT has been expanding its scope and its changing role. From being known as supporting business, IT started moving into space as a main driver of innovation (Figure 1-2). IT now impacts business strategies and even plays a role in driving them.

Figure 1-2. *The changing role of IT*

Conventionally, IT has played a role in facilitating the achievement of business goals. They have been the people, right from the 80s information center days, who provided the means to get visibility for required data: picture the back end of business running some expensive projects just because data is invested in so many disparate systems that they are required to consolidate it and then bring out prescribed details "as per business wish." With technical capabilities and most modern delivery methodologies supported by Agile and Lean, they could do it faster. With the latest technical advances in the area of databases, they could do so in a very lean and mean data model, but the crux remains the same—IT was and is the back end for business. They never had been thought of as contributing to business growth or expansion or reaching out to customers by themselves.

But then, with everything connected to everything (Internet of Things [IoT]), things changed. More and more use of the Internet in a globally connected society started to bring about customer preference patterns on the Web. Social media posts started to become guiding lights and have the capability to crumple products and companies in no time. Word against a product or service spreads like a forest fire. Any organization not geared up to manage this in near real time could face image issues that damage its reputation too much to be able to manage (e.g., how many would have known in the 90s, when the Internet and social media didn't have as much presence, that any company selling phones with batteries that caught fire would have a global issue, not just a local one?). Even if the impact back then were global, it would have taken time to reach people.

Now, one such event happens somewhere with even just one or two people sitting in two different continents. They post it on social media, and within a matter of hours this is a hot news item. Sales across the world drop to zero in a matter of hours, or people who already bought the product flood the customer care centers. If this is a genuine issue, it will ultimately help the company too, as painful as it may seem at the time, to recall the product for the safety of customers. But what if, instead, some mischief were afoot? Companies should have the capability now to have business intelligence manage this as well.

There are companies now driving their business goal setting completely utilizing IT resources (e.g., computers with human-like thinking and reasoning capabilities, as discussed in detail later in further chapters). There are examples of companies that are driving customer reach and planning expansions in a completely integrated fashion with their IT assets, and so the IT role is now essential for their success. IT resources were a major part of their success stories, running hand in hand with the business plan and even as the main executor. Worth mentioning is Netflix. The decision to put on board and invest even without watching a pilot for the complete TV series *House of Cards*, a show worth $100 million, was completely an IT-supported decision. Netflix does not depend on media houses to advertise but gains its footprint by internal IT data assets. So, Netflix has a ROI based on member subscriptions rather than on media house–based advertising expenses. It is an example of a company moving toward the optimized IT-driven organization of the future, which will be very capable of using extensive prescriptive analytics. This is a great example of the paradigm shift in the IT role.

Normally, where a TV show gets approved by any production house, it is submitted with an entire storyline script and thematic description, and then in the next level a host of pilots are submitted. But in this case, just the name of show and the lead actor names were taken as input, and without even going through any pilot, Netflix could judge the success of the show and invested into it, all based on smart predictive analytics. It analyzed these details with its huge customer base of about 81 million and viewership of about 125 million hours of content per day. The viewing pattern and behavior aspects of all its viewers and the likelihood of people watching a series with lead actor Kevin Spacey gave them solid predictions about its success. Not limited to the identification and confirmed prediction of this content, the analytics also divided the viewer base into ten different categories based on behavioral and content preference choices demonstrated, which helped them to promote *House of Cards*. Based on these analytics, ten different trailers were made to be presented to relevant groups of viewers (e.g., people who prefer watching action more should see the one with more action packed into it, people with a higher choice index for watching Kevin should see the one with maximum exposure of Kevin, and people watching mostly female-centric movies were shown the one suiting their taste). So instead of going to any media house for promotion data acquisition or execution of a promotion plan, Netflix took a decision based on user data and promoted back exactly based on their user preference. This is a good example of the changing paradigm of IT. Instead of just back-end data processing, ETL, and presenting to business, IT in this example is a great enabler of business for Netflix. They have a data-driven, and thus IT-driven, business model. The business expansion and product expansion details are taken very well considering the scope of business and with utilizing user data, and even promotions are handled that way. Before this, Netflix didn't utilize this aspect of the IT-business connection. Before 2002, Netflix had only suggestions running based on the geography of users.

By understanding user viewing patterns and other facts exposed via its vast big data collection, Netflix tries to push a new Netflix site visitor towards a subscription in 60 to 90 seconds. This particular time frame is important, since if an individual does not settle down in this interval to watch something he or she finds interesting or relevant, they might abandon the web site or if already a viewer may even plan to cancel their subscription. Even the videos uploaded on its Amazon AWS cloud servers have been watched and tagged into over 80,000 types of microgenres to be able to map to individual user preference across the globe.

Netflix also manages something called the continuous watch aspect. If a user does not watch about twenty minutes of content per session it is found that there is a high chance that he will abandon the subscription.

Figure 1-3 shows the high-level schematic diagram of how content from Netflix is presented to its viewers, from uploading media on Amazon AWS servers to making suggestions on the customer log-in dashboard.

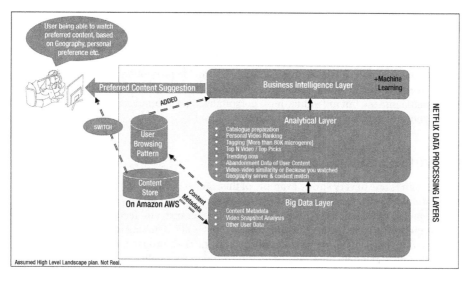

Figure 1-3. *Content management and presentation—Netflix (high level)*

So, the Netflix use case is one example of how a company is leveraging IT as a business enabler for its organic growth and sustainability. This is the start of an era where the equation of the IT-business relationship is changing from one of consumer and supplier to one of partners in success. The Internet and various facets thereof like social media are changing the way a product or service life cycle is managed. More and more customer service-centric approaches have changed the way businesses must operate.

Social media has a multidimensional impact on the businesses. Some of these are detailed in the following sections.

Customer Relationship Management

Word-of-mouth praise is good. It might take a thousand words of praise to get a good reputation with even just one or two customers. But it takes just one bad word to shatter this all. This has been never so impactful as now, and the reason is social media. One bad word in social media could go spiraling up and down to millions, maybe billions, of people in just a few hours. So, this needs to be tracked in real time. If we just talk about Facebook, there are about 1.7 billion monthly active users (MAU). There is about a 15% MAU increase expected each year. About 4.5 billion likes are generated per day (in 2013), about 10 million web sites are affected by Facebook likes or shares per day (in 2014), and 42% of marketers reported the critical importance of Facebook for their business (source: State of Inbound Marketing 2012). Other social media platforms also have big numbers, and the grand total of all these together is huge. On top of that, there are feedback web sites. So, there has been a tremendous effort from organizations to capture these, and moreover in real time.

Apart from this, the technology now allows outreach to individual customers and customized benefits and services for them. Say, a grocery chain customer in a subgeography might have expected a reasonable season promotion offer for the community there, which was the maximum possibility until recently. But with technologies available, it is very much possible to provide promotions customized or personalized for that individual customer. This may seem to have no direct relation to social media impact, but individual-level personalized promotions tend to help with damage control and can happen on the same channel.

Market Research Analysis

Netflix again is one of very strong example of this. Social media and all means of digital media should be ears for organizations. This brings in much valuable information about culture, preferences, reactions, lifestyle, age and gender mix, and feedback about self and competitors for the desired customer base. This is like reaching in a billion copies individually to each customer individually and noting their properties and preferences, which obviously can help in establishing best-in-breed surgically targeted marketing campaigns.

Loyalty Management

Customer loyalty management means plugging holes in the ship. Every business desires a heavier loyalty-based customer base. The target group of consumers registered as "loyal" do double duty: they bring in a fixed source of business, and they also spread good word-of-mouth to people around these customers. As a controlled group, these customers are also invited for new releases to get their first-cut feedback on whether a product is good enough to go further to target new audiences. Happy customers and their stories are considered trusted examples by prospective customers. An organization should ensure a healthy number of loyal registered customers equally in all categories of desired audiences. This will again in turn help them to reach out to further prospective customers with relevant examples; for example, a prospective customer in a low-income group would like to see and analyze a story which is relevant to his income level to gauge the benefits for him or her. He or she might consider the product or service too expensive if shown examples drawn from a story of a billionaire from the same state. Some people argue to keep the success stories free from social or financial grades. The reality is that this might work well in some cases, but a story from a similar grade always has more impact. Perhaps this kind of targeting was more difficult earlier with paper and billboard campaigns, but with technology for personalization it is very much possible. Research says that most people who tend to stick with a brand on social media even convert into businesses with that brand.

Product Release

The details about the prospective customer base provide exactly what needs to be released in a given geography. This increases the success rate of the released product.

Apart from these factors, after-sales service also presents a huge business opportunity. Companies have long understood the service-centric view of businesses. Car companies which used to denote themselves as manufacturing-centric companies now prefer to be known as service providers first. The research firm Aberdeen Group mentioned that in America, consumers spend close to $1 trillion every year on the assets they already own.

After sales, service is a big business now with very high margins. Companies know that the prices must be balanced with economical products and services with more fancy functionalities due to high levels of global and domestic competition. But service is the area that, if tapped, brings in continuous revenue flow from same customers and with a much higher profit margin. An AMR study in 1999 mentioned that businesses earn 45% of gross profit from the aftermarket, where it is only 24% of revenues. It is understood from surveys that customers are looking for a company and product which are more customized for their usage and could be fixed easily and quickly. They don't always bother about quality certifications of products, but of course they are impressed by a quick fix if their item isn't working well. In India, companies like Maruti have the advantages of specializing in country-specific products, having prices under control, and offering extremely efficient service. Conversely, some renowned European and American brands could not grab the market in India despite having otherwise-good names and the likelihood that customers would go for these brands, because they were plagued with bad reputations in the market about nonavailability of original parts and bad or insufficient service centers. Even dealer networks over time have realized the value of technology and a service-centric approach. Businesses like Kothari car sales in Pune, India, have been successful due to implementing technology and offering extremely good service. So, at every level of business the service-centric approach is the trend.

Research from *Harvard Business Review* (*HBR*) mentions that while this is profit making, normally the service supply chain must handle more stock-keeping units (SKUs) than the sales supply chain. Also, there are many more things to be synchronized to give a better and more professional service as compared to sales.

At one point in time, market research was focused on the maintenance of brands and helping in bringing up new products over time. Now the trend is to create brand value by connecting with customers in the long run after sales and to maintain this relationship. There are success stories of companies who went ahead to understand customers long before even creating a product. French car maker Renault launched the Duster model on similar lines. Their market research identified 30 families in their target customer group and developed the Duster from scratch, and it was a huge success.

So, to review the preceding part of this chapter, we understand that, from a very early time, from automated data entry until what is expected now, business intelligence has become mature and advanced in business and in technology.

With the change in market dynamics and so many new Internet-driven attributes and parameters in management of business, there has been a paradigm shift in how business intelligence is aligned within organizations and how it must be utilized.

Overall, the paradigm shift is in how business models have become more and more complex and how technology has become more embedded into business process management and getting or generating business rather than just producing red, green, and yellow dashboards on what has already happened. These days, IT has more of a role in the present and future of an organization, rather than only painting a picture of the past.

Companies like Netflix lead the way. Banking companies and retail business are also primary beneficiaries of this. From a business intelligence perspective, the paradigm shift is to move on a "maturity roadmap" toward optimization and churn out solutions in predictive and prescriptive mode. Predictive has been in the lead since 2015, but now prescriptive should have a chance to lead too. This is where cognitive and machine learning comes into the picture.

In further chapters, we will be talking more about them. The scope of this book is to talk in depth about this topic and how it is revolutionizing the way business is done. The book will not use core technical language. Rather, the aim is to bring deep understanding about cognitive-driven business intelligence for businesses and then guide them with defined steps to adopt these technologies.

Leading management consulting firms have already predicted that, if companies lag in these areas of IT-enabled growth, chances are high that these companies may just go away, -irrespective of present growth, size, or and current momentum.

Case Study

Let us now try to visualize whatever we have discussed up to this point with a hypothetical case study. The purpose of this book to bring deep understanding of the concepts, and this is better explained with good examples. At many places in the book, I will keep coming up with real or hypothetical case studies as examples. At times, due to data privacy concerns, I will limit the case studies to hypothetical case studies, but based on one or another of the real projects I have handled so far.

Here, I will discuss one case study of a retail chain in contrast with business intelligence before the paradigm shift around the start of 2015 and after. The case study will be first discussed under "BI Before Paradigm Shift" and then "BI With Paradigm Shift." I will not discuss older or more primitive examples here, where business intelligence was used just for data entry automation. The point I want to make here with these contrasting case study examples is how it would have looked as a business intelligence solution then and now.

We will now try to visualize a case study for a retail chain business. This chain runs shops in several cities. The challenges faced by the chain are as follows:

- Profit Margin Issues: IDC and other retail survey reports have repeatedly mentioned this as the major area where retail chains go for IT-collaborated environment.

- Customer Preferences: Ever-changing dynamic customer preferences affected by various parameters in due course of time, price fluctuations (especially for perishables), supply chain management, operational optimizations, competition, and many more factors contribute to this.

- Regulations: Compliance with government regulations is complicated and a 100% compliance is mandatory. This creates complications and delays.

- Quality Management: Quality management is not only about brand choice and taking cognizance of what was of poor quality in the past: it is helps customers toward warranty issues and coordinating intelligently and timely with concerned vendors.

- E-commerce and/or Omnichannel Challenges: Sales in either channel—whether brick-and-mortar shops, or online, or even both—have their own unique challenges.

- Going with Trend: Understanding changing pattern and following previous pattern in a scenario effectively is a challenge.

- Shelf and Store Level Out of Stock: This is very complex part of two-tier supply chain management. Determining what is going off the shelf rapidly and what its status is in inventory is a complex task (e.g., whether it needs to be brought from the store's warehouse or ordered from the distribution center, or whether an alert needs to be triggered in advance with one of the suppliers). Studies suggest that these kinds of out-of-stock situations cause retailers 4% to 8% annual sale loss.

- Outdated Product Management: The golden principle for stock to shelf in retail chains is "first in, first out." If this does not happen, older stock might have to wait longer and even expire or at best be sold at lower profit in a promotion offer (as selling as many perishables as possible at lower profit is always better than losing them to spoilage). Also, products which are specific to a time should have occasional price adjustments to ensure maximum sales in that time frame.

- Data Integrity Issues: A retail chain deals with a supply chain of thousands of products. Any mismatch, duplication, or defect in data could spiral into huge customer dissatisfaction and crumpled operations. Global estimates for loss of sales due to this are above $8 million. There are retailers who have even reported inventory record errors because of data integrity issues to the tune of 60% and more. Considering the number of items, how they handle it could potentially create millions of issues. Master data management is another challenge, and considering varieties and subcategories, it could be a very costly and uncomfortable situation for retailers if there are data issues here.

These and many more issues could surface together, one by one, or in any other combination for a retailer.

We will now discuss this further for our hypothetical retailer, which we'll call ABC.

BI Before Paradigm Shift

Let's talk about ABC's options before 2014–2015. Consider the possible ways they could have reaped benefits from a business intelligence solution.

Let us first put forward a bulleted list of issues discussed earlier:

- Profit Margin Issues

- Regulations

- Quality Management

- Omnichannel Challenge

- Going with Trend

- Out of Stock Management

- Outdated Product Management

- Data Integrity Issues

The technology until 2014 and the start of 2015, that is, just before the new paradigm started to prevail, was capable of answering these issues extremely well.

There were various products on the market providing retail-related solutions to cater to the back office, point-of-sale, returns, inventory, the head office, and supply chain management. By this point, there were off-the-shelf industry products available in the form of easily configurable products and predesigned reports to unpack and run with various degrees of customization. There were even mobile-enabled reports available.

Almost all areas were covered in the list of issues to different extents. Let's look at one issue at a time.

- Profit Margin Issues: This was an overall effect of customer management, operations management, and supply chain management. The IT solutions of these days were able to plug holes for losses in this area to a good extent. Predictive analytics running on big data could provide better insight into predicted possibilities based on past trends. Data slice-and-dice could give a vast array of visualizations of the data, which adds up to relief for these issues.

- Regulations: Regulations were easily monitored and managed, and alerts were available for the same via various products (e.g., SAP and Greenlight products). Automation saved businesses from violations by better monitoring and alerts on various thresholds or breaches. This would cater to better monitoring of internal and external regulation controls.

- Quality Management: Like regulation management. This also has internal and internal controls established, with these controls being dynamic and changeable over time. So, a proper record of what was done based on previous scales should also be there to differentiate and gauge benefits from the current situation. This was provided as a service and a product by multiple providers. Could provide a good monitoring and report to document for the same.

- Omnichannel Challenge: Products like Hybris from SAP, Teradata Digital Marketing Center, various Oracle B2B and B2C Omnichannel products, and many more were available. This would help retailers to use Omnichannel specialty services and products to provide customers a relevant experience and make them happier. For physical shops, this was not too useful, although there are products available to manage and enhance it to a certain extent in the shop environment.

- Going with Trend: Trend analysis and planning options were already maturing enough to be able to provide better planning and prediction results to have a smarter planning based on deep trend analysis. Big data and analytics made it easier to churn out information from diverse and huge data sources, whether structured, unstructured, or some combination. This in turn facilitated getting richer results out of data.

- Out of Stock: There were enough products already to cater to this need. Web- and mobile-based dashboards were available, and utilizing high-performance databases it was possible to monitor things in real time as well. Predictive analysis algorithms coordinated with point of sale data could predict the need to reorder.

- Outdated Product Management: This was also available in the form of various products to create customized configurations to manage this. Daily, weekly, quarterly, ad hoc, and anytime report dashboards were available to monitor and manage this. Workflows were in place for multilevel approval requirements. Technologies like SAP FIORI could provide decomposed transactions to the users in the workflow, where they would see very simple screens depending upon what they must do and what they should see. This UI technology also was very light, based on HTML5 technology, and easy to use on mobile devices. Moreover, underlying applications would take care of back-end updates to operational systems.

- Data Integrity: Best-in-breed master data management and ERP applications were present by this time to take care of this. Consolidated systems and high-performance data warehouses would provide harmonized data with one version of truth updated to real time. At times, this could mean a heavyweight time-consuming ETL from multiple systems, but in the end everyone was happy.

So, considering what we discussed in the preceding, it can be said that by this time we had all the needed capabilities in terms of technology, providing all solutions desired.

In terms of industry expertise, there were solutions providing off-the-shelf contents. IT was connecting all these advanced applications together with huge landscapes, providing answers to everything businesses were interested in. Memory-based databases could help to run a system so optimized and high-performing that every report could be in real time.

For e-commerce purposes based on user interaction, there were web sites which would customize contents dynamically as the user would navigate and present relevant content.

Predictive analytics would provide predictions about high-probability prospective customers from already obtained sweet spots. This would in turn move toward highly optimized surgical marketing campaigns. If I buy tomatoes and never bought potatoes from a retail chain, I would be proposed offers on tomatoes and rarely on potatoes based on my preference. This increased ROI on marketing costs. Marketing and sales would keep cognizant on their surroundings by peeking into posts and likes by prospective customers on social media and would bring out social-enabled campaigns and work on defensive plans immediately if negative inputs circulate.

Deeper understanding of text analysis would provide sentiment scores from consumer texts from feedback or even from videos posted.

Progressing along the analytics scale until reaching predictive analytics, in the "optimization" quadrant of Figure 1-1, would seem to be the final possible achievement.

But a closer look at predictive analytics would reveal the following:

- It is still a high level of automation with high complexity in play.

- Reports still need to be proposed by business and to be developed by IT as a fixed artifact added to the ecosystem first to be utilized later.

- Predictions do not always mean optimization; it's just a big complex algorithm running on data and is a static logic in itself.

- All the knowledge inhabited in the system logic is exactly equal to wisdom shared by business, which gets translated into technical terms by IT and realized. It is further used and enhanced over time as both contribute to it.

- The ad hoc data representations required by managers and leaders are huge, and this limits them to being two-dimensional representations that are generated by playing with data with only limited knowledge and scope provided to them in the IT landscape (kind of a playground area).

- As knowledge invested in systems is to be updated by the people using it, any changes to optimize or modernize must go via formal channels to IT, and moreover this process isn't free.

- The entire repository of reports is seldom required by users who make requests. Most of the time, these users might need just some part of it, and running the whole thing, which consumes a great deal of system resources, is not optimal.

- Trend analysis is possible, but considering trend analysis itself and modifying it or changing it is not possible using the same set of business intelligence.

- At the end of the day, while business and IT are employees of the same organization, they are used in different ways in this scenario. Business churns out business-related ideas and needs reports to increase revenue or plug leaks somewhere, while IT is strictly speaking a cost case, even though it's an essential piece, simply because IT departments don't generate revenue on their own.

- IT departments seldom contribute brain-power to ideas to expand business or churn out more profit, with the exception of data scientists to an extent. Instead, they simply translate business tools into technical terms, and awkward scenarios may arise in cases where IT seems to be unaware of the seriousness of one report out of a thousand others; they might feel surprised when someone says it's very important and needs to be fixed immediately. So, the situation is one of extreme dependency on IT resources, yet without IT being fully integrated into business case management.

- Reports provide predictions based on data input, but they need manual effort to be changed, including a formal channel of activities to tweak them when required. When changes are required, this isn't obviously apparent from the reports themselves most of the time.

- Managers on the ground are empowered with such advance tools to make swift decisions anywhere and anytime, but these tools still don't assist them in making such decisions in real terms. They still must apply 100% their own wisdom and thoughts anytime and in any external, internal, and personal situation. There could be checks at the process level on the validity of their actions after the fact, but there isn't any input on optimizing their thoughts at the time of utilizing that system-generated data.

- We have optimized solutions which read customers' geolocations and mood texts, and are even capable of understanding their sentiments and predicting quite a few things about them. However, these solutions aren't quite capable yet of providing specific and rational guidance to any given consumer on an individual basis.

- The dependency of IT in terms of knowledge management and share is huge. Despite good documentation and storage options, there is a disconnect between the systems and the documentations, and over time, it may become difficult to find the correct source of documentation. There have been instances where companies must invest substantial resources into solving this problem. They must then evaluate whether it would be cheaper to understand and fix the mess or just to start anew. This all can be attributed to bad documentation and/or to large volumes of knowledge management documentation (whether simple or complex). There are companies working on providing good knowledge management solutions, but knowledge management and actual systems still exist parallel to each other and never merge.

These and so many more thoughts, if applied to what was possible and deliverable via ERP and business intelligence systems, look primitive in the end. This is where we can talk about the paradigm shift, or more precisely, a second shift. The first shift is from automation of data entry and siloed data stores to business intelligence, as we know so well. The second shift is from systems produced out of thoughts to systems which could provide thoughts and even learn as well. As usual, this is something which is driven by the need for businesses to differentiate from their global competitors and run most efficiently on shrinking margins. This brings us into a world of collaborative competition, where multiple providers could become part of one seamless experience for customers based on their niche capabilities. For users, it is a system which interacts with them, understands them, and learns along with their experiences. The algorithms set earlier would not be constant; these learning cognitive business intelligence solutions would provide confidence by providing learned advice to users. These will provide seamless integration between the system to be used and the associated knowledge to be shared. These business intelligence systems would learn to autocorrect in cases of repeated failure. They would empower IT to equally collaborate in business welfare, as their role would change from being simple executors to being people who should know the business in depth to design solutions sitting right alongside the business users. The cognitive systems would take away the rigidity from systems where fixed requirements through formal projects would be required to produce a report or dashboard end-product.

Let us see the same retail example with this second paradigm shift idea. This book will be talking about this shift in more detail and making an effort to cover all aspects. This chapter, though, focuses on bringing up the most basic thoughts around this shift first; increased depths of knowledge will be revealed as the chapters progress. IBM Watson, a leading cognitive solution running on IBM WebSphere servers, will be discussed throughout the book.

BI With Paradigm Shift

Now, let's talk about options that are slowly becoming available for ABC from around mid-2015. We are talking again about possible ways they could have reaped benefits from business intelligence solutions in this era and with the same set of issues as mentioned earlier:

- Profit Margin Issues

- Regulations

- Quality Management

- Omnichannel Challenge

- Going with Trend

- Out of Stock Management

- Outdated Product Management

- Data Integrity issues

Let us again now first talk about the IT landscape. The IT landscape by now has best-of-class on-premise or cloud-based databases supporting any volume of data without any bottlenecks. There is now a cognition-based layer brought to this lean and mean (very simplified data model design) developed data platform. Data from all possible sources are harmonized and placed in a relational model. Most of the data is not even physically loaded into the databases, but open source protocols supported by these data platforms are now supporting virtual access to these sources. Data not immediately required or high-data-volume-churning sources are moved to low-priced commodity hardware running Hadoop on top.

There are operational reports which are available as usual as static reports. We by this time started to call all reports coming out of IT projects as fixed artifacts, a.k.a. static operational reports. These are the ones required for standard format reporting for general reporting related to accounting, auditing, and legal purposes.

Other reports, however, will utilize Cognitive solutions on top to provide reports. So, when a leader looking for a merger or acquisition suddenly needs to understand data from systems and ask nonroutine questions of it, he is not dependent on IT to generate the necessary reports for him. Before cognitive solutions, this would sometimes get so far out of control that the actual value would go down the tubes. Now, he also does not need to depend upon his assistant manager's technical skill in that system sandbox or workspace to try some new temporary model, but previously, his access to the system might even have been restricted by IT.

Maybe he needs to understand certain things at the last moment to discern the best reason for the merger he is suggesting to the board, and he'll almost certainly need some convincing numbers as well.

With such a cognitive system, all he'll need to do will be to ask questions in simple English (or whatever language he's comfortable in); in a flash, he will not merely see the data he requested onscreen but will have his choice of various graphical formats. All related trends will be aligned neatly on the same screen to enable him to understand the subject better (e.g., weaknesses they may be facing in a certain region in terms of financial numbers). The system throws a graph or graphs to show weaknesses in terms of product or service areas, and also throws many other graphs to show the true trends in multiple analytical dimensions. It automatically understands the context and shows categorized complaint trends from that region, and maybe comparative analysis with other surrounding stores. If it is connected and planned that way, it might even bring in real-time data for the store and any new publications related to the subject. If the leadere also wanted to consider staffing trends for the store to get even more context, he could also see attrition trends and most-frequent-reason-to-quit bubble charts.

So, there is a seamless integration of the user with the system.

The shift in retail is moving toward more personalization too. The consumer looks to the retailers with that expectation. A good example could be The North Face web site (`https://thenorthface.com/xps`). In near real time, this web site tries to help customers by using IBM Watson capabilities. In simple English, users can answer a series of relevant questions asked by Watson, and then from thousands of products, the relevant one is shown on screen. The three primary areas of customer engagement (i.e., engage, discover, and decide) are in prime focus now.

As previously discussed for changing volumes and patterns of data, the predictive models need to be tuned very often and cannot change their courses automatically, while cognition and machine learning are capable of self-tuning and self-correction.

Before the paradigm shift toward cognitive, systems were capable of good interpretation of results based on predictive capabilities, but they were not smart enough to learn. They could mix and match a variety of data like weather and other factors and come back with a broader-sourced data calculation to provide the precise details they were tuned for. There was some level of flexibility, such as the ability to change course based on algorithms, but this was limited to opportunities within the program scope of these models.

Conversely, cognitive has that element of being able to decide what to use and what conclusions to draw as a result. It can also notice new patterns and create new learning from it. This further evolves their overall scope of calculations.

The common issues we discussed for our retailer earlier are all effectively managed the very same way it was before the paradigm shift, but with cognitive in the picture, all of them became learning and predicting systems. The ease of a cognitive system's reporting dashboard made it more user-centric and unlimited in scope.

This magic journey started commercially somewhere around 2014-2015 and continues today, affecting almost every industry.

This book will cover this phenomenon in depth.

CHAPTER 2

▓ ▓ ▓

Why Cognitive and Machine Learning?

This chapter continues further in discussing why the cognitive option was a natural choice for the evolution of business intelligence. In Chapter 1, we discussed the various levels of evolution for business intelligence and saw that the more human-like thinking machines doing predictive and prescriptive analytics had become available by the 2000s. These were the cognitive and machine learning applications or machines. Though we intend to discuss these terms in coming chapters, let us first dig a little to see why this evolution was required.

▓ **Note**   Artificial intelligence (AI) and machine learning (ML) are connected. ML evolved out of the discipline of AI. Cognitive computing is a term originally made popular by IBM and is a level ahead of AI and ML.

Artificial Intelligence (AI) and Machine Learning (ML)

Alan Turing was the first person to raise the question "Can machines think?" [Turing, A.M. (1950). "Computing Machinery and Intelligence." *Mind*, 59, 433-460]. He created a test called the Turing Test. This was in simple terms a test scenario in which there are two participants, one man and one machine. The evaluator should interact with both using computer screen and keyboard interfaces, to ensure that the machine is not limited in the test by its incapability of speech. If the evaluator cannot tell the difference between machine and man, the test is successful (Figure 2-1). So, the question "Can machines think?" was raised by Alan Turing well before artificial intelligence as a discipline even started, but this was the fundamental question at the core of AI and ML.

© Rohit Kumar 2017
R. Kumar, *Machine Learning and Cognition in Enterprises*,
https://doi.org/10.1007/978-1-4842-3069-5_2

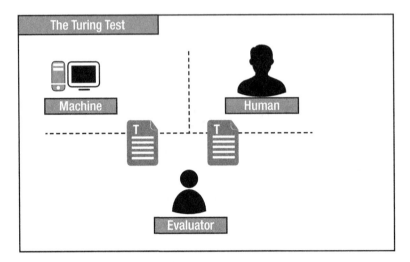

Figure 2-1. *The Turing Test*

Over time, AI and ML (a subset of AI) developed as distinct streams of study. The applications developed out of these applications were toward a more automated facility to do tasks by machines with less manual intervention. This was always thought of as the purpose of these technologies: to take the burden off human shoulders and automate things to have faster turnaround and fewer defects.

Why Artificial Intelligence and Machine Learning?

AI and ML differ fundamentally in that AI is focused more on just the making of intelligent machines, whereas ML focuses on taking this one step further by adding learning capabilities. So, ML talks about intelligent machines that could learn.

AI in any system uses a lot of rules already incorporated in the system; the system evaluates these to perform a response that looks like an intelligent response. So, it can be said that while they may have the appearance of intelligence, AI systems built this way are not actually intelligent.

ML systems are those AI systems which have learning capabilities. Furthermore, deep learning (DL) is a specific type of machine learning concept, a higher order which can learn from far more dimensions of information and combine results to generate an overall highly abstract result set (Figure 2-2). For example, such a system might look at a portion of an image which shows, say, a part of a car window and understand that this is a car. This term is dealt with in more detail in Chapter 4.

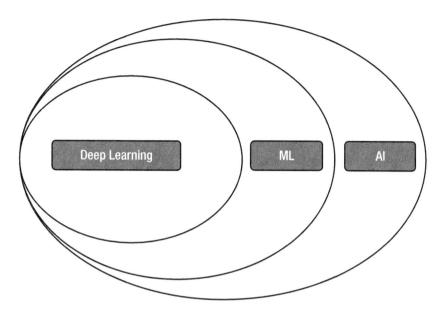

Figure 2-2. *AI, ML, and deep learning*

So, in simple terms, AI has all conditions handled by hard-coded rules, which are responsible for generating exactly the same experiences at all times provided that the same events are used as inputs.

Next, ML is said to be a program A which provides experience E with respect to some class of task T and with some performance P. With E, its performance P increases for task T.

AI and ML are focused on completing specific tasks or activities with limited functions using either preprogrammed scenarios (AI) or with learning abilities using patterns (ML). But they cannot think like humans or other thinking entities (e.g., an AI medical imaging tool might recognize and sort data input as various images into different cancer categories).

In contrast, an ML-based medical imaging system will also over time learn to increase its scope by identifying more new kinds of images and sorting them to predesignated categories by learning.

However, none of these machines could transfer their learning of medical specialization into another field (e.g., interior decorating). The machine is designed to work only in the areas of cancer detection and treatment; it could not help in other subject areas.

Some more prevalent examples could be the Google search engine for ML; not only does the search engine provide the user with AI-based results, it keeps learning people's search patterns and responds accordingly. ML has close proximities in association with statistics.

For more than 60 years, these ML solutions have brought about automation and better results in learning. AI and ML basics are described in detail in Chapters 3 and 4, respectively.

Why Cognitive?

Through AI and ML, we could achieve so many objectives, including smart automation and better and smarter machine responses/results. There are good data mining solutions available for business intelligence using these ML techniques.

Why then was cognitive computing required? If you focus on all that has been previously described here, ML and AI concentrate on the same problem, by reaching out to the solution using preprogrammed learning or extending learning with new experiences to enhance problem solving. But they are limited in the sense of being restricted to the same problem area.

Cognitive computing goes a step beyond in that it simulates human cognition-like behavior. It almost mimics the way the human mind works. Not only can it think using learning already acquired to respond intelligently (AI) or extend its knowledge in that area to solve the problem better (ML), it can identify new problem areas and then propose/build new solutions around them. Of course, it is limited to the knowledge sources it's connected to. But in reality, human cognitive capabilities are also limited in just the same way. So, if access to a new area of knowledge is given, cognitive computation utilizes knowledge from this new source or area as well. And since it has a high level of integration with natural language processing (NLP), it is easier to communicate with and the systems are also able to fill gaps between combining structured and unstructured data.

What it means for medical imaging, apart from just being able to read various images in a better way (ML), is that it could combine the data with medical research journals to understand problems. For example, a CT or MRI scan reading system with thousands of images could make more precise identifications with advanced ML systems, but cognition takes it into a totally new dimension by combining such images and anomalies of that patient with his medical history as compared to similar patients and all the possible medical research in that area. Also, in a weightage–based system where it could work on the question (e.g., what would be the best medicine and dosage for a particular patient), it will not give 5,000 or a million matching responses from some library based on word matches, nor only give a detailed report based on scanned images and some parameters predefined in the system and then provide a list of possible medicines and dosages. Instead, based on assessing a very personalized patient case history, understanding images, and reading all similar treatment repositories and all relevant medical journal articles up to that very moment, it will provide the single most weighted response with some more closely related options and with weightage and reasons. This is the power of cognitive computing: it acts as a tool in supporting the experts in collectively working with them as an enormous cognitive thinking pal.

Cognitive as a concept was already there the moment deep learning and machine learning were thought of. But without what we have now—enormous amounts of digitalized data to train these equally enormous computing capabilities—it was not possible practically to enable this. The gigantic corpus of digital data and the largely connected world helped to achieve this the very moment that massive computation for this enormous structured and unstructured data was possible. On top of that, connected devices and sensor data brought in digitally structured sense data from machines; this form of big data added an essential component to this new dimension.

In terms of our retail example from Chapter 1, it could mean not only training systems on data coming in from stores or various departments, but also mixing in data from various sources like weather, IoT sensors, and news channels to add a new dimension to store and warehouse management.

So, cognitive was a natural progression from AI and ML. This was conceptualized from the day that people first thought to ask "Can machines think?" It is now possible to have an ML system with the capability to run a million or so parameters simultaneously, a digitalized data corpus over Internet/intranet, IoT sensor data, and huge computational capability to bring the cognitive systems onboard as help. For now, IoT data application will remain a more advanced application of cognitive computing.

Figure 2-3 is a generalized representation of machine learning–based systems and how they are related to business processes.

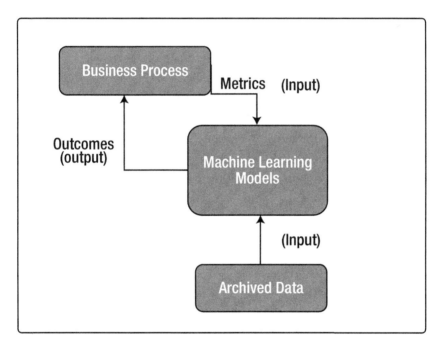

Figure 2-3. *Generalized relation between business processes & Other Data (including IoT feeds) And ML Models*

CHAPTER 3

Artificial Intelligence—Basics

The scope of this book is to build essential knowledge around cognitive computing and its role in influencing business and IT. But cognitive computing knowledge cannot be built up without having basic knowledge of artificial intelligence (AI), machine learning (ML), and deep learning.

Note Basic knowledge of artificial intelligence and machine learning concepts will help provide better understanding of cognitive computing concepts in later chapters.

Overview

The field of AI was born years after Alan Turing's research resulting in the Turing Test for machines. The field was started at a conference at Dartmouth College in 1956; John McCarthy coined the term "artificial intelligence." It was defined to be the field of computer science aimed to develop computer programs or applications which would have capabilities comparable in some way to human cognitive abilities (e.g., speech recognition, visual pattern or image identifications, language translations, natural language processing (NLP), or making inferences in decision-making).

AI was born as a concept too far ahead of the then-available computing capability. This was one reason it has reached to its peak use in only the last few years, from about 2012, when relevant computing capabilities were available.

However, there were earlier AI systems which had nothing like the functionalities of the cognitive methods we use now. These were mostly systems developed to make smart decisions based on knowledge maps and heuristic methods. So, they were relying on smart decisions taken in the direction of the most certain win or success and had nothing to do as such with cognitive methods (the way humans think).

© Rohit Kumar 2017
R. Kumar, *Machine Learning and Cognition in Enterprises*,
https://doi.org/10.1007/978-1-4842-3069-5_3

■ **Note**   Heuristics are also called "rules of thumb." While solving any problem as a human, we follow either procedural steps or some heuristic. The heuristic solution might not provide very optimized solutions, but it may provide a quick fix when needed. For example, you might have gone out in the sun in a new city hotter than yours and walked on the sidewalk to reach a nearby shop: you felt very hot. The next time you go out, you start walking close to walls and buildings to catch the shade. You have just followed a rule of thumb: the closer to the wall, the less direct sun exposure and so the cooler you feel. Similarly, heuristic methods are devised which run on a set of predefined rules, which help reach the solution faster than if rigid algorithm had been followed. So, heuristic models or methods follow a few wise predefined rule sets and reach a conclusion fast. An example was IBM's Deep Blue, which was used to play chess. Even most automated cars use this kind of artificial intelligence. This is also known as "weak AI."

AI systems capable of utilizing high-end ML and other capabilities comparable to human cognition are called "strong AI" systems (e.g., SAP Leonardo).

But weak AI systems are not artificial intelligence in the fullest sense. They are programmed to function in one kind of task with various consecutive options available based on previous input. So, it shifts through every input and finds the best-suited output to complete any action and traces its path toward one of the designated outputs as it is hard-coded to do. This is not how human cognition works.

Goals of Artificial Intelligence

Broadly speaking, AI has two goals:

- Engineering products/applications: This is required to create AI products to solve real-life problems in one or more areas. These products are the physical part of AI and are products used directly by users (e.g., Google search engine or a smart mobile assistant).

- Scientifically representing data: This is an aspect unseen by humans, and works to find ways that data could be processed and analyzed using various models and algorithms. This results in the smart representation of data for business intelligence purposes, creating patterns and graphs out of it (e.g., business insight dashboards).

AI borrows its knowledge from multiple disciplines like psychology, computer science, linguistics, philosophy, neuroscience, mathematics, and social science (Figure 3-1).

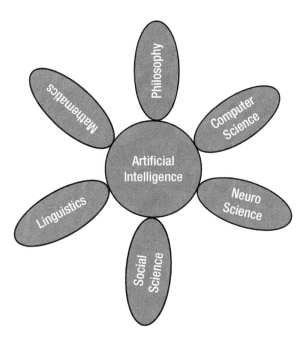

Figure 3-1. *Some AI components*

Components of Artificial Intelligence

AI has the following components:

- Learning
- Sensing
- Acting
- Reasoning and problem solving
- Interpreting language
- Planning

Each of these is explained in some detail in the sections that follow.

Learning

All AI systems are supposed to have learning capabilities at their cores. In weak AI systems, these learning capabilities are inbuilt via 'if-else' conditions of programming; along with rules, weightages and heuristic methods are applied.

In the case of machine learning, the learning capabilities are more prominent.

There are various types of learning:

- Supervised learning

- Unsupervised learning

- Reinforcement learning

Supervised Learning

This includes both "regression" and "classification." Supervised learning has all continuous data sets already present to come up with conclusions using these algorithms. For example, one may use an AI algorithm to decide if someone is suffering from diabetes or not (classification) or what could be price of shops in a certain area (regression).

Figure 3-2 shows an example of classification.

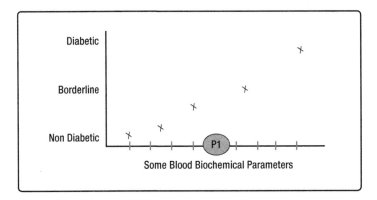

Figure 3-2. *Classification example*

Based on continuous value plotting of some biochemical parameter (e.g., sugar level) on the x axis and categories on the y axis, a graph is plotted. Any value of biochemical parameter is related to one or another category: nondiabetic, borderline, or diabetic patient. If for patient 1 (P1), the values lie at a certain point on the x axis, what is the probability of the patient being a diabetic? That is the job of classification.

This example has two distinct properties:

- Known biochemical value scales are available, and the classifications correspond to them.

- A solution or result is expected in each of the designated classifications. So, discrete values.

For supervised learning, then, the data set has all results available as a training set already, and for classification, the AI must put each data item into one of the brackets based on the logic of its algorithms.

Figure 3-3 has an example of regression.

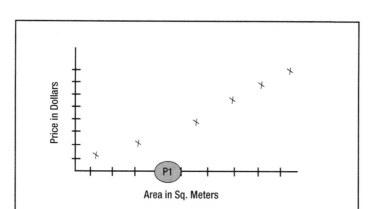

Figure 3-3. *Regression example*

In this example, price in dollars is plotted on the y axis and property area in sq. meters on the x axis. Based on this data, what will be the most probable price of property 1 when it is placed at a certain point on the x axis? This is an example of regression supervised learning.

This example has two distinct properties:

- Both axes have continuous relative values plotted against each other, and an existing set of values (area vs. price) is already plotted in the graph as X.

- The solution is expected for a new point P1; that point could be stretched out to the line created by Xs, and where it touches the line is the value.

Let us talk about these two types of supervised learning through use of a business scenario.

Planning and trend analysis could be executed based on archived and operational nonarchived data using a regression algorithm. For example, based on multiple such algorithms running parallel on sales data, a retail chain can decide the most competitive pricing for the day for products or the number of products on the shelf for certain days of the year.

A classification supervised algorithm may provide what items would qualify best for discounts.

It is possible to have multiple parameters to be run parallel to then tie the results together using weighting algorithms to get the final answer. Now, with high-end computation capabilities available, millions of parameters could run in parallel.

Unsupervised Learning

Unsupervised learning has no measured and/or categorized data preset as in the case of supervised learning. The common method algorithm used is clustering to churn out results. Thus, inputs are available, but based on certain parameters the data sets must be grouped (Figure 3-4).

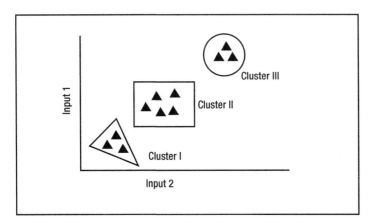

Figure 3-4. *Clustering*

In Figure 3-4, the solid triangles represent various unique data sets. There is no preclassified or quantified relation available as was the case in regression or classification supervised learning, so it cannot be ascertained how the data should be classified or have a result deduced out of it. But in deciding on how data are aligned with respect to certain predecided input parameters, algorithms could still identify clusters or groups of data sets based on their relation with these selected parameters. For example, in Figure 3-4, the triangles are grouped into three clusters around one central tendency with respect to input 1 and input 2 (the two parameters selected).

Business case example: Let us assume that the preceding triangles are amounts received from various customers and that we want to automatically group these customers into clusters based on amount spent and market segment. This will give a per-market-segment slice of customer purchase details.

Reinforcement Learning

This is one step ahead of supervised learning. It's based on the concept of how the output should be changed as input changes. In other words, any agent interacting with any environment keeps adjusting its output in relation to the changing inputs. The agent is not an integral part of this environment and is only interacting with it. Every state of the environment must be acted upon by the agent; the actions will receive a positive or negative feedback (punishment or reward) and thus will try to take a path gradually to maximize benefits by skipping negative feedback paths.

Reinforcement learning in a way mimics biological behavioral learning. There are not always manuals for learning every act (e.g., a kid trying to learn to walk will try, fall, stumble, etc., until with the cognitive feedback he will learn to walk properly). Reinforcement learning works the very same way.

Reinforcement learning has many business use cases in areas of finance, insurance, medical research, and so on.

Business case example: Investment policies could be analyzed with these algorithms to ensure maximum benefit analysis for a certain individual with a certain specific current state (age, remuneration, type of job, etc.) and expected future states.

Sensing

This deals with sensory aspects like visual, tactile, sonar, speech recognition, facial recognition, object recognition, and so on.

At the very start, computing machines were limited to inputs from keyboards only. But now a lot of options are available in terms of various available sensors, providing a full range of sensory perception of almost human quality to machines.

These data from sensors could be utilized in business intelligence reporting as well; for example, a major bank in Europe has implemented reports for its property maintenance including weather sensor–based data from Google. So, it provides not only details of lease renewal or such information but also what natural calamities are predicted for that bank location. This also helps the bank to warn their customers associated with that location to be secure or plan their activities so that they're safely away from the location.

Sensing or sensory detail provides a major contribution in business intelligence, and this comes from the core artificial intelligence branch of study. This is of great importance to machine learning and cognitive computing as well, as discussed in further chapters.

Manufacturing and aviation companies are utilizing these advanced sensor data for maintenance. Any wear and tear on important machine components in any of these industries (a machine in a manufacturing unit or an airplane part) could be monitored in real time, helping in focused and rapid maintenance, saving time, money and even lives.

Acting

Acting or providing required output is again a very important component of any AI system. The result should be output digitally or mechanically. In case of robotics applications, motion and path planning are part of this.

Reasoning and Problem Solving

This is a core component and expected from any AI system. Reasoning and problem solving are not expected from any other kind of computer program. Like in human thinking, every problem area is broken into subproblems and step-by-step action is taken. Concepts from probability are employed. Humans have other ways of solving any problem as well. They can solve it through context, previous learning, and intuition. But AI systems cannot do this unless they are a cognitive AI system. But that too is to a limited extent. Neural networks, sensory capabilities, statistical approaches, and learning systems together try to mimic humans to some extent.

Interpreting Language

AI systems are made to support people in doing designated tasks more efficiently and quickly. So, they should be then able to listen or read what people have stored and respond back to it in the same language medium.

Natural language processing capability is one of the most important for any AI system. The interfaces for natural language processing could be text based or voice/sound based.

A common way for machines to understand language is via semantic indexing. But this also depends upon how much the machine is trained, how much training data is available and how much input data can be stored and quickly processed. So, certain parameters are required: high computation capabilities, adequate (and cheap) storage space, faster Internet (in case an online reference library is needed to understand sound), and smarter algorithms. These capabilities have become more generally available only in this decade, and that's why they've mostly been used from 2012 onward.

Natural language processing is explained in detail further in coming chapters.

Planning

Automated planning and scheduling execution are yet other attributes. AI systems should be able to plan, schedule, and execute as agents in relation to the environment in order to maximize experience and utilization of resources. In a way, this also encapsulates the whole purpose of AI systems. Agents should be able to continuously monitor the world and keep changing the output based on it.

A few years ago, these were mostly used only in mechanical devices (e.g., unmanned vehicles). But such capabilities can be now built even into business intelligence reporting. Using cognitive applications (e.g., IBM Watson), an AI system can decide on its own to send some alerts to a selected group of people based on the current data flowing in from sensors from IoT devices. Based on its capabilities, it could also even plan a repair or remedy and provide the details directly to the users in time. Just using reporting and e-mail, it could not only plan a remedy but even alert and convey the correct steps to the correct people. Based on change-in-inventory critical stock data and sales/supply priority data, the latest business intelligence tools could be brought into place, which changes the production schedule for all orders being executed and results in a real-time report through the dashboard to relevant stakeholders.

Why AI?

Why was AI devised in the first place? Why did we collectively need it or think of it? The purpose was a quest to do more in less time and with fewer errors, and to automate things: to pass them on to be done by machines instead of humans.

AI brings machines closer to human operation but with the following superior properties:

- Quicker
- More accurate in action and decision

- Less error-prone in doing same task

- Always available to work with no need to rest

These were some of the capabilities which were much sought after in order for machines to do tasks as any human could but with superlative or superhuman capabilities. This automation was much-needed for industrial revolutions as well.

These were the most basic building blocks toward conceptualizing and creating AI-driven machines.

So, to get more output in industries including manufacturing, service, entertainment, and many others, we need AI.

Some prominent AI applications apart from industrial robots are Apple Siri, IBM chatbots, Tesla cars (other self-driven cars as well), Netflix (discussed in detail in Chapter 1), Amazon, and Pandora.

But the primary use remains manufacturing, where not only the previously mentioned capabilities are required, but at times, due to the job being too risky to be done by humans, AI-based systems are required. These machines work with the same level of precision every time.

Even though it has always been a worry for some that AI-based machines will completely replace human workers and that such supersmart machines could take over every bit of work from human hands, this is not the case. It might reduce the general workforce to a large extent, but the specialized workforce will always be required. Operators and mechanics to fix such machines will also be new group of workers with a new set of required skills.

As per IDC (International Data Corporation), the worldwide market for AI will grow to $16.5 billion from $1.6 billion in 2017-18, with a CAGR (compound annual growth rate) of 65.2%.

But until we have those supercognitive learning machines available, probably even utilizing the newly invented quantum computing, we have AI machines which are mostly of only narrow intelligence and programmed to do similar tasks only; they are still not even close to human intelligence.

Even advanced computing chatbots like Watson from IBM are limited in that sense. Watson, for example, is extremely advanced in the way it comes up with answers to problems and has applicability even in complex areas like cancer treatment, but it's limited to the training it goes through and updates to its corpus of knowledge for that area. Still, we can say we have not reached such computing capabilities where there could be a Watson which knows literally everything on earth.

However, this is certainly not to create even an iota of doubt about the capability of such technological marvels as IBM Watson or SAP Leonardo.

The quest to do more with less error and tirelessly around the clock led to the invention of AI. Now, the quest to make increasingly human-like machines is taking us toward cognitive machines, which we will discuss in further chapters.

Approaches

As I've mentioned, AI as a discipline is a combination of many subjects like psychology, computer science, logic, linguistics, philosophy, neuroscience, mathematics, cognition science, and social science.

These are some of the prominent areas or subjects connected with the study of AI. If we just talk about these and try to categorize them into two categories, we come up with the following:

- Group A (Nonbiological)

    - Computer science

    - Logic

    - Mathematics

    - Social science (up to an extent, e.g., classification)

- Group B (Biological)

    - Linguistics

    - Philosophy

    - Neuroscience

    - Cognition science

    - Social science (to a greater extent)

As it happens, Group A gives us weak AI and adding from Group B (both quantitatively and qualitatively) takes us toward stronger AI systems.

Based on the preceding arguments, the following approaches are prevalent:

- Symbolic: This is an approach to AI based on the manipulation of knowledge represented in symbols and their structures. All of the relevant meaning is explicit in this syntax-based structure. This uses hierarchical ordered logic and rules to derive meaning and results and is based on IF-THEN approach of written logic on human-readable symbols. The limitation was that it could only work in the scope of logic and symbols hard-coded into it.

- Subsymbolic: This approach was more influenced by human thinking capabilities. The knowledge potential in symbolic was reached once the right level in the hierarchy was reached, but not so for subsymbolic. This approach was inspired by neuroscience and used neural networks. These systems are also internally rule driven, but the level at which a single node result is reached is not the semantic level. However, it derives semantic through a lot of such parallel processing, making it more dynamic and seemingly less hard-coded.

- Logic Driven: This school of thought was driven by John McCarthy. He believed AI should not approach in the direction of human cognition but should rely on logic. Thoroughgoing use of abstract reasoning and problem-solving techniques are the core of this approach.

- Antilogic: This school of thought said that in fields of vision and natural language processing, there cannot be an AI which could work only on preprogrammed logic, however vast it might be. Advocates of this approach call it scruffy or untidy in the sense that it does not follow in the line of disciplined logic-driven AI.

- Machine Learning and Statistics: This approach is relevant to the logic-based neat approach which looks as scruffy as antilogic. The back end has a lot of mathematical models and tools to make it feel the machine is learning new things, but the logic is being modified, optimizing with the new state resulting from additional experience. A lot of statistical approaches are also used to reach out or derive a set of results from bigger sets of inputs received.

- Knowledge Based: This approach was developed at some time in the 1970s, when it was possible to add huge memories into AI-based expert systems. The only thing these systems could do was utilize the massive amounts of data loaded and respond using them. This was possible because of vast storage capacity.

- Cognitive: This is the AI which is inspired by human cognitive approaches. At its core, this holds human psychological and thinking capabilities to do problem solving. We will see this in detail in later chapters.

These could again be summarized into four categories:

- Symbolic Approaches

- Mixed Symbolic Approaches

- Agent-Oriented and Distributive Approaches

- Integrative Approaches

The scope of this book is not to get into the in-depth technical knowledge, but build knowledge toward understanding how current cognitive and other smarter computing aspects are changing the way business intelligence is built and used.

Still, just to do some justice to this topic and close the loop of knowledge, I will explain at a high level the preceding four approaches, and then I will describe a few tools, finally closing with an explanation of this topic from the business user perspective.

Symbolic Approaches

This was also named GOFAI or "Good Old-Fashioned AI" by John Haugeland. This was the primary approach to AI, based on the thought that AI could be built by creating systems which read and manipulate symbols. The symbols were read and processed by 'if-else'-based logic to provide an output. The inputs were also presented to these systems through designated human-readable symbols. This was predominant until the late 1980s. In a nutshell, such systems were AI created using programming languages (conventional) and had 'if-else' statements inbuilt to read and process such symbols into desired outputs.

A common analogy could be a person who does not have knowledge of a certain language. When he wishes to send a letter to his friend in that language, he first writes it in English and then goes to a language dictionary and grammar books to translate it. This person is thus processing the words in English together with dictionary and grammar rules for that language. He is simply processing the symbols to another set based on certain rules (rules of grammar here) and generates output.

So, this is not actual AI and not relevant to solving a clear majority of issues. This was one of the limitations of such systems. These systems were extremely rigid in nature and focused only on a very finely defined problem area.

Mixed Symbolic Approaches

This was a combination of the symbolic approach integrated with biocomputational or sensory abilities.

Mixed symbolic approaches provided a new capability to AI systems of being aware of the surrounding environment as a factor in decision making. After all, most basic human intelligence is supported by sensory inputs. This component in AI machines would make them more human rather than being just logical or mathematical computation engines.

This was an approach bringing AI from era of blackbox to a wider approach. Robots and machines with reinforced learning were created using these concepts (e.g., checkers-playing applications). The moves were decided based on actual real-time actions. The systems started to be built to learn and evolve.

Agent-Oriented and Distributive Approaches

With agent-oriented and distributive approaches, AI went a step ahead by involving the agent-oriented programming (AOP) paradigm. The agents were across a decentralized distributive system where they were programmed. These agents were very crude or primitive as compared to their human counterparts, but their programming was good enough for AI purposes, where the machine has to make decisions in an environment with multiple uncertainties. A good example could be an agent-based manufacturing control system where multiple parameters like task running times at various stages and overall scheduling are dynamic. Another good example could be a supply chain management controlled by such an AI where a lot of variables affect it: weather, road conditions, sudden route change, delivery plan change, etc. The hardware cost and capabilities were favorable for this, as massive parallel computing at lower cost was available by then.

Integrative Approaches

This is far more of a learning-oriented approach, with a concept of learning agents. Various sensory means are there to input state information into the machine. There are action-oriented systems inbuilt, which takes care of the next action toward the output based on all the symbolic and perceived sensory state information. There is an inbuilt learning mechanism which keeps learning the problem-solution pair with time for various event variations for different levels and types of sensory input. The system uses this corpus to bypass the main mechanism and directly use these learnings to act. Any negative response to such learning-based response, however, is also recorded and used to update or fine-tune learning.

The basic architecture of such AI machines was created or formulated to handle most basic operations and then elaborated to cater to a wider range of functionalities. The Soar project was one of the prominent works in this area.

The name "Soar" was originally an abbreviation of state, operator, and result, the basic cycle in AI computation. The concept of universal subgoaling was implemented. This used to start with an input for a goal. This input was supposed to be searched in a wider set of possibilities. Once one such possibility was zeroed out, the state of the environment was accounted for. This was further subgoaled into various subgoals to avoid a bottleneck of a single-output procedural step. Parallel firing of the processes would lead to multiple substate creation and subgoals derived. Recursively, the result process was applied to various such parallel goals, and best-fit solutions were applied. A reward is created and stored for best-case solutions, and this provides learning from the scenario. So, Soar could make the most favorable decisions almost as any wise human might have done, of course for a limited area of specialization.

Natural language understanding is a good business case example. Certain contents on the Web needed to be categorized into certain categories and published on a dynamic news page like Google News. The news channel crawls the Web in real time, analyzes the various contents, and then through a subgoaling process tries to segregate them into different categories. Finally, the news is categorized using the best-case scenario analysis and curated to a certain news category automatically.

This approach is closer to human or biological aspects like those seen in neuroscience and cognition.

Tools

With years of research into AI, some prominent tools emerged for various usages. These are generic in nature and could be part of many AI applications.

Logic Programming

The use of mathematical logic in programming language to create AI is called logic programming. LISP as software and mathematical logic in the form of lambda calculus was used initially to do such programming. Prolog gave rise to various logic programming languages.

Logic programming is a controlled deduction. Backward reasoning is used to determine an and-or tree, and this zeroes in on the solution space. Every condition is tried and tested for success, and once the best-fit solution is reached, it stops. For example, if alive and happy persons have to be listed, the data already present is Mr. A-dancing, Mr. B-sleeping, Mr. C-shouting, Mr. D-weeping, Mr. E-singing; and another set of information is happy (dancing, singing) and alive (dancing, shouting, weeping, singing). Then, the logic programming, upon checking these expression sets, would come back with A and E as alive and happy. It has done nothing but backtracked through all possible reasoning to zero in on the solution space.

It ideally is designed from a top root to multiple nodes and leaves. So, the result derivation from A, B, C, D, and E backtracking to the upper level like sleeping, dancing, etc., to higher level, alive or happy, is difficult to achieve in this kind of programming. But it could be approached further from any node for solving the problem. So, from the top down, we could start from "who is sleeping" or "who is eating" and easily get results, as top to bottom is still being followed. The logic is integrated with control statements to ensure that no undesired deviations happen, as is the case with more complex logic. Say we add relations and gender-related rules into the dataset. Then, if we say happy males, it would skip those branches where it hits a female token at the start and traverse the tree from top down only on the male side, skipping all female branches and individual names. Every branch has leaves or children grouped by and reached as individual choices by an OR clause. Prolog was a little primitive in nature and had no parallel processing capability, but only sequential backtracking was possible with the LIFO (last in, first out) approach.

Automated Reasoning

Closer to psychology and philosophy, this is a technique which helps programs to understand various aspects of reasoning using mathematical models or logic.

Automated reasoning was created to help computer programs reason like humans. The first such feat was "Logic Theorist," a computer program written in the 1950s to mimic human problem-solving capabilities. It was used to prove mathematical theorems from Whitehead and Russell's *Principia Mathematica*. It proved many theorems from the book through its reasoning capabilities. This was the first instance of any thinking machine and was the starting point of strong AI.

Search Algorithms

This is about achieving the possibility of having a good and intelligent search capability from tons of data. Logical reasoning and automated reasoning are included as well for a best-optimized search possibility. Simple symbolic comparison searches are not always very useful for real-life applications. Mathematical optimization concepts are used to reach a good result or good set of results.

The more the context of search is utilized, the more optimized the search will be. A good example could be Google search. See Figure 3-5 for an example.

Figure 3-5. *Google search example*

There are three examples shown in Figure 3-5. All three are search results from Google. The three different search phrases used are "tasty mango," "I wear mango," and "Mango," as shown via results A, B, and C, respectively.

All three provided three distinctly different sets of results based on the context of the search phrase and via the optimization models running on Google servers.

The first phrase, "tasty mango," provides strong context that suggests a fruit or edible mango which is tasty. The word "tasty" gives distinct context about something edible rather than the clothing brand Mango. So, all search results from the first position onward are related.

The second phrase, "I wear mango," provides strong context in the direction of it being some kind of wearable object, and so no result set provides any result related to edible mango, as for the first search phrase.

The third phrase is not really a phrase but just the single word "Mango"; this doesn't provide any context about the object being searched for, so the result set is a mix of results from both the first and second search phrases.

Although there is much emphasis on context-based searching, it has its limitations due to the parameters required for properly optimized search results.

One of the good examples in this area is IBM Watson, where it won the game of Jeopardy using such context-based and cognitive ability–based search capabilities. In addition to mathematical logic and optimization, Watson runs weightage algorithms to come closer to the context and answers with limited results in that area. A good commercial use of this is the Watson-enabled North Face web site (`www.thenorthface.com/xps`).

North Face has thousands of apparel designs available online. Based on some pointed questions, Watson then puts forward a catalogue customized for that customer. This helps not only the customer but also North Face by enabling them to provide the most personalized user experience to the customers.

Artificial Neural Networks

Artificial neural networks consist of artificial neurons or simple units of large neural connections. The artificial neuron is nothing but a mathematical function in the system. The neural network is analogous to the human brain, and single units or artificial neurons are analogous to a single biological neuron. Biological neurons have heads, or dendrites, and distal ends or axons. The artificial neuron, which is a mathematical function, has inputs (one or more) received which represent dendrites, and outputs represent axons. These artificial neurons or mathematical functions are single units of the whole artificial neural network. See Figure 3-6 for an illustration of this similarity. Such systems are trainable, and many complex problems can be solved using such networks. The following are some of the broad areas covered by neural networks: time series predictions, robotics, language processing, pattern recognition, face identification, and so on.

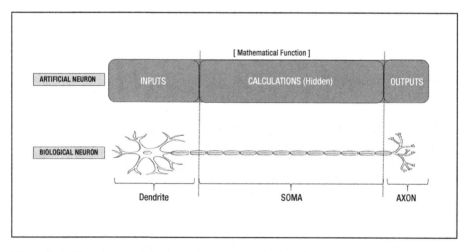

Figure 3-6. *Neural network (schematic representation) and neuron*

Summary

AI was created to automate many functions of business. Primarily, this had applications in factory line automation. With time, it evolved from simple symbolic iterative job machines to more human-like solutions. The human factors were added based on psychology, sociology, and neuroscience. AI moved further to machines designed more on human brain patterns called neural networks. These have units called artificial neurons, which are analogous to biological neurons.

Before we move any further, let us take a short pause and see what lies ahead in the chapters to come. By now, we have reached a point where we have already built the major required background technological knowledge.

So far, we have moved along the journey of knowledge building from BI to AI. Next, we will move on to two smaller but important topics: machine learning and then NLP. This will provide some insight on how these ML and AI machines and beyond use NLP capabilities.

We will then discuss predictive analytics and its business benefits. The chapter on predictive analytics will further connect with the central topic of this book, cognitive computing.

We will dive deep into principles used for such cognitive systems and then we will discuss parallel evolving IT business intelligence systems.

After this, we will talk about how organizations can move toward this transformation, pointing out various roadmaps but also roadblocks. We will further discuss more about these self-evolving cognitive solutions and the path ahead.

This book with all these discussions further intends to put forward views on changing IT scenarios, based on cognitive computing, Blockchain, and so on, which not only will change the IT landscape requirement for businesses, but will also have an impact on IT service firms and how they should operate from marketing-sales to delivery and what changes for consultants.

This book will try to address all these questions further for all three parts of its audience (businesses using these solutions, IT service firms providing these solutions, and consultants that work for them both).

CHAPTER 4

■ ■ ■

Machine Learning—Basics

Taking our AI discussion further from Chapter 3, we will discuss here further a special type of artificial intelligence called machine learning.

■ **Note** The primary audience for this book is business users and higher management (both business corporations and IT service providers). Still, a basic knowledge of artificial intelligence and machine learning concepts will help provide better understanding for cognitive computing concepts in later chapters.

Machine Learning

Machine learning is a special type of AI. This is the ability of machines to learn and work on new problem dimensions without being explicitly programmed to do so. The programs are changed as they are exposed to new data and scenarios.

Machine learning plays a very important role in the so-called industry revolution 4.0.

This revolution is centered around IoT (Internet of Things) and cognitive computing. Machine learning has an important role to play here, as this becomes an essential subcomponent in this ecosystem.

Google and lot of other companies are now even able to provide machine learning as a cloud service. This is in line with preparations to move to the industry 4.0 level: see the various industry generations in Figure 4-1.

© Rohit Kumar 2017

R. Kumar, *Machine Learning and Cognition in Enterprises*,

https://doi.org/10.1007/978-1-4842-3069-5_4

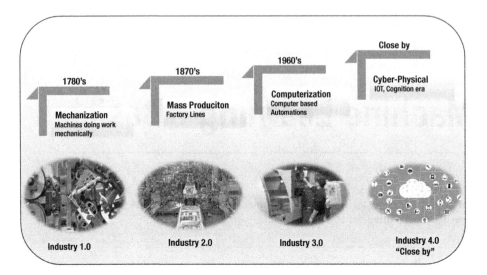

Figure 4-1. *Industry generations*

Machine learning has some similarity to data mining or pattern analysis. These activities help to search through data points to generate outcomes as outputs. So, the primary action for these functionalities is to analyze and understand data and then to use it to comprehend outcomes or outputs for users. Similarly, machine learning also keeps on understanding the data it comes in touch with while processing, but the result of such findings is not an outcome for the user but a continuous process of adjusting and updating the artificial intelligence program.

So, to compare patterns of basic activities between machine learning and data mining, in principle they both sift through mounds of data to get some coordinates fixed at desired outcome points. But the purpose of data mining is to display outwardly the essence of such mining activity with "fixed" outcome purposes and to help users see the patterns found as graphs or tables, while that of machine learning is to internally churn and derive multiple meanings out of it and internally consume it to evolve its algorithm to help optimize or upgrade different output somewhere else.

Therefore, data points consumed by data mining are the ones outputted as result, while in machine learning, the data points consumed might not be same data which is required to be output directly.

For example, rain and soil moisture data from a particular geographic region might be data mined to come up with some trend analysis using data mining, and so the same data is consumed and output, just in a different format as a result. In machine learning, this data pattern and forecasting might be used for running machines based on the weather to run irrigation systems in the most optimized way. So, this data of rain and soil moisture is still being consumed but to optimize the capabilities of a machine running irrigation in fields and influencing a different set of data to get optimized, say, ROI on running such a machine in the most optimized way.

The root of machine learning is in subjects like pattern analysis and various computational learning theories of artificial intelligence.

Tom Mitchell defined it as follows: "A machine learns with respect to a particular task T, performance metric P, and type of experience E, if the system reliably improves its performance P at task T, following experience E" (July 2006 CMU-ML-06-108) [http://www.cs.cmu.edu/~tom/pubs/MachineLearning.pdf].

Machine learning is a field of computer science which takes care of how computers could improvise their programs based on tasks and outcomes and in a way program themselves toward a better output.

Machine learning–based artificial intelligence was a late entrant onto the market, and almost no commercial applications were on the market until the late 1980s.

Some prominent applications available using machine learning now are speech recognition, face recognition, robotics applications, robot chat bots, self-driving cars, and so on.

The machine learning training of software candidates is an area where programming in advance could be difficult or even impossible. You cannot program a machine to learn all expressions of all possible types of faces or patterns of voice. Even if that were possible, it would be cumbersome and time-consuming, and it would come preloaded with a huge volume of program logic data, maybe in terabytes. A better way is to pretrain it to train itself based on certain vectors and then leave it naïve as a baby and allow it to learn for the user(s) using it. This is mostly how these systems work. For example:

- IBM Watson for medical applications can identify details from CT scan results for a patient and provide suggestions using comparisons with all such patients with similar CT scan results and other parameters. This data could be fed in as an example of multiple CT scan reports, and various label markers could be added, but it is definitely impossible to create such data for Watson via programming alone.

- A facial recognition or fingerprint recognition system could be trained to allow only authorized images through the system based on such recognitions.

So, there is a category of data which could be sent only via data labeling and feeding into the system and not by programming, mostly in sensory perception situations like those involving image, sound, or other sensor data. Data labeling means identifying individual data with various vector points to mark it as something unique and discrete and then recording it as learning for the system.

The special characteristics of an individual's voice (in the case of a speech-recognizing system) are extracted from training with the user. These are then repeatedly retrained with the same user, and all information is stored as possible clusters with a designated centroid vector position. This is the training data for the speaker. The extraction happens using digital signal processing (DSP)–related tools. All such user training data are then identified in the system with a unique user ID. The system may accept or reject a sample for testing based on certain thresholds like loudness, clarity, background sounds, and distortions. Finally, the system with all training data is ready with a reference model or template for that user identified via a user ID (Figure 4-2). The more it trains, the more precision it gains. That is the reason Google Assistant on your phone or Microsoft Word requests you to train the system with your voice at least two to three times. So, when the user is being matched on voice invocation, it is nothing but pattern or feature matching happening at the back end with the individual user's template as recorded in the system and identified by a unique user ID.

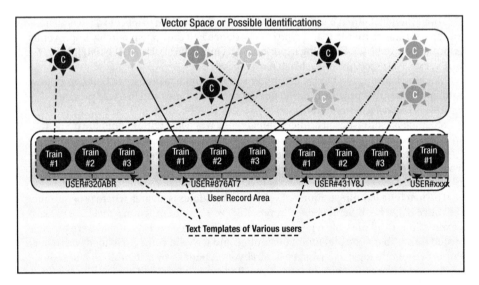

Figure 4-2. *Voice training models*

But there is a limitation: the learning is done according to the provided to that system. It cannot pick up new subjects to create a program related to a new subject area by itself. For example, a person proficient in singing might observe some street dance form over time and learn that as well. It could be willful learning, or he might observe it more passively and still learn it to an extent.

But a machine learning machine expert in cancer cannot just pick up music knowledge and become an expert into it; likewise, a voice recognition system learns voice wavefronts and not image pixels for facial recognition. Since this limitation remains, infinitely learning machines have not yet been created. What we have now is curriculum-driven machines which learn within their subject areas.

Conversely, self-initiated and –supervised learning would involve something like, say, a robot with the job of bringing tea and coffee to those working at a Recording studios also picking up some music lessons from people around by noticing and hearing them sing.

All these concepts are common in human and machine learning concepts. In fact, the latter tries to pick up everything from the former.

Some research says the human brain has one single algorithm to learn; if brain nerve connections from the eyes and ears are cut and swapped with each other at their primary connecting locations in the brain, the swapped locations learn the new perceptions. So, the hearing part of the brain when connected with the optical nerve starts to process the visuals and the vision-related brain now when getting connected with auditory nerves starts to process sounds. This is the basis for neural networks, which are very much a part of machine learning.

Machine Learning Tasks

Machine learning is a type of artificial intelligence. So, the types of learning tasks are as applicable for artificial intelligence and as mentioned in detail in Chapter 3 (supervised, unsupervised, and reinforcement learning)

Based on output, certain additional tasks could be listed. They are as follows:

Classification

This is an operation to predict into classes based on observations made. This is achieved using supervised learning only. So, the classification categories are already in place and well defined. The data so classified could be of any type, be it in normal text format or even images. See the previous example in this chapter on voice template creation for users and the image is Figure 4-2.

The training of the model is done to further classify any data into correct categories. The context of every word is calculated as a probability by the classifying program, and with this probabilistic weightage the whole connected content is moved under or labeled under one such predefined category of classification. The most common applications in this category are spam-detecting applications. Additionally, these applications could also be further trained by the user to identify more types of spam. The user manually designates some mails as spam, and the system further trains itself to use this criterion as well. Google search and Google news also fall in this category.

Clustering

Clustering is an unsupervised task. The inputs are divided into groups, but no predefined classification exists. These groups are called clusters. The clustering could take any of the multiple top-down or bottom-up approaches that are available. The inputs are marked with some values. The clusters are then defined based on all such objects present near or closest to this mean (K-means clustering). Every cluster defined could be related further into a tree, or else all objects may first be considered as a big blob slowly divided into clusters and related with the other clusters as a tree (hierarchical clustering) (Figure 4-3). Online e-commerce shopping applications like Amazon work on clustering principles.

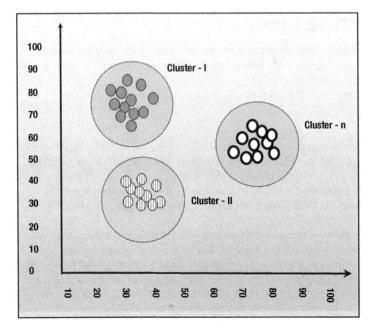

Figure 4-3. Clustering example

The online stores have millions of products in connected inventories for sale on their web sites. There could be two major issues here.

- The products for sale on these web sites could be so numerous at a given point of time that quickly grouping them into correct product groups might become difficult.

- If a user is interested in a specific subtype of product, the method by which the group is determined should be flexible or intelligent enough to help that customer make the purchase.

This is where clustering helps. While uploading details by the seller, there are certain questions asked to have a quick tagging. For example, a supplier might upload a shirt which has details like men's apparel; formal; sizes M, L, and XL; material cotton; and colors red, white, purple, and yellow. Based on these properties (tags) and clustering algorithms, the system automatically registers it under the men's apparel category.

Now if a customer is interested in buying blue formal shirts, the system should be again able to do a clustering of products based on the specific search terms, earlier buying patterns, or clone customer properties (any other customer with a similar pattern, e.g., geographic location, search term language, age, etc.).

There may not be a "blue, men's apparel" category as such. But based on the tagging and smart recommendation and prediction clustering algorithms at the back end, the e-commerce site starts to show relevant products on the screen, and this should increase user satisfaction and sales.

Regression

This is a supervised task. The relationships between mean values of multiple outputs are compared, and corresponding values for other connected outputs are predicted linearly. Training data is used to predict (regression) using statistical analysis. A famous example is predicting house prices from related training data. It does not group objects as clusters around mean values as seen in clustering or classify them under different labels as seen in classification; instead, it predicts values for individual candidates (Figure 4-4).

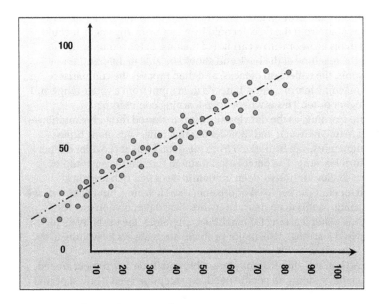

Figure 4-4. *Regression example*

Connected Key Concepts

Machine learning has many key concepts associated with it. These could be considered as approaches to machine learning and are applied to achieve machine learning solutions. Some of them are described in the following sections.

Deep Learning

This is also known as deep machine learning (DML). Artificial neural networks (discussed in Chapter 3) with multiple hidden layers, when studied together with algorithms, are called deep learning or DL.

A quick differentiator between machine learning and deep learning could be an example of image recognition. It could be both, depending upon what is required. Imagine that there is a factory-based robot whose purpose is to learn and stop defective parts from going to the packaging unit. It has some sort of image variations and original expected images fed into its system. This robot could use a full mug shot of every article finished and running on the factory line and quickly do a comparison to see whether it's defective or not. These machines could do this with extreme speed and accuracy. This is classic machine learning.

Now let us look at another example: in a crowd, moving trucks, buses, cars, cycles, cats, dogs, and people are all there together. The requirement is to only find people's faces and compare them with the mug shots in a database of criminals to see if someone is fleeing the law and then to arrest that person immediately. This has other challenges apart from those the previous example had.

In this case, there is no specific image or images that could be captured with calibrated focus adjustments and arrangements; it could be a lot of things captured in the surveillance cameras apart from the face. It could be a face from any angle; it could be a man with a big cat in his arms or with a cart full of melons. Before comparing the face and the mug shot, the machine at the back end should be able to differentiate from continuous exposures, the collection of faces, and then process the comparison exercise. This is where machine learning fails. It needs data input from a wider range and processing of a much higher order. This is where deep learning comes into play.

DL is more in-depth learning, as the data learning is transferred through a multilayer artificial neuron–based neural network, and thus deeper meaning, with many times more variables and components, can be derived from the data. Thus, it provides deeper understanding and in turn learning. The percolation through this multilayer complex neural network can turn shallow or not-so-deep input into deep and rich learning.

This could be used for either supervised or unsupervised learning, but the best usage is for unsupervised learning, as this deep neural network–based percolation provides richer inferences and thus richer learning for machines. Therefore, the usability factor fits more with unsupervised learning. Also, major problem areas always lie waiting in the unsupervised area.

In simple languages, multiple dimensions of possible details on any subject are fed into the system, and then the system can get the needed perception even if only a partial dimension of information is available. This is the technique behind face recognition systems used around the world (one recently in the news is that being used in the Gold Coast by Australian federal police in preparation for the Gold Coast Commonwealth Games 2017). An array of CCTV cameras will be using such algorithms to capture facial images of people in the crowd; in turn, their facial features will be mapped, measured, and compared with terrorist image databases.

So, the deep learning machines are a step ahead of machine learning machines. The machine learning applications start to fail when the dimensionality of the information becomes too high. In other words, the more complex the problem, the more it becomes dimensional. Deep learning, which uses neural networks to help it break the problem's dimensions into various abstraction layers and then to solve them one by one, combining the result at the highest abstraction layer, is used for all of these applications.

Facial recognition from partial face images and being able to detect a known terrorist in a crowd is a problem too complex and multidimensional to be solved by machine learning. It has so many dimensions: the edges to understand that this part captured in the image is a nose, partial lips, and some part of eye or some other combination of facial features captured. There are dimensions of skin color, skin texture, eye color, proportion of the eye or nose to face, and so on, along with everything related to movement of muscle stretching it while laughing or even full-face details of people to be compared with. The neural networks help here.

The neural networks follow the Markovian hidden model concept and have an input interface, an output interface, and in between multiple hidden layers. Every layer processes a different dimension; then, all of them are combined using mathematical models to come up with an output result at the highest possible abstraction level, and the face is recognized.

See Figure 4-5 to see the same example there.

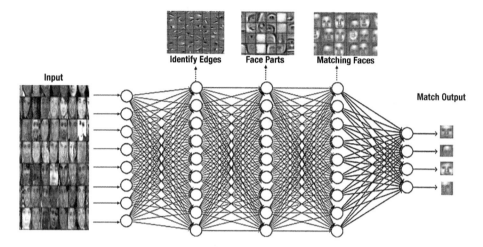

Figure 4-5. *Example of deep learning*

The figure shows a neural network with multiple hidden layers in between. The input and output layers are at both ends. The feed of images from cameras is entering from input, and then every layer of the neural network is processing the various properties and goes to higher abstraction layers with increasing closeness in terms of output or the reach toward the resolution. The first layer looks at the various edges and contours of images and then tries to resolve them as understanding of face parts in the next layer, which is a higher layer of abstraction. The next layer then matches these identified attributes with the database images and could differentiate faces from background in the original images and compare them easily with the database images, identifying, say, four people from the database as matches in the crowd.

This is how deep learning works, as shown in one very famous and simple example.

The deep network combines the various simple networks doing multiple simple tasks together with increasing levels of complexity of result, and then formulates the result. This could be very thick in terms of the number of layers in real-life applications, considering the dimensions of information that need to be processed.

Genetic Algorithms

These are algorithms that mimic the biological genetics theory of natural selection. Where biological theories talk about various crossovers and mutations of genes for a sustainable species, these algorithms use heuristic concepts to find better solutions. The genetic algorithms have genetic factors for calculations and success parameters to judge the success of each possible variation hypothesized and simulated. Machine learning algorithms use these to optimize their efficiency, and genetic algorithms are refined using machine learning.

Decision Tree and Association Rule

Machine learning uses data mining like computation to get the most structured learning to improve its program. So, decision trees are exactly like data mining decision trees. These trees are helpful in predicting solutions better and structuring data for learning even in unsupervised learning.

By comparison, the association rule helps machine learning machines to create combined learning from deducing associations in data and further bringing combined learning out of the scenarios to add more complex and effective changes in programs.

Bayesian Network

There are two major problem focus areas in engineering, and managing both together is a challenge always: complexity and probability or uncertainty. This could be modeled using graphical modeling and random variables in Bayesian or belief networks. This graphical model is a combination of smaller graphical components. Each smaller component is a representation of a smaller subset of the whole problem. Graphical models have always been considered the most intuitive way of representation by humans. This makes it a more interesting subject for artificial intelligence and machine learning areas. Bayesian networks could be simple or even dynamic.

Speech Recognition

These applications are unique in a way; they're shipped and then trained afterwards by users. Speech recognition isn't something which can be preprogrammed to recognize all speech patterns; Instead, it must be trained for the use of specific users. Even aside from regional accent differences, all people produce slightly different sounds when pronouncing the same word. With more than 6,900 living languages across the world and even with thousands of dialects in just one country or region, it is impossible to have the software to be trained in advance in all these. It is again the physical configuration of the person that influences how he or she speaks that language in that dialect, and this of course makes it much more complicated.

Even this would have been impossible to do: just consider the amount of training data needed to put into this. For instance, imagine a smartphone coming with 50GB or even 1TB of data preloaded just to have a training content for such a voice recognition system.

All this combined makes the speech recognition task a perfect candidate for machine learning, where a system based on preset training and rules is shipped and then does its training with the specific user to interpret his voice.

Biosurveillance

Many countries globally now use machine learning for biosurveillance of hospitalization data to understand admission patterns for many infectious diseases. On the basis of already understood patterns, the system detects any anomalies. This helps in the setup of biosurveillance to help stop the spread of such diseases.

Machine Learning vs. Statistics

The similarities and differences between machine learning and statistics have long been a topic for debate. Some people refer to them collectively as the statistics of computer science, while others prefer to consider them as two distinct areas based on origin: statistics coming from mathematics and machine learning from computer science (artificial intelligence).

Both machine learning and statistics work on data to derive patterns and churn out some meaning.

One major difference is that while statistics looks for data with a predefined pinpoint to discern any number of tendencies, machine learning must jump into a complete new data scenario and deduce meaning out of it. But if we consider that machine learning is an application for one just subject specifically, then this is equivalent to predefining data pinpoints as seen in statistics.

To explain this: say the machine is primarily designed to respond to problem A. Over time, the machine develops some new learnings about the environment and starts to develop meaning out of it. More specifically, let's say that the machine was required to bring a glass of water or cake or an apple from the kitchen to some user's desk in a specific room, and the user says "bring water [or cake, or an apple, etc.] to my desk." Now, the user has moved to other side of the desk and calls by saying "bring water to the other side of the desk." This will require adjustments in the path. Subsequently, when the user calls for cake or an apple by using the phrase "other side of the table," the machine will know that it must go to the other side and thus will calculate its path of travel to take it there. The machine has learned. But consider the scenario in which a natural and normal statement is made. This statement could be made in any number of tones, styles, and other variations by the same user or a different one, and yet all would mean the same thing: bring water to my table. This works at the back end exactly the same as statistical analysis, and the mean value of weightage of statements for the same scenario is being used. The learning curve brings in nonstatistical behavior by shifting the central mean to another locus, where again its multiple variants with same meaning at the other side of table would be there. So, for the same situation and to understand that routine input, it works in a statistical pattern, while a new one is to be generated for new learning and it must deviate from that basic behavior to be able to generate new training data which could be stored further.

There is also interrelation between these two. Statistics has given means to machine learning for it to write algorithms, while statistics has also gained from machine learning usage.

One very nice representation of the relationship between statistics and machine learning can be seen in a publication from SAS (http://blogs.sas.com/content/subconsciousmusings/2014/08/22/looking-backwards-looking-forwards-sas-data-mining-and-machine-learning/).

Statistics is only concerned with data points or results coming out of the data set under consideration, while machine learning has a purpose to generate further meaning out of it and use it to upgrade its program and in turn the complete system.

So, it is very difficult to come up with a conclusion no matter whether both are the same, one is a subset of the other, or they are complimentary to each other.

In my opinion, statistics, a well-established subject for hundreds of years, is more into pure mathematical modeling or deduction of data for various sets of data. It is a tool to play with data. It is said to be a branch of mathematics dedicated to collection, analysis, interpretation, presentation, and organization of data.

On the other hand, machine learning a newer field of computer science, or rather a sub-branch of artificial intelligence, and uses most of the techniques of statistics to solve its purpose of inferring meaning out of data given to it through various means. So, the end stage for a machine learning application is to get data organized through statistics and then also to make some conclusions in the form of learning. This is then used to create changes in programs or to create new ones based on rules to do so.

However, statistical methods could also do lot of analysis using various machine learning applications to generate relations or test such relationships.

In other words, they are complimentary to each other. But machine learning is based on (some part of) statistics, but the reverse cannot be true.

Also, machine learning is not only statistics. It is lot of other subjects also combined to come up with such a solution.

Business Use Case Example

Netflix is one good example of this. The Netflix Prize is one of the famous competitions in this area; its purpose is to understand how user data could be utilized to train the system in predicting user choice in advance and propose the most probable options to them.

Even part from the publicity from the competition itself, it was a very smart business idea to have a competition or challenge brought onto the market using sample data. By paying $1 million to the winning team, they had paid only to for the winning idea and saved themselves many hours by having multiple teams research all the options and select the most relevant and suitable. So, it became a very low-cost affair relative to going only to a selected team in house for the same purpose. Also, the restrictions of knowledge reach-out were overcome due to this. Anyone who is eligible and could think of something could compete, removing all limitations to work only with people selected via recruitment limitations.

However, there was one problem: there was a lawsuit filed against them for disclosing private/confidential customer data to third parties without any prior consent.

But to return to our business use case topic, let's look at how Netflix runs on an extremely advanced recommendation system. The bases for this system are as follows:

- People are unique and every single person using the same subscription in a household is unique.

- People respond positively by liking a solution or service when it provides them with favorable solutions.

Netflix wanted this kind of machine learning solution for its viewers. Starting off as a store-based DVD movie supplier, they had moved to being a completely web-based business.

The biggest shift in this from a client interaction perspective was the missing store-level personal touch. Even though the library was so immense by now, a store-based service might still have advantages in helping individual customers select the right stuff, since it was still possible to interact with or even know a customer personally to recommend something relevant for them.

But the online store environment at times works as a black box from this perspective. You come to know who liked what if the customer provides feedback and again if the customer hits the right content by searching and browsing through the sea of content and multiple genres.

This was the problem solved by Netflix: to deliver content even better than they might have done in store with the human touch.

The system was designed from the get-go so that it would recommend the right stuff to people based on their prior interactions and on rule-based recommendation algorithms.

So, a smart system would need to make recommendations based on the actual person from the household who is using that subscription; that is why Netflix recommends adding individual subusers from the household to the subscription account.

Not only the videos but even the trailers for movies are handled that way. For instance, one person might be interested in watching war movies, and another in the same family would rather watch comedy more; in such cases, trailer versions shown to each might differ by emphasizing the more interesting factor for him or her.

So, this takes care of everything from TV serials to movies to trailers that are to be recommended and presented to individual users as per their choice.

This is all within the scope of machine learning. The system algorithm was first designed in the Netflix Prize. At one time, the algorithm was designed for a smaller set of data; about 100 million user ratings. It was then recreated to accommodate billions of records. Once the system was ready with this algorithm and trained with this data, a baseline intelligent system was ready. This was based on understanding these customers and getting inferences from this learning to make recommendations for other customers, even new ones.

Over time, this system learned from both perspectives. One perspective is of the overall preferences of the various customers, and this is to help make recommendations even for new customers when it has not started training itself about their preferences. The other perspective is more of a continual and complete learning process to identify the preferences of existing customers to be able to recommend relevant content to them.

This is how machine learning works: getting trained via data to be able to create outputs more and more preferable to that event and in this case to individual customers or members using this subscription at home.

■ **Note**   As we saw in Chapter 1, Netflix went a step ahead and started producing movies based on such choice patterns. Based on customer base matrix and their choices, Netflix could understand in advance or predict what kind of story and which artist combination might give a superhit program cocktail. The result was a show like *House of Cards*.

The genres for content were also divided into subgenres. This was required to be able to make recommendations with the benefit of additional parameters. For example, a single genre like comedy was divided into subgenres like

- Dark comedies (e.g., *Look Who's Back*)

- Mockumentaries (e.g., *People Just Do Nothing*)

- Political comedies (e.g., *War Machine*)

- Sports comedies (e.g., *Chalk It Up*)

- Satires (e.g., *Tropic Thunder*)

There are about 12 such categories in comedy itself. So, Netflix broke every genre into subgenres to fit every subtype of viewer identified and recommend relevant stuff to him or her.

The recommendation system is such that it takes care of recommendations based on preference and popularity. Popularity, though, is in some senses just the opposite of preference, since it refers to something being watched because one likes it only, rather than because others are watching. But this important factor too is counted while training the system for that individual from a group or category, as ascertained by machine learning algorithms.

It also takes care of users' social data to see what is popular among the users' own networks.

So, Netflix is a well-running and successful example, and a model like theirs is my personal choice, since its lets organizations not only to successfully implement it and reap its benefits but also to bring in a new era in the entertainment industry: a shift from the physical CD/DVD renting business to online content streaming.

CHAPTER 5

Natural Language Processing

Taking our discussion further along from Chapter 4, on machine learning basics, we will discuss here the next topic: natural language processing, or the way machines and computers process and understand natural (human) languages.

Note   This chapter presents an overview of natural language processing and its associations with artificial intelligence and machine learning. The purpose of covering this relatively smaller topic is to gain a good understanding about interaction media and methods in human encounters with machines.

Natural Language

The kind of language which evolved over time and is used by people is called natural language. These languages are not developed under any premeditated plan or project but instead evolved with continuous usage; over the years, and with repetition, many changes were ingrained. Such a language is native to a certain group of people using it and is the most natural way of communication for them (e.g., Hindi, English, etc.). There could be dialects as well for a natural language based on its geographic location. Natural languages came about first of all in the form of speech, but writing or script also developed for most of them.

Note   The Toda natural language of Nilgiri tribes in India does not have an associated script.

© Rohit Kumar 2017
R. Kumar, *Machine Learning and Cognition in Enterprises*,
https://doi.org/10.1007/978-1-4842-3069-5_5

Natural Language Processing—Overview

This section presents a field of computational linguistics and artificial intelligence that deals with language processing by computers. This field of study is about how machines/computers process natural language commands, whether written or verbal, and then engage with any action as requested. The output should be through written or voice response in natural languages.

Since the 1950s, when Alan Turing published his work "Computing Machinery and Intelligence," natural language processing started to evolve as a subject. The whole purpose was to have a machine automatically doing actions that previously humans would have done, with more accuracy and speed—but also could interact with the user in natural languages. The very first moment that the seeds were sown for artificial intelligence, or a human-like machine, the communication perspective or natural language processing perspective was already expected.

A machine in a Turing Test is successful if the user has difficulty in differentiating whether he or she has communicated with a human or a machine. This is highly effective if the communication modes followed by both the human and the machine are in sync, and both are talking in the same language. So, if you are chatting with a chatbot at the other side, it's more convincing if the chatbot has enough intelligence to answer your questions and good and seamless natural language processing capabilities. In simple words, seamless communication is a must. Intelligence could be lower as that could be the case for real human support as well, but communication is a must for good machine-to-human interaction.

A machine should be able to make meaning and context out of the sentence input to it in a natural language and should be able to respond or output communication similarly and seamlessly in natural language.

So, this is about machines being able to listen, perceive, and respond using natural languages or capability being integrated in machines to achieve the same.

The initial works were very basic and ran simple and fixed rule sets. But with the rise of machine learning in the 80s, there was a revolution in natural language processing as well. So, if we compare both scenarios, it is like a person sitting behind a curtain and passing translated slips back to the person requesting based on his own memorized knowledge of language. This is equivalent to machine learning machines that have fixed rules. The knowledge fixed via rules (if-else) itself is a limiting factor. But on the other hand, if a person has access to a library and thus can translate anything back referring to the books there even if he originally didn't have that knowledge; this is an example of higher-degree machine learning. The learning capability is not limited to the rule sets fed into it, but with new inputs it could create new associations in its algorithm and generate new program parts to upgrade itself, the very same way our person in this example is upgrading his knowledge by reading books required further to translate languages out of his actual knowledge area.

Decision tree algorithms started to mimic the initial fixed-rule translation algorithms. The decision tree algorithms were nothing but graphical representations of fixed rules and their translation into mathematical models to recreate the logic steps mathematically. These are still part of algorithms in most cases but are intermediate tools and not the only ones.

Then came some new computational theories, including probability theories such as Markov's model.

In a nutshell, Markov's model says that in a probabilistic dynamic environment where a precise inference cannot be made about a future state, the future state depends upon the current state and not on any stages or events that happened earlier. But all the states are hidden.

So, the important aspects covered here are the following:

- We take into consideration an environment which is stochastic in nature, which is the case in the real world. Every action is part of bunch of multiple possible actions.

- Like mentioned in previous point, as this is a dynamic-probabilistic environment, no inference could be made in advance with absolute certainty about the next action, so it's a black box in a way for the next possible state or action.

- The current state and actions applied are connected. The action applied is in relation to the current state and for reaching to a next stage, so the current state decides the next stage and mostly not on the basis of any previous states.

- All states are hidden until they are achieved.

Language processing always needs one or another form of Markovian model to be used.

The various voice waveforms in case of speech recognition have multiple voice vectors generated, and the probabilistic model using the Markovian hidden model then determines what could have been possibly spoken. A single word could be broken into smaller sound vectors, and with the highest probability of inferring the meaning of that vector via the highest-probability possibility, the right path from start to end state may be taken; the probabilistic model discovers or reveals the overall sound path to decide the placement of the sound into a particular word pronunciation area. Please refer to the details and Figure 4-2 in Chapter 4 regarding speech recognition voice template generation for multiple users.

When we command Google Assistant to dial a number and call a name, all these activities happen at the back end from differentiating between two names and putting the correct one on; however, this happens only with as much accuracy as the system has been trained to with that particular user's voice. This is done using machine learning capabilities by training the system for a specific user's voice waveform.

Later, more complex statistical models were created by IBM. The Georgetown Experiment by IBM is famous in this regard.

■ **Note**   The Georgetown Experiment was a famous experiment done by IBM in collaboration with Georgetown University. In it, Russian was translated into English at high speeds for the first time by IBM's then-famous vacuum-tube-based 701 computers.

NLP and Machine Learning

Taking the story further, natural language processing with time started to use many formats of statistics and machine learning algorithms to ensure growth in this area of computer science.

Part-of-speech tagging was one of the main concepts.

Taking English, for example, there are nine parts of speech:

- Nouns

- Pronouns

- Verbs

- Articles

- Adjectives

- Adverbs

- Interjections

- Conjunctions

- Prepositions

But for computational linguistics, there could be tagging for even 100 parts of speech to bring out context from English sentences.

This tagging would help machines understand the difference between sentences like "This is mine" and "The boy works in a mine." The word "mine" is a possessive pronoun in the first sentence and a noun in the second. This understanding is not only achieved by parts-of-speech tagging; some other techniques are required as well. They are mentioned further in this chapter.

Parts-of-speech tagging was developed over time into a massive corpus of knowledge to be used for machine linguistics. A combination of parts-of-speech tagging and Markovian hidden modeling was also used.

So, the big corpus of such parts of speech, together with Markovian models, would help machines to determine the path to be taken for understanding the real meaning in the context of a sentence.

These corpora of real-world examples, together with statistical tools like Markovian hidden modeling, were used with machine learning techniques to train machines to understand and learn language better.

These machine learning algorithms would now refer to the corpora of parts-of-speech associations and, together with statistical and probabilistic methods, would do a weightage analysis to achieve better natural language processing.

Together with clustering algorithms (clustering is discussed in Chapter 3), the machine learning algorithm would be able to determine the most relevant set of data from the corpus of parts of speech and then would know to proceed further in a certain direction.

The more the system gets data, the more it gets trained over time. Many massive corpora like this have been created; one example is Brown Corpus compiled at Brown University.

A robot that could go from point A to B and pick up a glass and return using artificial intelligence became a machine learning intelligent robot which could even overcome hurdles between A and B to pick up and return a glass. But with natural language processing capabilities, this robot could take verbal commands like "fetch a glass of water" instead of needing a button to be pressed or some similar manual input. This is the power of the potential combination of AI+ML+NLP (artificial intelligence + machine learning + natural language processing).

Just as a combination of machine learning and natural language processing brought machines into a new age, machine learning was also helping natural language processing to evolve.

With the advent of deep learning, it has become easier for natural language processing to complete more complex tasks of language processing.

The statistical approach had its own limits, but together with Markovian hidden modeling supported by machine learning and later by deep learning, it reduced the fail rate to a large extent.

How NLP Works

Though the purpose of this book is not to get into technical details of technologies too much, we still need to understand some basic core concepts at a high level to reach out to our core topic of the book, cognitive computing (and we are close to it now).

The natural language processing machines must deal with multiple aspects of language to come up with a final output or understanding, be that written (text input) or vocal (voice inputs).

Some of these are the following:

- Phonetics (sounds of words and letters)

- Segmentation based on morphology of word

- Syntax rules

- Semantics

- Pragmatics

We won't get into too much technical detail about how these are implemented; instead, in the sections to come, let's look at an overall summary of how language processing happens.

Words and Letters First

Understanding the sounds of letters and their composite formation into words is the first step. Unless these are not resolved into what they actually were and sent toward the NLP system, nothing further could happen. Phonetics is the study of the structure, recognition, and classification of sounds made. The elements of phonetics are not only understood by sound but also by context in an NLP system. The sound might be similar but context helps to zero in on which one to select.

Single phonemes are easier to detect. The sound wave for a single phoneme is easy to map, and all possible resultant waves for that specific phoneme are already well-identified.

But understanding a word in a sentence is far more difficult.

A word in a sentence should be first understood distinctly and then categorized as one of the designated parts of speech for further processing. In cases of speech, it must be figured out from the overall waveform of a sentence via various segmentation models. The speech segmentation helps to cut these waveforms into pieces which are equal to a single word unit. This is difficult, as in spoken language there is a one single waveform for one or more sentences.

Breaking up sound waves is a high-order probabilistic operation called segmentation, which breaks the complete waveform of the sentence into various words, using not only the morphological sound of the word identified but also the context. I will discuss morphology a little later at the end of this section.

The context of a word is a very important aspect. Say there are two sentences: "Mr. E. Hunter is dead now" and "Mystery Hunter is dead now." These make almost identical waveforms which are very difficult to distinguish.

Take another example. "I bought this rabbit fur coat from the sweatshop"; the word "sweatshop" rhymes with the word "pet shop" as well. But then a context-based understanding ensures that we are talking here about the "fur coat" made up of rabbit, and so it should be sweatshop and not pet shop.

Another aspect of speech recognition is to understand the morphology of the words. When learning a language, people learn the vocabulary of that language. But vocabulary, which is made up of words, also has morphological characteristics. The words are not only known by their literal meaning but also through relational knowledge coming from similar usage. Let me explain by a simple example. The word "blue" (pronounced as /blu:/) means a color between green and violet in rainbow. But "blueish" means something with a blue tinge. Now consider any color you might add the "–ish" suffix to: it will mean a tinge of that color. Even if a new color, zup, is discovered tomorrow, zuppish would mean zup in tinge. This is the morphological understanding of language (i.e., how the words are formed and how relationships are established among them). This is also utilized in NLP to understand words.

Sentences Come After

After correct category tagging for words, now a right inference from the whole sentence must be found. The sentences "Time flies by quickly" and "The eagle flies by rapidly" should be able to be distinguished via inference, and it should be understood that time is not a type of bird. Terms like synonyms and polysemic words are important here. It takes care to understand the right meanings of words in the context of whole sentences and also to understand if a synonym is used. Word sense disambiguation (or WSD) techniques/concepts are used to solve this problem. A wordnet is performed to understand the correct inference of a sentence. Thus, the correct meaning has to be considered.

Web sites like `www.conceptnet.io` and `http://wordnetweb.princeton.edu/perl/webwn` are interesting in that they show how NLP functionality breaks down the various meanings of a word which is polysemic and traces the correct meaning using weightage.

An example could be the word "Dash." The wordnetweb web site provides details as shown in Figure 5-1 about this polysemic word.

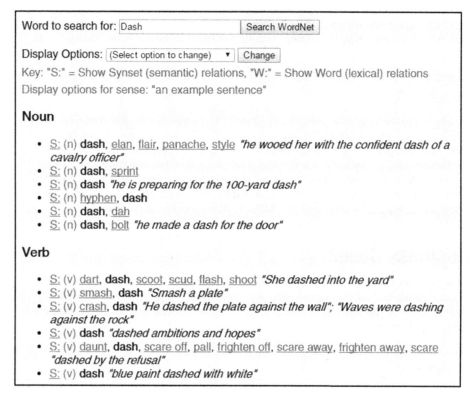

Figure 5-1. *"Dash" on wordnet*

Similarly, a search on conceptnet would reveal what a word could mean in different contexts. "Dash" here would have many headings of categorizations, some of them as shown in Figure 5-2.

Figure 5-2. *"Dash" contexts on Conceptnet*

Each example listed in the "dash is a type of..." category leads to a different subcategory of information, in turn leading to a different possible meaning of the sentence in the context in which it is used.

This is how natural language processing happens and how words are used in determining the overall meaning and context of a sentence by using various algorithms and Markovian hidden models. Deep learning machines make this easier and less time consuming.

Pragmatics

Pragmatics follows this as a type of revalidation of the whole meaning or context to be derived from the sentence. For example, A says to B, "You are a good man; you can do this." Now after the whole inference using all the techniques mentioned earlier, the processing machine should correctly tell if B is being appreciated or this is just A being sarcastic. Or take a sentence like "John saw Kelvin with spectacles." Does this mean, "John used spectacles to see Kelvin" or "John saw that Kelvin was wearing spectacles"? This area is important, especially in applications like text analysis and sentiment analysis.

Business Cases

Now let us talk about some business cases where this is used. I am sure that in this world of smartphone and Internet connectivity and devices, NLP is no longer an alien word. But just to follow the general trend of this book, I'd like to mention some of the prominent uses or applications.

Chatbots

This is one of the most important applications used nowadays, and it relies heavily on natural language processing. IBM Watson chatbots are worth mentioning. These take support services (technical mostly) to the next level. With the smart answering capabilities of Watson and the chatbot interface on top, organizations can see huge savings by implementing it.

These chatbots could respond to individuals just like any human chat support or technical support would have done, and with proper training corpus it could resolve lot of issues just as human support might have done. Moreover, this is done rapidly and tirelessly.

There are some other famous chatbots like Mitsuku, Baidu-Melody, and Duolingo available online.

Spam Filters

Mail spam filters also are natural language processing applications. The false-positive and false-negative detection of words could save a good e-mail from being counted as spam just because of a few words mentioned in it; in other cases, a spam could be so intelligently written that it might by pass the filter by not using any word pattern present in it. So, this smartness of the mail spam filters comes from their natural language processing capabilities.

Sentiment Analysis

In the world so well connected online and with a huge presence on social media platforms, it has become very important for companies to tap sentiments flowing around about them and their products or services. The quicker any negative response is caught, the quicker damage control can happen. This is the core of marketing and customer relationship management nowadays. With a lot of tools doing this for companies, worth mentioning would be SAP business objects data services text and sentiment analysis capabilities and SAP Hybris marketing solution. These are pioneers in gauging individual customers' sentiments and finding social media–distributed messages with such sentiments.

This is required not only for damage control, but to measure the effectiveness of marketing investments as well. This could also help to conduct precisely targeted marketing campaigns, again increasing return on investment (ROI).

Natural language processing also helps here in differentiating between false-positive and false-negative statements.

Search Engines

Search engines like Google and many others are among the foremost of these highly popular applications. In Chapter 3, we saw an example of how the Google search engine understands the context of three different statements and provides relevant search results.

Question Answering

IBM Watson won the game of Jeopardy in 2011 by competing against former winners Ken Jennings and Brad Rutter.

This is just an example of question answering. Nowadays, there are lot of such devices or applications which could provide single weighted answers to problems instead of providing a host of answers like any search engine. Of course, this is not something wholly owned by the natural language processing domain, but it has a major role in understanding the question sentence and coming up with single most weighted answer.

Summary

Now that we've reached the end of the chapter on natural language processing, the only technical topic remaining is predictive analytics. This will take us right up next to the main topic of this book, cognitive computing.

The knowledge gained up to this point and additional knowledge about predictive analytics will equip us very well to be able to understand the concepts of cognitive computing.

Once that's done, we can start diving deep into various aspects of cognitive computing and show how it will be the major game-changer in industry.

■ ■ ■

CHAPTER 6

Predictive Analytics

The subject matter of this chapter continues on from artificial intelligence, machine learning, and natural language processing. Now we will discuss predictive analytics, which uses all of these to predict valuable information from both present and historical data sets.

■ **Note**   We already have discussed artificial intelligence, machine learning, and natural language processing in the last three chapters. This is prerequisite knowledge in order to discuss predictive analytics. This chapter talks about technical aspects and then business use cases.

Overview

Predictive analytics is a form of advanced prediction system which comes up with highly probabilistic, intelligent, and relevant pinpoint predictions for a business case or focused area utilizing both current and historical data.

It is a branch of study which uses techniques like artificial intelligence, machine learning, statistical and other mathematical models, data mining, data modeling, text analytics, and sentiment analysis.

The predictive models are nothing but mathematical models applied to specific sets of data to come up with specific result sets as the conclusion. There are a lot of applications already available on the market, with very rich sets of applications and in-built libraries having prepackaged models for almost all the typical business scenarios (e.g., customer relations management, marketing predictions, sales predictions, risk predictions, fraud predictions, etc.).

Both current and historical data sets are undoubtedly required. In a way, this kind of analytics looks through heaps of data to find patterns. A pattern specific to a specific business prediction goal is the specific mathematical model pre- or custom-programmed into such an application. This makes it essential to have specific minimum sets of data to be input into these models from various sources.

The data could be coming from a specific time frame (e.g., from specific past business areas, stored historical data, etc.). There is always a challenge, though, how

© Rohit Kumar 2017
R. Kumar, *Machine Learning and Cognition in Enterprises*,
https://doi.org/10.1007/978-1-4842-3069-5_6

much should be retained, what should be retained, and what happens to data after the retention period. These cannot be controlled just by corporations' own rules and regulations. It also always has to be within the framework of rules from relevant governmental and nongovernmental regulatory bodies. This makes it more complicated. We will discuss these aspects as well in the scope of this chapter.

The data is harvested from various kinds of sources depending upon the kind of data. It could be a big data distributed file system as well, which has a huge impact on the growth of predictive analytics.

Certainly, when we talk about predictive analytics, we are talking about obtaining data from as many diverse data sources as possible and mixing it into the right cocktail to get the best predictions. This means huge, at times beyond huge, data volumes, even in petabytes. So, the emergence of cheap and commodity server–supported open source applications like Hadoop played a vital role in the emergence of predictive analytics. This enabled it to get the most vital part of such analytics, which is big data. The enabling of such simple and cheaper data storage platforms thus is a major help to this technology.

Analytical predictions could be done on specific application packages, but considering licensing costs for associated databases, the use of cheaper data sources should always be considered. There are some other reasons as well to do so:

- Conventional data storage systems are mostly made for storing structured data in tabular format, while the data sources relevant for such analytics might provide data in unstructured formats (e.g., text files, videos, audios, etc.).

- In situations with unstructured data, the actual data harvested from the supplied data might amount to only a very small fraction. So, analytics-usable data could be in single-digit percentages from terabytes of data harvested from such unstructured sources. For example, a video file with 700 MB worth of data could provide analytics-worthy information in some KBs only. In cases like that, it is extremely important to have a cheaper and more cost-effective storage option.

- Ease of storage is also considered an important aspect. The conventional data bases are very particular about checking the integrity and format of data before loading or writing. But unstructured data is always a mess in that regard. A system storing such big data should be quick enough to ensure quick writing. The data volume is enormous anyway: for instance, a system capturing Facebook or Twitter feeds is supposed to store billions of such transactions per day in unstructured format (e.g., comments on feeds).

- It must be easily extendible. Considering the simplicity of data storage and simple application interfaces, this is easier to do so.

These data storage options, which are cheap, easy to write, easy to extend, and mostly freely licensed, have contributed greatly to predictive analytics in many ways. These file systems (mostly called so, e.g., Hadoop Cloudera) could also be used directly as the reporting environment for certain pieces of information from the data stored within it.

The statistical methods used are mostly time series analysis, regression analysis, and predictive modeling.

So, in a nutshell, predictive analytics has the following:

- Data identification and storage for a purpose

- Running mathematical models of designated data points

- Derivation of data point results

The reporting scope of predictive modeling applications includes the following:

- Historical perspective of problem areas (e.g., how and why something had happened) for when historical data is utilized.

- Current status (e.g., what is happening currently and why) for when present data is utilized.

- Future predictions (e.g., what action should be taken or how something should be done) for when mathematical-statistical models are used.

Figure 6-1 further summarizes these aspects.

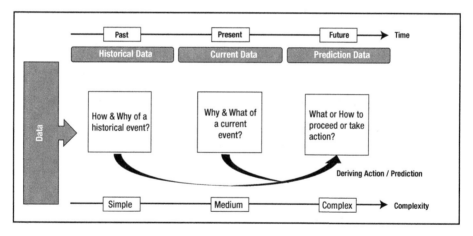

Figure 6-1. *Reporting scope predictive modeling*

Data Relevancy

A very important aspect of predictive analytics is data. We discussed some aspects in the preceding section, but there are other important aspects as well. One of them is what is relevant to be stored.

Research from many consulting firms has highlighted that even up to 99.99% or more of data stored or harvested is not relevant (as per IDC). This is in addition to the fact that only a small fraction of relevant stored data boils down to relevant analytics data.

So, if 100 gigabytes of relevant or good data would have given 50 megabytes of analytics-relevant data, a selection of nonrelevant data would again make this a bigger ratio gap.

There are various aspects that should be considered while considering the data to be selected for analytics purposes. Gartner (cited in Chapter 1) mentions that "only 31 percent of business and IT leaders have metrics that contribute to strategic KPIs (https://www.gartner.com/newsroom/id/2650815)."

The data so acquired should be stored based on some quick test scores. Only if it satisfies such test condition scores to a good extent should it be considered as good data for the purpose.

The test conditions are as follows:

Fresh and Genuine

There could be sources that are not trustworthy or not up to the mark. Picking up data from just anywhere simply because it's of one specific type could be a big mistake. Remember, the cheapest commodity server storing big data still comes at some price, and this will still show up somewhere in your accounts and have an impact. So, a CIO and team should be extremely careful about sources used.

As an example, let's say that customer voice data is needed. People normally go and consider sources as Facebook, Twitter, or some other relevant and popular social media discussions or customer forums. Say that there are 200 such web sites running with these kinds of data for customers with various hit percentages distributed among them.

Now it should not be the case that all data sources should be considered just because they have a few customers who have posted something there or might use it. This is an unnecessary burden to design and cost. The web sites which have major hit rates and are the most popular are good enough to be used for trend analysis; the reason is that they have quicker updated details from the majority of customers or targeted audience. In that sense, the freshness is also guaranteed due to constant and more recent hits there.

Putting effort into consolidating data from each of them and designing a system to catch records from each could be overkill to system performance and your pocket as well.

See Table 6-1 for the stats of users across some famous social media web sites (as per www.brandwatch.com).

Table 6-1. *User share across famous social media websites*

Web Site	%Total Internet Users (Approx.)
Facebook	23.53
WeChat	15.24
YouTube	13.60
WhatsApp	12.24
Weibo	8.98
LinkedIn	6.12
Instagram	5.44

(*continued*)

Table 6-1. *(continued)*

Web Site	%Total Internet Users (Approx.)
Twitter	4.35
Google	4.09
Flickr	1.52
Pinterest	1.36
Snapchat	1.36
Myspace	0.69
Airbnb	0.68
Reddit	0.49
4Chan	0.15
Periscope	0.14

So, if we trust this data set (which seems quite well researched), the first four web sites or applications provide more than 60% of social data. A combination of the first six to nine listed also has good numbers. And this is just for these 17 sites/applications; there are thousands more that could be listed.

But actual quality, from the perspective of the individual corporation, should also be considered via good market and web research. So even if the 17 in Table 6-1 are considered, the permutation and combination of good data relevant for that corporation might differ markedly from the customer base strengths shown in Table 6-1. The reason is simple: the table shows only total customer numbers active across these platforms, and for a specific corporation, such customer numbers might be quite different. So, despite all standard market research about the quality of data and the number of active users across these platforms, still for a specific organization it must be rechecked; not all should be targeted, but rather only major chunks. Normally, organizations would go for between two and six such platforms.

Avoid Noise

One person's music could be another person's noise. So, not everything from relevant sources ascertained from the preceding point should be used, even after you know how many of "your users" there are across that final list of platforms you would like to go for. Again, a quality recheck might be required.

There might be the following user counts across multiple platforms:

- 8% platform A,
- 20% platform B,
- 34% platform C,
- 30% platforms D and E together

This is the final list of platforms based on the number of users across many such platforms. A further drill-down investigation, though, reveals the following facts about data quality.

- A has 60% or more data quality

- B has 5% data quality

- C has 80% or more data quality

- D and E have 60% or more data quality

If the noise or quality threshold is fixed at say 50% or above to ensure good data quality, the trend in Figure 6-2 could be seen.

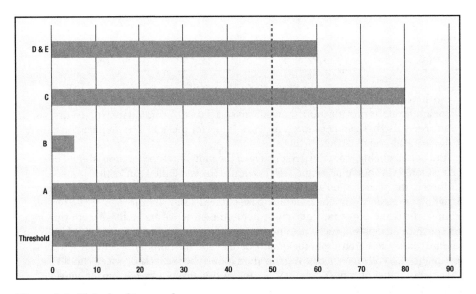

Figure 6-2. *Noise level in sample*

Based on this, despite having about 20% customer hits on platform B, the data quality is extremely low. In this case, it would be wise to drop this platform from the list.

However, this is just an example scenario, and real-life decisions might be a little more complicated. But until and unless corporations and CIOs are aware of what they need to target, this two-step drill-down should be able to cut the waste or flab and increase the usability factor to a respectable level.

Avoid Personal or Sensitive Data

There are extremely tough legal norms for this kind of violation. So, only harvest what you should and are authorized to. Legal and regulatory sensitization is a must. Personal data should be kept up to date if you are authorized to use it. Data should be well secured or encrypted to avoid misuse or release to others. This should be deleted or removed as soon as it's not to be used any more. People should be well notified about their data being used and the purpose for the same. Consent should be acquired before using it. Breaches should be stopped, but if any do happen, all regulatory bodies and users should be notified.

The drill for ensuring that only required, authorized, and relevant data is harvested is good not only technically (system performance perspective), but also from a cost and timeline perspective. This adds up into overall ROI benefits and more confidence in the system and in turn in the predictive analytic results received. The purpose should be to have the lowest volume of haystack to find a needle and not to put whole worlds of hay in one place and make an already complicated exercise even more complicated and costly.

Data Retention Period

Another aspect of data relevancy is the time factor, or in other words, how old data should be acquired or retained in systems. This is also a good aspect to keep in mind for all the reasons mentioned in the previous section.

It is very much evident that any information is only useful if used or applied at the right time; otherwise it has no usability or importance. This is a function of time.

The following are some test conditions to be kept in mind:

Past, Current, and Future Value

In terms of the timestamp of any data, it should be well considered whether it has some value in the scope of current problem solving to generate predictions and where it could be used as a parameter in the mathematical/statistical model. If it does not fit into this, it's not good historical data.

For example, for predictions of seasonal sales patterns for a retail shopping chain for one location, it would be good to harvest data on customer sales details, customer master data, and customer membership details for categorizing customers based on gender, age, employment type, and so on. By itself, it would hardly be of any use if we were to combine data from all cashiers' rosters and shift details during that period. These two details might be present together in sales information in transactional tables, but picking up only the right subset of data is correct, suggested, and most effective. Taking cashier data from historical data aside from predictive analytics is not even close to the purpose of the prediction process.

The same is true for current data. Only current data which is required to work with a problem scope and/or mathematical predictive model should be picked up.

Once this is done, and when the right data set or rather subset is used from historical and current data, automatically we have a data set which is of future value, the future here being the output coming out from the predictive models using these data records only.

Consistent and Not a Liability

The data should be consistent with need and should not be a liability. Even private data from a timeline perspective should be considered. Sensitive data should be removed as soon as possible.

Outdated or Out of Purpose

The big data systems provide us the capability to store even hundreds of years' worth of past data. With tools like Apache Spark on Hadoop or HANA Vora, it could be sifted easily to understand it.

But will it be relevant? Businesses change with time as civilizations go through various societal and lifestyle changes. This is affected not only by social changes on the personal level but also by overall change in social norms over time. The political situation also has an impact.

So, companies should be wise enough to demarcate what data would be of good quality from the time perspective by understanding how far back in time the data will be good enough to be used with current models and whether it was created in relatively similar social scenarios.

Something once very fashionable could become a thing of shame or criticism with time (e.g., smoking).

Corporations should be very sure and have a benchmarking process to determine how far in the past they could go for certain analytics to be in play.

Predictive Analytics—Process

From the time it started until now, it has been mostly person skill intensive. Data scientists and business analysts work together to run the show.

A good knowledge of statistics, programming, and business sense has always been required to be a good data scientist.

More recently, however, machine learning and cognition have started to replace data scientists due to their superhuman capabilities, like working with extremely minimal error and coming back with new results for new requirement dimensions after mere seconds have ticked by.

But the million-dollar thing is that tools and methods should not be ruling the predictive analytics result. It should be the purpose first. Big data and tools do not provide good predictive analytic solutions; it's the other way around. The approach should be first defining what is expected, then refining it and seeing the value outcome by doing this. Then, the data sources should be finalized and fine-tuned. Next, the models should be tried and tuned. Finally—poof!—the golden result.

There have been examples where data scientists are caught in the trap of their very own tools and the charm of the trade, and some unreasonable analyses were worked upon with superficially fantastic figures, graphs, and charts that made no sense in the end.

To continue and conclude the previous argument: the technical aspect of predictive analytics is not the important part. What is far more important is at the organizational level, namely, the defined purpose for going for it or the need for it and then a clearly defined list of what would be required to achieve that organizational goal.

In spite of all machines with superhuman effectiveness (e.g., IBM Watson), the need for human involvement remains. This is the reason additional skills like taste or experience with similar business and a very scientific approach toward problem solving are important attributes to be looked at when hiring a data scientist. Data scientists cannot work and should not be expected to work in silos with some requirements on paper. Data science should be an organic activity and should be closely monitored too, with close cooperation and scrutiny from stakeholders in management. It is more of a strategic initiative for an organization.

Putting the process in place for predictive analytics after business case finalization is mostly technical. But the pilot and expansion approach mostly monitored by C-Level is a must for being on track; if not, deviation is all too easy.

The data scientist's efforts are complex, since the needed correlations could be a combination of multiple areas and so it cannot be done solely by him. These correlations should not be just a mastery of any machine learning or statistical models. They should be fine-tuned over time with help from managers and analysts, also measuring that there is no deviation from the initial purpose.

The process is not very complicated. A high-level generic depiction is presented in Figure 6-3.

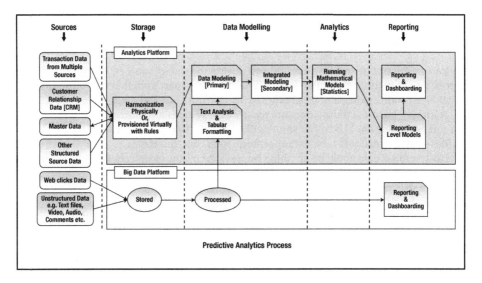

Figure 6-3. *Predictive analytics process*

This is a typical predictive analytics process, and the scope of high-level usage of designated analytics platforms (e.g., SAP HANA, BODS, etc.) and big data platforms (e.g., Hadoop) is shown.

Remember that good data does not always lead to good predictive analytics, but it is a combination of that as well as good planning and organic environment as mentioned before.

A culture of data-driven management or business needs to be ingrained. So, predictive analytics runs from the top. The people in this value chain all should be working as closely as possible to the heart of the organization. They should be fully aware of business areas, problem areas, and strategic long- and short-term plans for improvement. Mathematics, machine learning, and tools do not run businesses or successful predictions, but if they are invested with the right purpose formally planned and monitored, they run the show together.

Now to summarize what is in Figure 6-3, I will present a small further discussion at a high level with essential inputs (mentioning again that the purpose/scope of this book is not technical).

There are five areas under which we will describe the process:

- Sources

- Storage

- Data modeling

- Analytics

- Reporting

For the sake of convenience and relevance I will take sources and storage together.

Sources and Storage

The sources are comprised of structured and unstructured data sources. By structured sources, we mean the proper table format data; anything apart from that is unstructured format. Even audio, video, and other types of files are unstructured data.

Normally, business transaction and master data systems are sources of structured data sources. There could be other sources like flat file systems where XML, Excel, and text files could be read into tables via specific adapters and interfaces.

Unstructured data could be anything from sensor inputs to web click information and social media harvesting.

While structured data normally sits in relational database tables, unstructured data sits in distributed file systems like Hadoop. These data should also be processed to be converted into meaningful derivatives, and that is taken care of by specific applications (e.g., Hive).

The volume of unstructured data is mostly very high as compared to business transaction data. But there could be some business transaction data that could be at a tremendously high volume as well, and it might end up sitting in big data platforms (for the sake of having it all) but be of low utility for general and analytical requirements (e.g., telecommunication network data).

The data from the same business areas but coming from multiple sources should be harmonized to ensure they are in the same type, size, and business term format.

Text analysis for the big data content is also processed and stored on analytical platforms.

Data Modeling

Data modeling is done for multiple purposes. Some modeling must be done to create data marts to store certain subsets of data brought in for use in prediction models. These are called primary data models. The primary data models have harmonized and cleaned-up data subsets required for limited problem-solving purposes. Now it is also possible to connect with data from multiple sources remotely. This means instead of data marts or containers made to extract and store data physically, a metadata structure and an SQL-like query are created and stored, which at runtime gets the data from connected sources on demand. Once the reporting requirement is done, the data does not exist anymore. For this, virtual modeling is done.

Primary data modeling must be done (physical or virtual) for all types of data entering the parameters of the analytic application platform. This is to ensure the presence, physical or virtual, of all such subsets for further use in the predictive mathematical models and at the end for reporting.

There might be some further modeling required for integrating certain subsets of data coming from the same or multiple sources for the sake of better preparation of data for presenting to the predictive models.

This is called intermediate or integrated modeling.

Analytics

This consists of the actual models required for prediction generation. Mostly, these are supplied as prepackaged models/libraries covering all generic and typical business scenarios. There is always a possibility to create or extend the existing ones.

The analytical models could be done via single or multilevel calculations, again creating some new intermediate subsets of data or results.

These make up the action part or heart of analytical solutions.

Reporting

This is the final visible outcome. There might be some sort of modeling layer in between to store the results and further use them in reporting applications.

Reporting on certain data could directly emerge out of big data platforms as well.

Types of Analytics

Predictive analytics is related to predicting based on scoring achieved using statistical methods on specific sets of data. Basically, predictive analytics, according to its "textbook" definition, means predictive modeling put into practice, which in turn is largely a discipline of machine learning. So, the origin of predictive analytics is from predictive modeling techniques.

This modeling, when created in a transaction system or a separate system containing transaction and other data (as mentioned in previous sections), is a system which churns out predesignated prediction; then, this commercial business application is known as predictive analytics.

Nowadays, the majority of the reporting apart from operational reporting is done to create one or another type of direct or indirect predictions. Direct predictions would be something directly indicatating that something might go wrong (e.g., prediction with color codes about customers who might be on the brink of jumping to another telecom service provider or a machine's chances of crashing in a few minutes if not maintained).

The indirect ones could be some clear inferences from various data to show current patterns of data and also prediction patterns based on them as possible outcomes or trends (e.g., financial forecasting reports).

These series of predictions could then be summarized as a single dashboard to provide a general health trend about the organization from one or another dimension.

The major areas of usage are in finance, sales, marketing, cross-selling, customer relationship management, process optimization, and product research.

Natural language processing is an important tool in predictive analytics. The application uses this arsenal from the toolset to understand or make inferences about the meaning of data from big data coming out of social media interactions, be it text comments, audio, or video. These capabilities are near real time and targeted to record a hit in the system to update predictions based on this.

The biggest challenge is use case understanding for these analytics. It should be handled in the way mentioned earlier in this chapter. This type of analytics is good for problems related to optimizing operational as well as strategic capabilities.

Unlike direct predictive analytics, indirect predictive does not provides any absolute result or prediction. This only provides a pattern about what could happen. But there are three more important questions.

- What has happened? (What has brought us to the situation we are in today?)

- Why did this happen? (Why exactly did this happen or what went wrong exactly?)

- What should be done? (What should we do once we reach a potential situation?)

These are not answered by predictive analytics, as it mostly focuses on answering "What could happen?"

The preceding three questions are answered instead by three other types of analytics.

- Descriptive (What has happened?)

- Diagnostic (Why has this happened?)

- Prescriptive (What should be done?)

They are shown in Figure 6-4. They are shown with a data timeline perspective and use case or applicability.

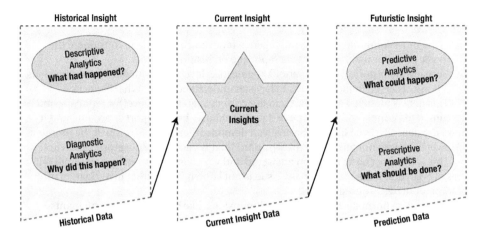

Figure 6-4. *Types of analytics with regard to timeline of data consumption*

The maturity level progresses in the following sequence: descriptive, diagnostic, predictive, and prescriptive analytics.

This shows the degree of value it brings to the organization and in the same sequence. As the maturity and value increase in this sequence, the skill and effort required to implement them also increase proportionally.

Figure 6-5 again depicts all types of analytics from the perspective of maturity achieved and skill level required to achieve this maturity.

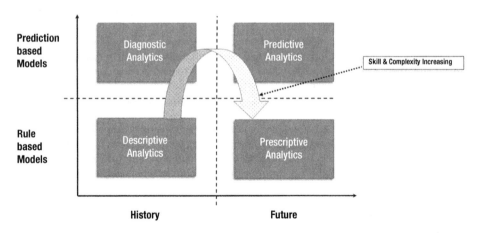

Figure 6-5. *Types of analytics with required skill and maturity level*

Let us discuss each of them one by one:

Descriptive Analytics

This is the most common business intelligence reporting done, and is considered the most basic or preliminary analytics via reporting on historical data.

By using the historical data at various aggregation levels and with different dimensions, the KPIs are observed in these reports to have an understanding of "What happened."

This data is modeled and brought to the correct aggregation level for reporting and watching. This is most common type of data warehouse–based report at present, and it shows the dent size from impact. Basically, it demonstrates how big or small the problem is. However, it does not talk about the why part. That is covered by diagnostic analytics.

This is the most basic question answered and which is then an entry gate for all other types of analytics. If the reason for any issue is not known, any further investigation or solution is out of the question.

So, the data normally here has some dimensions, like business area participants (e.g., customer number, document number, company code, etc.), dates (e.g., sales date, purchase date), and some KPIs (e.g., sales amount, order quantity, etc.).

A tabular or graphical representation is common. This over time could help users understand the pattern changes, and these pattern changes could then be understood as the issue area highlighted. Dashboards combining such multiple reports are created as well.

■ **Note**   Descriptive analytics makes the base for a further plan of action.

For example, imagine that a company supplying telecommunication equipment wants to check and plan for better understanding of all the parts they are supplying to their customers. Now, this company has at least 50 variants of antennas and other smaller parts up to the level of a screw and which are considered a unit bill of material. Some components are used across multiple variants. The details of sale along with last year's sales records will help the company to understand the pattern of consumption or use of all the components individually; then, it can decide to go further and see what to plan to make, keep in inventory, and sell, and also what is not required at all or only very little and should be discarded. This report on historical sales and material data would be a descriptive analytical reporting providing clarity and describing what has happened to the sales related to this.

Or let's look at another example: before launching a marketing campaign for all of its customers, the company wants to analyze the existing customer base. The products launched are seldom for all classes and age groups of customers. They are mostly more appealing to one class and a certain age group of customers or another based on usability, price, etc.

They did a descriptive analysis to determine data on the current users based on three parameters—education, income, and age—in order to see who currently buys their product the most (Figure 6-6). They see four major segments: the major segment is younger subscribers in the category of medium spending level, and the second-highest is middle-aged subscribers with a low spending rate and a high level of education. This gives them an age to understand how to design the campaign better to address the same segment or even a new segment consisting of a highly educated, young, and high-spending group.

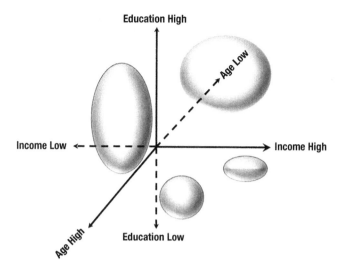

Figure 6-6. *Telecom campaign user analysis*

Such a report to describe the customer base based on such parameters would be a descriptive analytic report.

This needs only the most basic modeling and reporting skills and could be done by technical developers with very little guidance or monitoring from business users or managers.

Besides this, the complexity of these reports is the lowest, as these are mostly rule-based and not dependent upon any probability mathematical model.

Diagnostic Analytics

Now that the problem area has been defined by the descriptive analytics, it's time to run some diagnostic analytics to find the root cause of the problem.

■ **Note**　Diagnostic analytics starts where descriptive analytics leaves off and provides inputs to predictive analytics.

It should be noted here that these analytics in real-life use are not separate operations running on single or multiple applications one by one as separate and sequential activities or processes. They are presented this way in this discussion only because it's necessary to explain each type of analytic analysis and its properties separately. This simply means that the application used in the organization could be taken to that maturity level by adding some more complexity into the models to be used. Every model upgraded to a higher level comes from its previous version, and so in batched format, once all the related reports are there, organization has that level of

89

reporting enabled. So, when I say that it starts from descriptive and goes up to predictive, it simply means that the reports developed in this maturity level will use most of the same back-end technical models and furthermore that the reports will be based either on the same models or on some new added models or some more complex models created out of them. It does not mean that there is a report which is taking data from the previous one and passing it to the next.

Coming back to diagnostic analytics, this is the slicing-dicing and drill-down/drill-across functionality usage. These functionalities and other supporting ones help reach the root cause of the problem. Even macros are used in Microsoft Excel on such report dumps commonly to run some user-level rules to diagnose.

As the diagnostic analytics lies in the quadrant of probability-based rules, it also uses some such mathematical and statistical models.

But the probabilistic part is not mandatory. This limit itself trains the data calculation using machine language concepts and techniques to correlate previous trends and the current state to zero out to a certain problem focus area and that's all. To give an example, let's say a machine is showing a certain malfunction or lower productivity, and under similar conditions or visible symptoms, the diagnostic analytics with probability would show what might be wrong and would need to be checked using similar lessons learned or trends from similar symptoms earlier which had led to a disruption. So, the probability-infused diagnostic algorithm might not necessarily pinpoint to a root cause, but it might bring focus to areas related to such an issue, based on previous events and states leading to the same kind of issue. Indeed, the non-probability-based diagnostic analytics based on drill-down might be equal or stronger in pinpointing the current issue exactly. This might be more time-consuming then the other one (i.e., probabilistically based), as focusing more broadly to analyze a larger area might take time. Additional time is a negative factor, but precisely pointing to the root cause is more possible via manual drill-down. A combination is best: a focused zoom into a few specific areas, which are highlighted and then validated.

Prescriptive Analytics

Prescriptive analytics could be considered an extension of predictive analytics. Predictive analytics does prediction on problems highlighted at a high level by descriptive analytics and pinpointed root causes by diagnostic analytics to provide forecasts based on probabilistic methods to answer the question of what might happen. Prescriptive analytics goes a step beyond this to answer how to be prepared about this and how to handle this.

This is the highest order of analytics and the most mature one as well. It includes additional concepts and techniques like the Internet of Things (IoT), cognitive computing, and deep learning.

The relation between predictive and prescriptive analytics is deep, as prescriptions must start from an examination of what might happen. It has a close relationship with descriptive and diagnostic as well to recursively come to conclusions on the best solution and timing predictions, because it answers not only how to fix an issue but also when that can happen and what happens when it is fixed that way.

Figure 6-7 depicts the possible relationship among predictive, descriptive, and diagnostic analytics within the scope of prescriptive analytics.

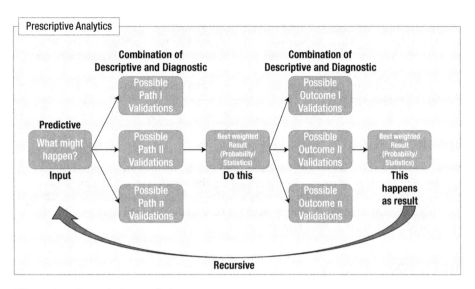

Figure 6-7. *Prescriptive analytics ecosystem*

These analytics do have a particular shortcoming, however; kind of a nonunitary solution. It might come back and point out *n* number of options, with each one having a different path. This is what is handled in newer applications using cognitive computing (covered in later chapters).

By talking about these types and especially about prescriptive analytics, we have already covered the foundation knowledge required toward understanding the core subject area of this book, which is cognitive computing. In the next two chapters, we will discuss the concept of cognitive computing at length, and then we will return to our discussion from prescriptive computing onward and see how cognitive computing concepts contributed to prescriptive analytics to further shape up business intelligence.

Tools

There are plenty of such tools available on the market. I am pointing out a few famous ones here. The purpose is not to justify by mentioning here that they are the best or that others should not be considered. Rather, the purpose is to present a small collection here and provide some details on some of them, showing just a bit of the variety available.

SAP HANA Predictive Analytics

This comes with in-built libraries for predictive analytics. Additionally, it has libraries and standard template data flows for some famous social media harvesting as well to use with predictions. Text analysis/sentiment analysis libraries are there as well. The ETL capabilities are in-built to be able to connect to all possible types of databases or data sources including big data lakes. Besides, it has in-memory–supported capabilities for supercomputational speeds.

This is available on premises, in the cloud, and as a hybrid and runs on various Linux and Unix operating systems.

Apache Mahout

This is from the Apache Software Foundation and so is an open source application. It comes with highly efficient machine learning capabilities. It is mostly deployed over Hadoop installations but could be run without using Hadoop as well, using some other applications like Apache Spark. This is relatively new on the market and is a totally new type of product from the Apache Foundation.

IBM SPSS

This is a statistical analysis tool from IBM. It is also capable of text analysis and data mining activities. It runs on many operating systems like Mac, Windows, and Linux and is written in Java. It is primarily used in market research and social analytics. It is a simple-to-use application and is used by individual researchers as well. Mostly, a freeware license is provided for this.

SAS

This is also one of the pioneers in predictive and other analytics. This application is written in C language and runs on most of the operating systems including IBM mainframe.

Statistical

This is a Dell product. This runs on the Windows operating system. There are six product lines available for various activities from data mining to predictive analytics. Data visualization capabilities are included. It has the capability to integrate with the open source R programming environment.

Oracle Advanced Analytics

Considering the competition between Oracle and SAP, I considered keeping them a bit more separate. The sequence is not a priority for me, and naturally either of them could come first, so I hope I haven't caused any offense.

This is also one of the first-in-league kinds of software, with a combination of Oracle data mining and Oracle R Enterprise. This gives it a capability to do data mining inside the Oracle database; together with machine learning algorithms, it is very effective.

With Oracle R Enterprise, it allows R capabilities to be used inside Oracle databases.

Actuate

This is a product from BIRT, the open source Eclipse BIRT company. It has three lines or areas covered in this direction: business analytics, embedded analytics and visualization, and customer communication management.

Mathematica

This a three-decade-old solution written in Wolfram language. Finance, statistics, and business analysis are the three major areas. This even has applications talking to the IoT.

There are some free applications available, like Orange Data Mining, RapidMiner, KNIME, R Software Environment, Dataiku, Apache Spark, Anaconda, HP Haven, Scikit-learn, H2O, and Apache Mahout.

Some Applications

It's worth mentioning now some business area applications of predictive analytics.

There could be a million options or ways in which predictive analytics could be used for single or multiple lines of businesses. It is limited only by one's imagination and understanding of businesses, and of course having engineers to implement one's ideas. I will mention some important applications in the following.

Manufacturing

Predictive scheduling of machines/jobs and preventive machine maintenance are the two prime areas.

How much could machine usage be optimized with respect to oncoming orders and predictions of future demand increase? Do we need to buy new machines now, or instead do we need to use the current ones in a way to enable us to push the buying decision for new machines to sometime in the future? Can we do well with smaller versions, or do we need bigger-capacity ones? These are some questions which are not related to production planning only but even to the overall financial management and financial reflection of a company.

Another aspect of the problem is preventive repairs. Companies must be alerted before a machine or important equipment is going to be down. This is done through sensor data streaming and notification about a probable error in time, which would help effective repair/maintenance and result in less downtime. The target is to have minimum machine downtime and overall machine effectiveness, in turn increasing ROA (return on asset) and profit.

A good example could be usage in the microchip or semiconductor industry. The industry has a difficult and complex order, manufacturing, and supply cycle. The silicon wafers used are cut and fabricated on high-tech machine lines. The number of sensors on every machine and the details generated per machine are huge. The order, sales, and supply also work in silos. So, what if a company could combine all this? The result would be amazing. The distinct data heads here could be machine state sensor data, product manufacturing process steps data, inventory of raw material data, near future production plan data, and current order and sales data. The machine would be designed to predict in the following areas:

- Machine real-time predictive maintenance, so no frequent maintenance downtime would be required.

- Product manufacturing step sensor data and finished product processing data with machine state data would help combat yield failure or degradation. With advanced and smaller tools and complex processes, yield failure is common. The increasing die size also leads to more defect density. At times, process variation is required to overcome more than 80% of defects. There are already many separate control charts available for manufacturing line engineers and controllers. But if all are connected via one predictive analytic application and even better through a prescriptive application, the results would be unthinkably awesome.

- R&D and sales are two ends which seldom strike a good balance in this industry. In this case, betting on the right thing in the market or what is likely to come in the market always helps in taking product and productivity optimization R&D into right and productively focused directions. So, the spending on R&D is controlled to a larger extent. This could be far more optimized by prediction-based marketing, CRM, and trend analysis.

Marketing and Demand Management

These days, business talks about individual customers and their choices: not only about customer journey analysis, but also about customer journey manipulation.

The predictive models could be used to further predict, based on buying, searching, social interaction, and sales history, which sub segments of customers out of previously worked out segment of preferable customers would most probably respond positively to the current product sale or related marketing campaign. The journey of customer and multichannel presence history would predict the ideal mix for campaigns where there would be much higher ROI on advertising cost. It could predict more precisely and help put every penny into a clear investment to get customers and not into blind bets. This is the power of marketing with predictive analytics.

The tools of today are well equipped to even mix and merge live social media and forum data to further sharpen ROI strategies.

Another aspect is demand management: keeping the right stuff in inventory at the right time so that

- The customer gets what he wants readily available and without waiting much;

- Inventory is not overloaded with things waiting around, which can be a huge cost (even if it avoids pure wastage, there is still the chance of wear and tear at the seller's expense).

With the e-commerce boom, it becomes more crucial to have the right goods stocked at the right inventory level and at the right place. This is being achieved using predictive analytics models nowadays, and these models have created a lot of savings in this aspect.

This all gives so much in the way of information and predictions about the choice of customers that products based on their choice could be brought to the floor, and the customers would be almost compelled to buy those, as if it was their idea to get them in the first place. This is the manipulation of the customer journey. Many times, a customer buying product A might keep buying A and all its later versions or the similar product B. But if one understands the individual customer's buying habits and virtual interactions, the customer might be offered product C, for which there is a high probability of purchase due to the predictions based on customer data. And then the customer buys C instead of A or B; his journey has already been manipulated. Take the example of Netflix. Let's say I want a free version—the month-long trial—as I saw that certain movies I wanted were already there, and of course the video quality is always good, and streaming is excellent, even for a free temporary account. Now the magic happens: I keep seeing recommendations from Netflix about various kinds of content, not only movies. Now Netflix is offering me things which I would probably like or even couldn't possibly reject based on the statistics its smart recommendation system could generate about me in a month's time. So, the free month's end comes, and I still have 10 contents on my watch list. Not only was my decision to use it free for a month hijacked, but now I watch content recommended to me by Netflix. Good for both. I got a good site to watch entertaining content at a good price and with good quality. But the site is also exploring itself in front of me instead of me going ahead and saying, "Hey, tell me what you have for me." For them, this of course means one more customer for their coffers. Ultimately, it's a good ROI for Netflix from the Netflix Prize money spent and all that program adoption/adaptation.

Also, North Face's Watson page is a beautiful example of this (as discussed in Chapter 1).

Predictive Maintenance

This is in principle two things:

- Awareness of the need to repair something before it might fail;

- With help of Prescriptive analytics, reducing the number of scheduled maintenances, which is like a black box thing. You stop everything to do a routine check to go and see if all is up and running.

Predictive analytics in areas of tool or machine maintenance is not a new thing for airlines; they have been using it for some time now. The more snags can be known, the quicker the fixes and the more time in air, and so more profit or income. Therefore, it becomes necessary for airlines to go into predictive maintenance mode. There are thousands of sensors already on a flight. This makes easier to have predictive maintenance for aircraft. There are many companies and airlines themselves as well that are optimizing MRO (maintenance, repair, and overhaul) using this. Also, airlines could combine this data to analyze the part supplier and maintenance contractor performance.

Another place where it is important and is very much integrated is automobile manufacturing. The term "manufacturing line" is given to this section of industry. A line stall due to a snag could cost a lot and bring the entire production process to a halt. Moreover, the greater the frequency of this happening, the higher the cost. So, somewhat like airlines, automobile manufacturers are going for predictive maintenance, getting the benefits mentioned in the preceding bullet points. The results are already very encouraging.

Flexi Pricing

Flexible pricing is very important in e-commerce. There are web sites which let people know that a product may be purchased for less on a completely different web site now. And businesses themselves keep looking at the customer journey, tracking the virtual path to propose the best price. If a customer has visited web site A, where the price was $2, and web site B, where the price was $2.10, and I have a pricing possibility between $1.5 to $3, I need not put a hard-coded price of $1.5 to degrade my profits or to keep at $3 to put out a general impression that I sell too high. I will use analytics and first produce a cluster of recommendations which apart from the original one gives me more profit margin. I could sell to the customer at a much cheaper price, and I will price that exact article at maybe $1.90 or $1.80. This will be a 5 to 10% discount compared to the first web site (web site A) and 10 to 14% compared to another (web site B). Check and mate; the customer is happy and so am I. Please notice, however, that this could not be achieved except via virtual footprint tracking and putting out a competitive price. It might be that the customer has somehow reached my web site first: then what? That's where predictive analytics pitches in. Now, what options do I have? Maybe the following:

- I try to catch his browsing style, geography, and all possible details and do a prediction to put most relevant (usage or need and price) choices in front of him

- If a known customer, then I have better chances of prediction, including buying patterns and browsing history, or maybe I have access to the customer's social interactions

So, in any case predictive analytics takes the lead.
Airlines and power companies benefit a lot from this flexi pricing.

Weather Forecast

This is not only for the weather report coming at the end of a news program, even though this is a very important aspect of it. Weather reports help in too many things to be left entirely out of the picture. But there are companies who are now doing weather forecasts for businesses. What does this mean?

You'll notice that "weather forecasting for business" has two parts. One is "weather forecasting" and the other is "for business." The first part remains the same as compared to that television news hour tail part where you learn how the weather was everywhere today and how it is predicted to be tomorrow or further for some days or even some highlights predicted for a year in advance (e.g., early monsoon expected, etc.).

The other part, "for business," is not for the report after the news hour. This is for your specific business. So, the solution with understanding of your business, possible geographical scope, and supply chain live data and combined with weather forecasting could predict the best way to do supply, or prescribe using prescriptive analytics a fix for any consignment already on a troubled path. Either way results in saving money.

Weather forecasting in general is important, but combined with individual business it saves a lot of money and also preserves reputations.

Epidemic Management

In these times, many governments across the world are using this together with healthcare agencies to predict various disease outbreaks and epidemics. This is based on historical data, weather, and trend of disease together with the present vaccination status of that population. Also, demographic migration is considered. This helps in keeping good control and in some cases even helps educate people by showing predictions through these tools.

R&D

The statistical model in applied science has always been used. Predictive models help in going through the data bases of known research and predicting some results virtually. This saves time and money. Also, repeated effort in the same direction is saved.

Corporations doing it for the sake of product development save a lot of money by predicting in which direction various product features should be taken, considering predicted demand for the same.

With this, we come to the end of this chapter, which has presented an overview of predictive analytics, types of analytics, tools, and their major applications.

We will now move toward the core topic of this book: cognitive computing.

CHAPTER 7

Cognitive Computing

This chapter talks about cognition and cognitive computing concepts. These machines simulate human thought process through computational capabilities.

▮ Note   With all the basic knowledge required to understand something about how artificial intelligence, machine learning, natural language processing, and predictive analytics work, we are ready to explore details about cognitive computing in this chapter and those that follow.

Cognition

Searching for the meaning of "cognition" throws the following onscreen:

> "The mental action or process of acquiring knowledge and understanding through thought, experience, and the senses."

This primarily lies in the areas of psychology and neuroscience, however. There are even newer fields of study like neuropsychology, which combine both these disciplines. This new field of study focuses on both neuroscience (i.e., study of structure and activities of various parts of the brain) and psychology (which talks about the functioning of the brain in processing information and learning new things with experience).

Cognition is a vast area of discussion: we will cover here only areas related to our continuing further into the topic of cognitive computing.

Artificial intelligence, machine learning, natural language processing, and predictive analysis, as discussed in earlier chapters, all have their roots in human cognitive studies. They follow it. The effort is always toward making machines as close to human intelligence in learning as possible and as autonomous as humans: self-learning and evolving. In the recent past, we could have reached something close to cognitive computing, but we still had a way to go as compared to humans' intrinsic cognitive capabilities.

The major difference between human cognitive studies and cognitive computing is that the former is based on something already in place and is attempting to learn about it more in depth, maybe to help a brain recover or train better if it isn't working well;

© Rohit Kumar 2017
R. Kumar, *Machine Learning and Cognition in Enterprises*,
https://doi.org/10.1007/978-1-4842-3069-5_7

in other words, a bit like reverse engineering. But the latter, cognitive computing, takes input from the former and tries to recreate the same cognition phenomena in machines.

So, where human cognitive studies talk about measuring cognition and developing it or understanding it to improve it, cognitive computing tries to simplify the knowledge gained from these studies and convert it into algorithms to implement in machines.

Cognition in animals (including us) is a very complex subject. But in simple terms, the understanding could be as follows.

After birth, a baby starts learning. The brain has preprogrammed functionalities to perceive and respond to senses via sensory inputs. These are the five gates of raw information coming into the mind. Additionally, the sensations from inside the body (e.g., internal sensations like pain, full stomach, etc.) flow to the brain from the central nervous system. This makes the raw fresh system ready and well-equipped for learning. The learning is stored as experiences from physical sensory inputs, including the ones coming from the central nervous system as well as from the external world (Figure 7-1). The experiences are good or bad, and later some more finely distinguished feelings which are somewhere in between would evolve, but not just yet. To get to that level of degrees of feelings, a lot of learning would be required over time.

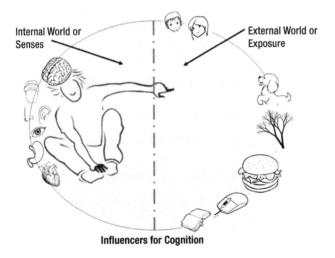

Internal World or
Senses

External World or
Exposure

Influencers for Cognition

Figure 7-1. *Human cognition influencers*

So now the brain will start recording these experiences as good feelings or bad feelings and responses would come as outcomes of smiling or crying, as per the basic programming present in the brain: a very binary response indeed. The responses between a smile and cry as output (i.e., intermediate responses are developed) via the long learning of the brain after birth. So, if the baby sees momma approaching, it relates this with good feelings like cozy care, love, and food in the stomach; then the baby smiles or at least does not cry, depending upon whether it was busy perceiving something at that point or was free to react. This is a very important and interesting aspect of behavior which starts to develop. This aspect is, "should I react or not?"; the prioritization part is picked up by now.

The whole world is a learning platform; everything is new. After basic visual, auditory, olfactory, and nerve perceptions from within, speech recognition starts to develop. This is also very interesting. Any machines doing this need a grammar and algorithm to perceive a language, while the human brain is a machine which just based on basic sensory interpretation and results obtained, together with emotions experienced, is able to learn language after birth, when no capability to read or learn academically is there yet. This is one reason people learn any foreign language better when they are in that language environment and surrounded by native speakers, as compared to sitting and learning it through examples and grammar written in books. This is all because we are programmed to learn better that way.

Consider the idea that every person on earth has his or her own experiences and sees the world through these experiences and the resulting perspective.

This is the way we are programmed. The brain is said to have a conscious area and a subconscious area. The subconscious part is the major part, which is like the hidden Markov model. This is the part which records the memories and experiences biochemically. So, people are programmed continually every day, and that is stored over time into a complex set of associations in memory for even a single subject. The initial experience related to any new subject is linear detail; with time, the more it is experienced it keeps associating information from various experiences together, which might be stored in various parts of the brain.

Let us try to understand this from a simple hypothetical experiment. Say there is a kid who is blind from birth and at a very early age is exposed to people smoking around him, but apart from knowing one simple fact about cigarettes, that they're smoked for fun, he has no other information. The brain would have certain specific information stored recording these experiences. So, the next time he smells this familiar smell somewhere, associations say that this is smoked, burned, and gives pleasure. This is his experience about smoking at that point of time in life.

Over time, this kid gains sight. Now, visual exposure for the first time creates experience and is stored somewhere in the brain. But associations are automatically made with previous experiences. Either the previous or the new experience gives him all the feelings about the overall learning stored.

Now the kid himself smokes when he becomes an adult. One more dimension is added, maybe stored somewhere else, but associations are made nevertheless. Over time, more and more experiences happen and are added with the corresponding associations also made. At times, the brain just records things without even actively knowing it is doing it and creates corresponding associations within itself.

So, association with all learning and with all aspects are created in the brain; over time, any related information is also associated together. For example, he might become a science student and come to know all the medical disadvantages and diseases that may happen with smoking. Even mention of such a disease, say, throat cancer, or exposure to such a patient may trigger all information related to smoking to flash in his mind.

This associative memory makes learning complete and extremely powerful. The kid has various degrees of acquired knowledge at various stages of life about the same subject. The associations were either adding up new informational dimensions and changing the response of the kid for the same, or the associations with new experiences and inbound knowledge took away some associations and replaced them with others. So, at one stage of life the pleasant association was deleted and replaced with bad feelings toward the subject.

This associative learning is a very important concept, and it is crucial for cognitive computing.

We will see the same experiences of this kid mentioned further in this chapter as it correlates with cognitive computing.

Research says that the brain even records experiences and reacts or learns when we are sleeping. A very interesting experiment to help people quit smoking was done at the Department of Neurobiology, Weizmann Institute of Science, Israel [*J Neurosci* 2014 Nov 12;34(46):15382-15393. doi: 10.1523/JNEUROSCI.2291-14.2014.]. People were exposed alternately to smells of their favorite cigarette flavors and the smell they most hated multiple times and during multiple nights. This made the brain make new associations with smoking as an unpleasant experience. This has helped many people quit smoking.

Another aspect is to derive details from existing knowledge and predict new results. For example, when we grow up from infancy we see lot of things in singular variants (e.g., books or trees). Books could be of many size and colors, and the same is true for trees: every species on earth has a different look. But then how do we see and recognize all of them irrespective of type? The brain stores some peculiar snapshots of information at the back end in the subconscious, and the moment we see something similar with matching information points, we perceive it to be that. So, anything tall, with a thick trunk below at the base, and with a lot of green leaves is a tree, and any object with multiple pages is a book.

The brain goes through various levels of maturity as we grow from infancy, and later in life, similar exposures would give different perceptions of truth.

Sometimes this creates illusion as well, like how it is difficult to perceive from a distance whether steam is hot or cold, until some hint like water droplets or snow confirms that it is cold rather than hot.

The brain overwrites some information or discards it completely. It is said that early morning, around 2am and up to 4am, is the time when the brain does this. So, the information which could have multiple associations today might be replaced completely with new roots and associations tomorrow. So, let us assume tomorrow we come to discover some chemical component that when sprinkled on cigarettes and smoked, gives better health and longevity, and it is made mandatory for people to smoke. Boom! The brain will overwrite the previous negative experience, and the same smell might suddenly seem divine. The brain discards information with less associated experience and/or almost no associations at all. So, things read once or just read for the sake of reading will be lost over minutes, days, months, or years. This is the way for the brain to do a cleansing and keep precious computing space free for good new or old information and to make some sense with associations. Until such associations are made, information taken in might not make much sense.

The other interesting feature of the brain is its ability to pick up on something unusual or unique. This is stored at a higher-order place in memory with some unique experience or feeling. Slap memory is one of the ways to achieve this. Einstein used to talk about this. If you slap someone very hard during a session of discussion, that session and discussion at that point remains engraved for a longer time. This is because the associations are made then with multiple distinct areas of the brain together (e.g., for learning, curiosity, pain, shame, fear, etc.).

It makes one big complex association across the brain for this, and so we call it imprinted in the brain. This is what is called associative learning. Human (or animal) brains tend to lose details or complete information from the brain if it is not associated.

Therefore, scattered information in the brain which is without any associations tends to go away soon and become difficult to remember.

There are lot of educators nowadays talking about this. The people with left or right major brain activity, especially the kids, must be taught or trained based on the way their brains are physically created at birth, not in the same way for people with their brains created with the opposite pattern. This is actually working wonders for lots of kids, and the same is true for personality improvement workshops or sessions. Book - Brain-Based Strategies to Reach Every Learner by Diane Connell [ISBN: 978-1-58390-205-9].

All of this is required background to discuss cognitive computers, the thinking machines.

Cognitive Computing

This is nothing but trying to mimic maximum human cognition properties in a programmable machine using various computer science technologies and mathematical models.

This attempt to mimic human cognitive abilities thus comprises a myriad of areas of science, technology, and other subjects as shown in Figure 7-2.

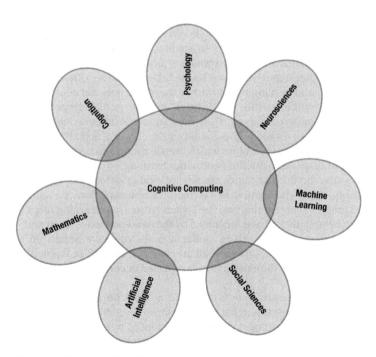

Figure 7-2. *Main disciplines of cognitive computing*

So, the series of cognitive abilities simulated in these systems from human cognition aspects are as follows: perceiving, sensing, analyzing, problem solving, weighing a decision, simulating the possibilities to get the best one, learning, expressing, responding, and so on.

As mentioned in a previous section, this is engineering of thinking machines from reverse-engineered details from human cognitive studies.

So, in spite of having a host of technologies and disciplines coming together to formulate the concept of cognitive computing, subjects like human cognition, neurosciences, linguistics, and anthropology take center stage.

And then, the disciplines of studies related to human behavior, interaction, and neural engineering take center stage right alongside. Many other disciplines help create it: mathematics, programming, hardware accelerations, artificial intelligence and machine learning, and so on.

So we can safely say that this is driven by biological sciences and limited by computer sciences and mathematics. The biological studies present an unlimited scope of possibilities by disclosing the way it works, while computer sciences and technical subjects must become more and more capable of mimicking it flawlessly together. This was why the there were limitations in technology, which led to delays in actual first implementations, even though the concept existed from the time of the conceptualization of the Turing Test. The Turing Test is explained in detail in Chapter 2.

So, the machines should be able to perceive the world with an existing knowledge corpus programmed and loaded into them, and they should be able to take a final, unitary, and maximally appropriate decision and then act on it, again appropriately.

For example, imagine that there is an egg and a potato. A picking-up task should not only be perceived by understanding about which one is which, but should also know how to handle each one. So, the egg should be handled softly while the potato does not need that. Even if it doesn't know this at first, the machine should be able to learn and act properly after the first egg was picked up in the potato way. Thus, the cognitive abilities should not only be in perceiving things but also should be present during the course of action.

Thus, cognitive computing creates machines which keep learning and keep modifying their behaviors or responses with this continuous learning.

Remember the discussion on the associative memory of a kid at various phases of life toward the subject of smoking. The learning of the cognitive systems follows the same pattern. The knowledge progressively coming into the system creates new learning maps and associations to generate meaning. This is facilitated by the new knowledge input and training the system to understand this data. Along similar lines, the cognitive system too makes a huge association for every subject area and all the available knowledge input to it. This either gets updated with a new dimension or gets replaced or completely removed with time.

One precious capability of the human baby is to be able to "feel": the good, the bad, and then all intermediate feelings. This is nascent behavior shown by almost all animals, most clearly expressed in humans. Learning is very much influenced by emotions as well, and even Emotional Quotient is now considered a better parameter than IQ to grade how able people are.

Cognitive machines have quite a struggle here as well. Emotions change in the human for the same experience with the passage of time, as mentioned in the "smoking" examples in the previous section. For machines, this difficult task could mean identification of pitch and facial point distortions which it's programmed to perceive as emotions. And this could be difficult to detect due to hardware and software and other performance limitations. While a computer could be made to learn these emotions as training models within them to an extent, then this is again a very black-and-white solution for a problem that is not very clearly demarcated most of the time.

Getting the context of a statement said to a machine is also difficult. The statement can be sarcastic, happy, or angry, and it's difficult for the machine to perceive the context.

As humans, we have an assumed purpose from the world which takes priority before input stimulus is processed and perceived. That could be influenced by factors like our own agenda and purpose or expectations. Machines do not expect. The expectations are there but only as expected output and changing expectation toward a new output is again a challenge.

These perception- and emotion-driven actions are simple for a human to do but programming this capability into a machine is a mammoth task. These are the limitations which current cognitive computing scientists need to fill in order to obtain a cognitive system of a higher order.

The hardware is cheap and state of the art and so is the abundance of software available. Also, the business use cases for doing this are abundant. All this is driving cognitive computing.

■ **Note**   I would rather that cognitive computing were called super artificial intelligence instead.

The discipline of natural language processing is very important for cognitive computing. This makes it

- Natively interactable with humans

- More human-like

The aspects of human learning, as described in short in the previous section, could be categorized into genotypic and phenotypic.

- Genotypic: Inherent capabilities as programmed in genes (or DNA)

- Phenotypic: As induced by environmental interactions or experiences with the external world and the world within (sensations of the body)

So, twins separated into two different cultures and parts of world would perceive things differently and act accordingly. The basic nature of the act remains the same, as governed by genotypic programming, while developed secondary behavior and response stem from phenotypic learning. So, if one of the twins is brought up in a culture where fire is worshipped and the other one in a culture where it is not, the basic response toward not touching fire remains the same and it will also burn in both case. But seeing fire and then feeling divine bliss and kneeling would not happen for one of the twins.

Similarly, the machines have their one basic corpus of intelligence fed in and then learnings are added to the algorithm and as new code extensions from experiences.

The learning can change the people's purposes, but for machines of whatever level, the purpose remains the same. So, an IBM Watson might be trained to be a good cancer-diagnosing expert but it would never pick up music lessons from the same doctor singing in the same room, even though it was receiving the singing through the microphone. The purpose remains static or fixed.

So, one limitation for cognitive machines is that the purpose remains as fabricated for that machine. Indeed, arguments have been made that no such machine should be made which can show all cognitive properties of humans, as they might compete. With superlative hardware as compared to fragile human body and speed, computers with cognitive capabilities may cause human extinction if they wish to do so.

But that is not possible in the near future, so let us get back to our discussion of cognitive computing. The limited application of cognitive computing so far remains as something assisting humans in making decisions. This is not really a limiting factor, however. Their assistive capabilities are superhuman; they are very intelligent and can help make the most informed and best-calculated decisions possible.

For example, an IBM Watson for cancer assists the doctors in making the best decisions for critical cancer patients where a small deviation here or there might be fatal. The application cannot replace a doctor; so then what is the utility? Let us see what should be the true capability of a doctor doing this diagnosis. This expectation is not any scale given by any organization and considered mandatory to qualify as a good or bad doctor. Rather, the expectation is that of the doctor herself to be the best in her field: to do the best diagnoses and patient consultations and to treat patients with the greatest probability of success in the shortest time. In short: best treatment. There are about 30,000 to 50,000 research papers published every year just on cancer treatment. That is something like 80 to 140 papers per day. There are millions of cancer cases diagnosed every year across the globe. On top of that, there could be millions of pages within medical textbooks on the same subject across the globe. So, any doctor determined to provide the best consultation should want to go through all this knowledge, be able to refer to any part of it for details relevant to specific patient cases (as there are various types of cancers), and then decide on treatment. This isn't humanly possible. This is where Watson for cancer jumps in. With its cognitive capabilities, it relates to the right sources, including an organization called bestdoctors.com, to get the latest diagnosis details by the top physicians in this area. The machine learns the patient's current stats and sifts through all the relevant details (even almost in real time), and then suggests weighted paths of treatment with the probable result.

So, cognitive computing with all its capabilities partners with humans to add value to the processes and actions to be taken. It works as an advisor, as depicted in Figure 7-3.

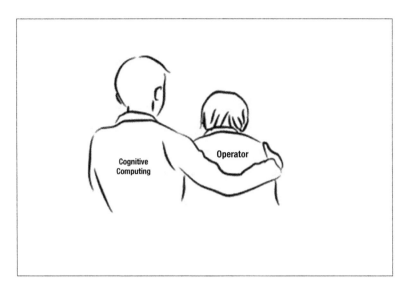

Figure 7-3. *Cognitive computing confidence building*

For businesses, this could be even a bot upgrading itself with each outage and bug and maintaining the system tirelessly round the clock.

Cognitive Era

The current era is considered as third-generation computing. Computing started with basic tabulating computers in the 1900s and proceeded to the next generation of computers, called programmable computers (1980s), moving to programming capabilities in conjunction with the Internet by the 1990s. I will keep both programmable and programmable with Internet in the second generation. The second generation's later phase with the Internet was perceived as the ultimate generation until the 2000s, when cognitive computing started to come into existence (Figure 7-4).

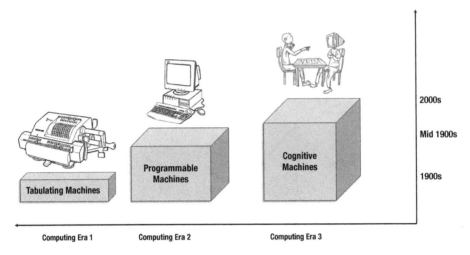

Figure 7-4. *Computing eras*

The concept of computing was redirected from fast calculations to highly complex machines deriving rule-based answers in programmable machines.

The tabulation machines were limited to achieving big calculations speedily and with more precision, much like a calculator.

With programming-based computers, we were already into a world of machine learning and cognitive in later stages, but then it was mostly pseudocognitive learning.

With the advent of and demand for cognitive computing, we moved into an era where machines would answer like humans, based on confidence in the machine's existing knowledge corpus. As with humans, the answers are judged to be right or wrong based on current knowledge and experience. The answers might not be straightforwardly an A or B, but could be C as well based on the experience learned by that time. Another aspect was that if these machines could learn, they could even make mistakes in case of little or no knowledge in that area.

The cognitive era came up with machines which could learn from huge data and information under the hood and would generate their own learning maps from that. It was also thought at times that this huge data necessity could become a limiting factor. The system was using capabilities to interact much more effectively using NLP. The synergy between human and machine became more complete.

To reach to this era of computing, we needed high-capability hardware with feasible prices. This was achieved almost fully by the 2000s.

So, the era of human-machine collaboration in the realest sense started with cognitive computing. This is yet not the era of machines; rather, this is the era of human-machine collaboration. A man who is assisted by such a superhuman capability could then perform higher-order tasks in decision-making and would be free from basic preparation steps in performing any task best.

The data requirements for these systems to process to reach out to conclusions would be enormous. The enhanced capability to store and handle such big data went along with the ability to make such machines.

Table 7-1 displays the major differences between the traditional computing and cognitive computing. This table will explain what was new and came with the cognitive computing.

Table 7-1. *Traditional Computing vs. Cognitive Computing*

Traditional Computing	Cognitive Computing
Mostly mathematical and logic resolver	One step ahead; goes further to generate relations and conclusion derivations
Gives discrete data results or pattern projections	Answers questions like What if? How?, How best?, etc.
Rule-based computing; covers only the sets of answers fed from programming	Creates or reaches out to answer in form of weighted conclusions; also, might answer the same question differently with knowledge gained through experience
Mostly executor of actions	Mostly advisory in nature
Fixed inputs and outputs (maximum decided for each)	Could have unlimited variables
Planned for preplanned activities and scenarios	Also for preplanned activities, but scenarios under that may change or vary

The number of cognitive applications is increasing day by day, and huge numbers of new developers are trying to explore all sorts of new ways to achieve cognitive computing. IDC forecasts that by 2018, half of the development teams will be engaged in such developments.

Cognitive Architecture

This is the structure of the thinking machine, either a brain or a human-like computer. In the case of cognitive computing, the architecture and plan together allow it to act as a cognitive thinking machine. So, basically a model must be created, and this model is the cognitive model. This could be of various types. The model should be always based on ideas based on human cognition and then expanded and generalized to make it possible to convert it into mathematical models working in tandem and written in a specific language.

There are many such architecture models available: Google DeepMind, Soar, ACT-R, CMAC, CLARION, and many more.

Let us discuss some of them in length and then conclude with a summary about the architecture at the end of this chapter. All these models are principally trying to describe the way brains process information and then converting this description to an algorithm or mathematical model.

Soar

Soar was originally created by John Laird, Allen Newell, and Paul Rosenbloom. It tries to create programmed cognitive models to do a vast array of intelligent actions mimicking thinking, decision-making capabilities, and so forth.

The base theory talks about the problem space from which every current state drives to the next possible single state, and so on and so forth until an intelligent action is concluded.

The graphical models display the state and stage combination, and processing happens by combined efforts from procedural and working memory functions.

Soar is written in C, C++, and JAVA languages. The primary uses are for gaming and robotics.

ACT-R

This stands for "Adaptive Control of Thought—Rational" by John Robert Anderson, Carnegie Mellon University. In terms of technology, this is an interpreter written in a specific coding language, and it processes information to then sequentially demonstrate the resultant cognitive responses.

This is based on psychological and neuroscientific research findings.

Any developer can use this technology, language, and interpreter to create various mind models.

This is influenced by works of Allen Newell in creating Soar models.

CMAC

This stands for "Cerebellar Model Articulation Controller." As the name suggests, this is a machine designed along the lines of part of the brain called the cerebellum. This was first proposed by James Albus in the essay "A Theory of Cerebellar Function" (*Mathematical Biosciences* Vol 10 No. 1-2, February 1971).

The cerebellum is related to motor control, imaginary activities, language perception, and so on.

The whole concept was derived from deep study of nerve fibers inside this part of the brain and seeing how messages are passed over these cells to finally record a sensory perception by the brain.

CLARION

This stands for "Connectionist Learning with Adaptive Rule Induction On-Line," and was proposed by Ron Sun's research group. This talks about the subconscious and conscious parts of brain, which are called the "implicit" and "explicit" parts of the brain, respectively. This is closer to a model from psychological studies. Every cognitive module is a combination of implicit and explicit parts and is driven by motivation. This could be thus considered the way humans (or animals) respond, with every action being driven by some motivation and action coming from implicit and explicit combinations of brain response.

So, the various architectures for cognitive computing are influenced by brain functions. Different models have their basis in different aspects like sociology, anthropology, neurosciences, neuroimaging, brain functioning, psychology, and so on. All these biological sciences are used to reach out to conceptualize one or more of the models to be considered as the way the brain processes information. These various architectures are then generalized mathematically to convert into computation models. These are then converted into real machines by various choices of hardware and software.

There are numerous such models available now and counting up in numbers with more and more participation of companies in this area. There are many commercial products coming up every day.

Cognitive Chip

There are various computer chips available now which are not based on the conventional architecture of Von Neumann but are designed to very closely mimic neurons and their network in the brain; these are called neurosynaptic chips or cognitive chips. IBM TrueNorth is one such chip. Because of this structure, such a chip consumes extremely low power as compared to conventional chips. These chips do not have a clock and instead follow events to run the flow of signals through their cores. Being event driven, they do not run continually but only when an event occurs.

Why Cognitive?

Any technology need is due to business need and is limited by technical knowhow and resources.

Cognitive computing is a much-awaited technology marvel which was conceptualized a long ago but is only being realized now.

The need for cognitive computing is not recent but has been around for quite a long time, and with the ever-greater usage of data and its bulk generation it has become much more needed now. We are in a world now which generates a quintillion terabytes of year. As described by IBM CEO Ginni Rometty, data is the next natural resource to drive business.

Cognitive solutions address current needs because they go beyond systems which can be programmed to act only on fixed inputs and provide fixed outputs. They should be smart machines and think. They should be working as assistants and not as tools.

The IT infrastructure was once considered only as a set of tools supporting some decision-making or supporting some activities. Now, with the advent of cognitive computing, this becomes a driver of business; this is the need and expectation of the current age businesses.

A machine has the upper hand in reading a billion book pages in seconds, creating a knowledge corpus out of it, and using it in decision-making. These machines and humans together could do wonders. This will help not only in doing pattern analysis or presenting reports, but also in optimizing business process and generating opportunities.

For example, as mentioned earlier in this chapter about doctors treating cancer, this technology extends the capability of a seasoned doctor to make better decisions. This does not take away the expertise required from people, but extends it beyond all previous expectations.

Again, this is the era of IoT (Internet of Things), which also contributes considerably to big data. The cognitive systems work wonders with IoT data to help make quick decisions. A thinking machine understanding the language of machines communicated through sensor signals could help these two worlds, the real world and the machine world, converge to make better decisions, which itself is a need naturally arising out of the velocity and volume of data coming out of these machines using IoT. In fact, the use of IoT has made cognitive computing more needed than ever.

This is because it can read and make sense from a vast array of data which is normally not possible for humans. It must be processed one piece at a time by a human operator.

The understanding and learning from such a variety of high-volume data are better used by machines than human operators. There is an effectiveness gap in using these resources (see Figure 7-5).

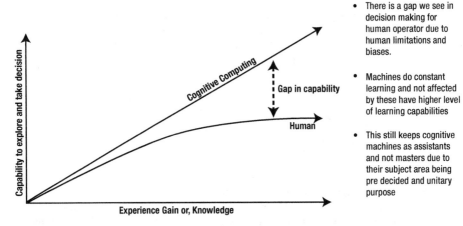

Figure 7-5. *Human vs. cognitive utilization of data resources*

Decision-making is a very important operation for any business. Conventionally, decision-making with business intelligence is still dependent upon management and business dashboards and reports. This means that someone must still sit back and collect and compare these and then come up with a conclusion to achieve this.

This is affected by the various capability levels of participants, their ability to consistently adhere to standards, how busy they are, and so on. We can say that humans are limited by these factors and more. However talented a person, he or she is often limited by situations and various other factors, and these may have dampening effects on the results. Again, the dimensions of data needed to be compared to derive any conclusion could be too many (e.g., finance, logistics, material, project plan, etc.). It is really time-consuming and still with no guarantee that even a talented data scientist would be able to consider all dimensions required to reach a given conclusion. If the result is not found relevant and another combination is thus required, extending the effort and time could again extend the activity. Also, there is at times, in fact mostly, a lack of deep business and organization strategy awareness within the data scientist team and a lack of technical knowhow for doing such activity within the management team. It is nearly impossible to reach out toward any possibility to have a set of people working with such huge volumes of multiarea data and still to be able to keep changing these combinations to try to get a good conclusion or even meaning from the data. Then there is something called learning from the past. That means that any such scenario or data point available now should be able to help optimize the current work in hand.

The decision-making process is thus standardized, optimized, of high confidence level, with all relevant data (structured or unstructured), near real time, and extremely rapidly done. That's the power of cognitive computing, and that's why it's needed.

The decision-making activity for business strategy is just one aspect. Even the knowledge level gaps of people working in projects are filled by these machines. They help to provide the required knowledge to do a task immediately and in the right context to these people. So, not only do the reporting, monitoring, and management aspect with a high volume of multisource data create a need for cognitive, but also the high utilization purposes of human resources could be achieved using this.

The data which could be analyzed is not limited to the organization's business data only. This could be data from all relevant and trusted sources to be used in analyzing to further come up with better decision-making capabilities. For example, an organization making decisions about price adjustments could also see global benchmarking data and data from competitors and also use sentiments derived from social and other web sources to make sharper decisions and to get maximum possible win rates for these decisions.

All these reasons and many more boil down to certain specific reasons for having cognitive systems. They are as follows:

Was Always Desired

The very first assumption or theory made for having an artificially intelligent machine was for a machine which is like a human. But technology limited this. Now, since we have all the technology needed to achieve this, it is a natural choice. A very shallow argument, but one that I am sure makes sense.

Big Data and Insights

The volume of data is being generated everyday is huge, whether it's the business transaction data of an e-commerce or logistics company or a trading firm, the data from sensors, or the data from web sites in the form of text, video, or audio. So, this massive volume consists of both structured and unstructured data.

Sitting on this heap of data makes it much more difficult to analyze with fixed reporting and tools. Correlation between connected data and real-time data is a must to understand the right patterns for decisions. The cognitive systems not only generate patterns but also churn out weighted insights.

Advisory

The cognitive systems help primarily as advisory systems, and with gathered knowledge and experience, they offer apt advice for any situation. What has happened? How do we manage this? How was this handled in similar situations earlier? All these and many more questions can be answered in seconds. The evidence-based answering with the weighted most probable answer is provided, going beyond just a yes or no.

Where there could be a challenge to combine multiple facets of data with external data to come up with a conclusion, cognitive computing comes as a magic wand solution.

IoT Leverage

In a world of connected machines and their sensors, communication should be understood and even analyzed with correlated business data. This is leveraging the IoT data. Otherwise, it would make no sense to have a dashboard separately to monitor only. This will only help in device maintenance.

Business Continuity

Chatbots are the new support agents available all the time and accessible from all devices equally. These chatbots are important not only for external customers but also for employees working in the organization. This helps to give information not only to the customers about products and services but also to employees about solving any problem where there could be a knowledge gap and quick assistance is needed.

Utilize Resources

Resources can be utilized most optimally with cognitive computing capabilities. Some oil and gas firms are already using this together with sensor-fitted submersible pumps and devices to read through the survey data and utilize the natural resources to the max for extraction.

Even farmers with soil-embedded devices and IoT-connected pumps can manage irrigation with minimal usage of water and as required.

The computer chips running on these models are not always in power consumption modes and are triggered to act on the basis of events.

Efficiency

The world is becoming a smaller place with each passing decade. Businesses are competing with shrinking margins. Cognitive systems not only help in margin improvement by optimizing a lot of processes but mature with the organizations and become more and more knowledgeable about all the data there. They leverage external data in any form and then become an asset to the organization to be able to take much better decisions and find more and more meanings from data over time.

These systems help to improvise and optimize the core of operations and remove unnecessary processes from organizations.

Customer Satisfaction

Since they are experiencing shrinking margins and fierce competition on a global platform, businesses cannot afford to have bad customer relations. The advent of social media has made things worse for them at times. A bad word could spread like a forest fire and spoil the overall image of that firm or its product or service.

For example, one of my friends recently made a Facebook post about the postsale service of a very famous domestic water purifier company. He had a bad experience with the service technician. In a matter of hours, there was a response appearing on his timeline from the company representative asking about the details and promising to have a dedicated support to fix the issue faced.

This is the level of customer support possible with the cognitive-assisted applications.

Another aspect is recommendations and customer journey manipulations driven by such applications. Netflix and Amazon are good examples in Chapter 1.

Customized Care

Whether it's the retail customer standing in the store and being helped by a cognitive assistant to find what he needs and suggest what he should take or custom medical solutions, cognitive computing is a big help.

More Ad Hoc

Reporting capabilities before cognitive were limited by being planned, designed, developed, tested, and sent to production. The cognitive-driven models are far more capable. A simple natural language sentence could be used as the query to get the desired results and data.

As an example, let's imagine a company that's in the process of acquiring another. At that very point, the CXO-level leadership wanted to have a quick evaluation of their assets that may be relevant to the current acquisition, along with details of associated products and services. Now, the organization has two reports existing for these. One is assets reporting and the other is on products and services. Though the first report had some details of assets and products associated together, the other one had all finer details of products and services. This now becomes a challenge: someone must play with the data. Developing a new report even using self-service applications is not as easy as it's often promoted to be. The resulting situation is a "run, run" situation with many goof-ups possible. The business intelligence system is not flexible enough to bring in a new report immediately when required, and moreover doing this requires additional people like technical developers to be involved, which is not always expected or even possible.

With a cognitive-based system (e.g., IBM Watson), a simple English statement, "Hello Watson, I need asset data with all product and service details with sales information," should enable the system to quickly summarize the required data onscreen, not only in tabular format but even with a myriad of graphs and associated data.

I would say that this need was always there, but can be fulfilled only now.

Generate What's Required

We already have capabilities now where a computer can create music through cognitive abilities. So, what about food and movies being made according to taste? This is the future of cognitive computing. Netflix is already moving in that direction; some food companies would come up with recipes that are most appealing to certain groups of people and even individuals. So, assume a pizza company knows what proportion of vegetables and meat would be right for you based on your taste preference history, what you buy from the grocery store, or even what you store in your refrigerator. This might even include data from your Fitbit and allow you an additional amount of cheese. This is the future of the food business.

Look Inside

The exhortation to "look inside yourself, rather than looking outside" used to be only a theme for meditation. However, it's applicable now even for today's businesses that use cognitive computing.

Cognitive computing has the very basic capability of being able to play an advisory role. As seen in Figure 7-6, this means we have achieved the highest possible capability: prescriptive analytics.

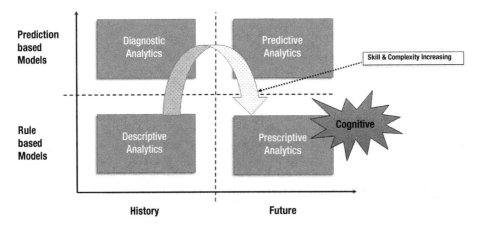

Figure 7-6. *Analytics capabilities*

This is the reality of businesses now: such a high level of prescriptive capabilities is not "good to have" but "mandatory." Looking outside for winning factors is no more considered the only act of success. In going out and searching the forests of markets for footprints of customers and prospective customers, looking out for all the competitive factors cannot be the only strategy any more. In the globally competitive market where margins are thinning, only looking out would not at all be the deciding factor for determining winners or laggers. I am not using "losers" here, as I understand that all companies try to do their best in survival, competition, and customer relations, but if the cognitive edge is missing this would become their lagging end. The laggers would lose.

There have been many areas of performance and process optimization that companies were always trying in order to make a difference. The top leadership, the drivers of the organizations, and the CXO level all were looking into this straight from the top to see where they are in the market. The efforts were worthwhile. There was a rate of success which is commendable, and this happens every day in the life of such an executive body in any organization. But still, are we missing something or could we make it better?

Google displays the meaning of the term "bias" as "inclination or prejudice for or against one person or group, especially in a way considered to be unfair."

We are not talking here about biases about people or groups of people by some person or any group, so let us convert this into a sentence relevant to the decision-making process.

We all know the "decision" is equivalent to success or failure for any organization. Bad decisions put a new hole in the bottom, and mediocre ones hardly get good profit. So, the goal should be more toward having more decisions hitting the right spot to maximize success rates. Biases play an important role in making things difficult.

Let me first reframe the earlier definition of bias I mentioned before.

Bias in decision-making is "a clutter in thought or inclination or prejudice toward any probable decision to be taken by any executive affected." And such problems come about because of human cognitive limitations or emotional pulls, and which may be intentional or at times not even known to be happening by the person affected and making decisions.

The decision-making person or even a group of people may get affected without even knowing that this is happening. There could be bias because of

- too much information or information presented in a certain way

- overconfidence

- distraction or attraction

- lack of clarity

- lethargy, tiredness, or stress

- reciprocate some goodwill

- getting influenced by people, groups, or situations

- personal experience or choice or not liking something

- earlier handling of such situation (we assume and think the current one could be handled exactly like the earlier one)

- cultural or traditional beliefs

- not understanding something from deeper insight

- having unwarranted "assumptions" about the subject and not considering facts and opinions

- gut feeling

- no time or time being too limited to make decision while considering all aspects

- being corrupt or some malicious purpose

- change of focus from subject (maybe I have another offer in my mailbox and plan to resign next day)

- being favorable to some parties affected by decision

- being too defensive in situation or by nature or style of work

- some facts are missing and no time to gather them

These are only some of the reasons why bias in decision-making may occur. In addition, this can happen from the top to bottom. At the top, bias hampers strategy, and the bottom, it hampers the operations. There is another aspect: the top and bottom levels of management aren't considering the same level of facts and not connecting every time or in fact mostly never seeing if the same strategy is being taken as the guideline to run the business at the bottom.

So, biases and lack of direct monitoring of strategies and their realization at bottom comprise a risky gap. This cannot be left unattended (Figure 7-7).

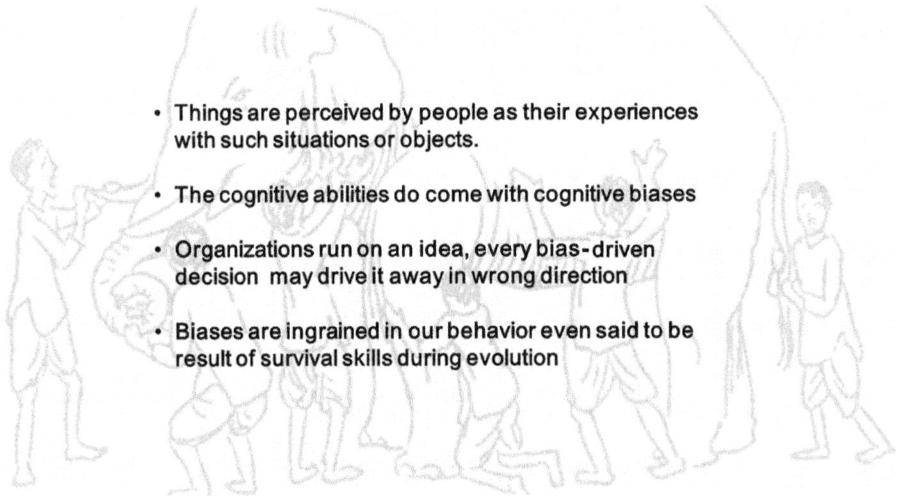

- Things are perceived by people as their experiences with such situations or objects.

- The cognitive abilities do come with cognitive biases

- Organizations run on an idea, every bias-driven decision may drive it away in wrong direction

- Biases are ingrained in our behavior even said to be result of survival skills during evolution

Figure 7-7. *Cognitive biases: some highlights*

This is another place where cognitive computing helps. It does not take decisions at the moment and replace the CXO level currently, but it empowers decision-making and "grades" the decision on the basis of probable biases that might be creeping in. It provides assistance and raises concerns if it sees that the simulation of a decision shows negative results if the decision were actually implemented. This covers a lot of risk.

The overall organization-level monitoring of policies and strategies and correlating day to day with such decision by lower-level management gives a clear picture if from top to bottom the decisions remain valid or are drifting in a different direction and causing loss of momentum and policy loss.

Let us take an example and see the difference.

A group of top management executives sits and reviews a situation for frequent raw material supply issues. There is a chain of suppliers involved. It happens that this meeting is being conducted on Christmas Eve. This is one of the regular strategic meetings. Since it's Christmas Eve and holidays commence the next day, it is necessary to finish this and move on to everyone's vacations. Although the purpose is never to be delinquent in decision-making because of this, still this factor is at the back of everyone's mind, causing its own effect (Bias 1: negligence driven).

Now, it happens that the suppliers are all from region A, and four of the five executives sitting on the board are also from region A, while the fifth person is a new person on the board from region C. There are two biases here, hidden but acting (Bias 2: some sort of prejudice): the two groups are from two geographic locations, and it happens also that they are from regions not sharing good rapport with each other, say due to football rivalries. The other bias (Bias 3: assumptions) is in play due to a newer person being on board: there could be mixed feelings on the part of the others, for instance, that he might be better at the job than them, or that they don't trust his capability as they have not known him for long.

The data support team also has some people on leave, so there's no access to the data that's been mined and presented to the board unless it happens to be available from previously created reports (Bias 4: irrelevant or incomplete information). Now the discussion begins and it happens that the new board member wants to put a new processing unit in region C, as he believes his gut feeling that this would help them to be safe if for some reason location A has some political or other issues; the data points to analyze his gut feeling aren't available fully, as some data personnel are absent, but he believes he saw some data that might have proved the point better (Bias 5: not enough evidence data). The board concludes finally with a majority not supporting the new idea and goes with some minor changes in the long relationship with the region A suppliers. They all go happily after the meeting for their vacations.

Now we see the human effect on the decision in the preceding scenario; on purpose or not, the decision was affected by several biases. The people were all dedicated and experienced masters in decision-making but the defects were there in decision-making due to biases. This is just one such example; there could be hundreds of such decisions during the year and of greater complexity too. The overall impact could be multiple changes at top management level that could even be disastrous to some extent over time. This is where data-driven culture supported by cognitive computing and supercomputing analytics could come to the rescue.

How does the situation look when there is a cognitive assistant helping there? The biases would be there but then there would be an evidence-based cognitive guidance safeguarding against this interfering with the decision-making process. Let us see how the decision-making would be different when a cognitive assistant was present to limit the effect of biases in decision-making.

The team of these five executives sits for a discussion on supply-related issues creeping in. The executives take the help of cognitive assistant, which has access to all relevant business data plus the latest data mined from news feeds, which it has extracted and understood. The cognitive assistant lets the executive board know about the situation in a very detailed and evidence-based way with one or two possible good solutions along with some assessments of the near-future impact of the solutions. It also tells them the recent impact on businesses from ongoing political news, and that they might have to face strict business regulations in doing business with suppliers from region A in the near future, so it would be wise to mitigate by having a processing unit at location C or D. Then, it points out that C qualifies better for this, being the closest to the manufacturing unit and raw material mines. It shows based on trends and evaluations that some suppliers are frequently missing deadlines and that this needs to be taken care of. Now, with this all detail and a prerequisite assessment with advisory details up to a future vision, things are more reliable and clutter-free. The executives are free from these preparations and ground assessments and could focus on only the following:

- Understanding the evaluation in more depth

- Reading the options and supplier evaluations presented with facts and evidence

- Taking corrective actions immediately about the suppliers as needed

- Comprehending the political issues that might affect the situation and possible necessary actions in response

So, in spite of being human and prone to such biases, the executives are not required to put them or mix them to business decision-making, knowingly or unknowingly. Business is kept as "straightforward business," and biases don't get the opportunity to get mixed into it. The culture is in a real sense data driven and evidence based. Simulations help them to reanalyze with evidence the "What-if" scenarios. No data support team is necessary. Not only has the system advised them, but it will in fact learn from this scenario based on final results and in between also keep track of the decision.

This is how cognitive computing could help get rid of decision biases to a large extent and limit the human cognitive bias–based quality defects in decision-making.

After this, the team could leave, satisfied with the decision made as they have much more confidence in decisions that are data driven and evidence based.

The other aspect, namely, that top-level management decisions should trace down to day-to-day management decisions at the bottom, could also be taken care of through these applications. So, every bit of the big puzzle is oriented in the right direction to sum up into the larger image for the organization as planned and decided by the top level. This is strategy orientation in a real sense. No need to have multilevel town hall meetings every quarter, which are even being skipped by some or else spent in daydreaming and looking at their watches by others, since it's just jargon to those at the bottom. They would mostly understand what relates to them in their operational language. A salesperson on a car showroom would find it rather difficult to understand and utilize in his operational sales activities sentences like, "The aim of organization is to sustain in market with a call to focus on sales spectrum expansion with collaborative business line sales and service portfolios." But it is easier for him when in an operational day a cognitive assistant guides him to do so. So, when he closes a deal to sell one expensive car to a client, the cognitive assistant tells him to cross-sell certain accessories based on (if possible) the customer's tweets and Facebook posts, and suggests that a comprehensive service package would be a good choice to be proposed to her, seeing that she has a long drive that she takes every year with her family.

Thus, every transaction at the ground level enforces or echoes the strategic goal of the organization without confusing employees or bombarding them with jargon. This level of engagement made possible by cognitive computing has tremendous benefits, perhaps even beyond explanation. It fills in the gaps and drives the business from policy to execution and with a possibility for each transaction.

The organization becomes equally focused at each level and drives uniformly toward its overall goal (Figure 7-8).

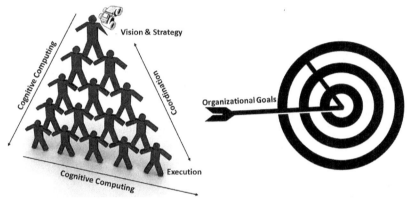

- Cognitive computing drives the wheels of organizations to have better decision capabilities and as a result better results

- It also drives the policy from top to bottom at all levels uniformly and consciously without fail and even with every transaction even at bottom of hierarchy

Figure 7-8. *Cognitive capabilities driving an organization*

This is the organization revitalized and rediscovered, an aspect of business management that was previously only a dream but that's now delivered by cognitive computing assistance. Many HR firms are already doing cognitive assessments of executives at every level to validate their role fitness, grooming, recruitment, and progression in career.

Cognitive + IoT

Let us talk a bit about IoT and its relationship with cognitive computing. Wikipedia defines the Internet of Things (IoT) as "the inter-networking of physical devices, vehicles (also referred to as 'connected devices' and 'smart devices'), buildings, and other items embedded with electronics, software, sensors, actuators, and network connectivity which enable these objects to collect and exchange data."

This means machines talking to machines and to people. The machines are the things and their electronic addresses are on the Internet, all connected via networks.

This means a lot of data every second. The sensors are connected to everything: factory machines, glass in windows, articles in stores, on people, on cars, and many more. All of this constantly generates loads of data. This could be any type of data, be it be audio, visual, text, or electronic pulses. This is beyond the coverage of conventional reporting for business intelligence in the following ways:

- They are constantly coming, mostly in real time

- They are too high in volume and velocity

The data must be rapidly understood and utilized with business data to make some sense in driving certain aspects of business. This is where supercomputing capabilities and cognitive computing help. Supercomputing capabilities help to capture and process data in any format, and then cognitive capabilities derive meaning and value out of it.

Cognitive computing works to get desired actions out of sensor data. It could combine it with the unstructured data to get more insight and generate necessary action recommendations. It could even use these data together with subject knowledge and historical experiences to generate more real-time monitoring and recommendations to overcome bad situations.

So, cognitive computing should be married with IoT.

Some of the business cases mentioned in the next section will elaborate more on this.

Use Cases

Let us discuss some cognitive computing use cases and benefits at a high level.

Cybersecurity

The entire world is getting more and more connected day by day. The initial devices on the Internet were PCs; now, we have many new kinds of devices on the Internet like health-monitoring wearable devices, smartphones, tablets, IoT devices, and even pacemakers.

The economy is going global; entire countries are going toward intelligence-based industries; everything is connected.

Early hacking incidents were immature and were more individually operated attacks. Attacks were mostly file based then. A file needed to plant into the machine to work. Normally, this used to go into the machines through executables or script injections. Now, given the way it is done and the massive scale, this could truly be termed a black industry.

Countries could also use this as the winning edge over other countries to get valuable military, organizational, and public data. They could use it to disrupt public services and organizations like banks.

Cybersecurity needs to be a vigilant eye keeping itself updated in real time, not only learning from previous attacks but also detecting events, incoming signals/messages, and even global alerts.

Firewall antivirus programs would need vulnerability patches and code fixes sent across to subscribers in the event of any new attack to enable them to control it.

This paradigm needs to be deeply built into the IT security landscape to

- Have a learning security system which gets sharper with time and increasingly able to detect mixed types or hybrid methods of attacks in any permutation or combination

- Keep an eye open to find suspicious patterns in events, signals, and behaviors to immediately send an alert

- Help the security workforce with all the needed information and fighting formulas based on past and current trends and experiences

The answer for all this is a cognitive security solution fighting cyberattacks. Such a system would keep an eye even on current global trends and start to focus on the vulnerable areas and increase security measures as needed.

Cognitive security is not a planned gate with all type of defense gadgets attached to keep away the attackers, which is changed every now and then to ensure they are kept at bay. Rather, it keeps itself updated and almost in real time tries to use all available knowledge within and outside to find a solution. So, rather than being only reactive, the cognitive solutions are proactive.

When it makes sense to have digital core and cognitive abilities in business, government, and all other types of organization and increase the dependability of this new precious resource, data, it makes sense to go for cognitive cybersecurity solutions to save them. These cognitive systems are intelligent enough to even monitor inside security threats as well. Someone logging into high-value systems at odd times could also be a threat that the cognitive systems could detect and then alert designated people.

Oil and Gas

Oil and gas exploration is a very challenging business niche. The costs and risks are extremely high. These resources have always been scarce and are becoming scarcer due to depletion over time. The places of exploration also are frequently difficult to access (e.g., explorations are common in the middle of the desert or the ocean). The political and business challenges are making it yet more complicated. Margins are thinning due to price changes, and so operating costs need to be reduced.

Exploration in this area is not new. So, a lot of stuff is already present in the form of

- Previous experiences in this direction

- Research papers and journals on the topics

- Engineering and other fine textbooks with all knowledge required for the procedural and engineering aspects

The tools are already heavily monitored using various sensors. The pumps submerged inside the tubes for exploration, the rigs, and the supply and machine pipelines all have sensors to monitor functioning. Still, some extremely important things, like weather data and machine failure predictions, were not connected.

Cognitive computing helps give a computer the eye of a technical expert and also that of a seasoned manager working on such projects together.

All the sensors, together with the unstructured data like weather forecasts, messages, notices, worklogs, and so on, could manage the work efficiently. They could easily predict mishaps or failures based on learnings from the previous experience knowledge corpus and real-time data from sensors.

The skill level has never been uniform across the floor. All do not have the same level of skills, maybe due to lack of exposure or experience at times. This aspect is also crucial as crisp information with relevant action points is necessary at times and can save a lot of time and money. This is also being taken care of by cognitive systems.

Predictive maintenance saves a lot of time by avoiding scheduled regular maintenance, and it is done when alerts are created with different priority levels by the cognitive system. Before sending the alert, the system is already ready with spare parts, maintenance options, and service technician details and passes on the relevant information to the correct team for fast and timely action, reducing overall downtime.

All devices talk with each other in the oil fields, and together they are connected with the cognitive assistants as the central interpreter and executor.

This saves a huge amount of money for these companies.

It also gives a high level of confidence about instruments' running condition in the field in real time. The cloud of uncertainty is reduced as the instruments now autonomously give status reports to the cognitive system. The system in turn can make sense of the huge amount of constantly flowing data.

Risk management and operational efficiencies, like little need for downtime and avoiding scheduled downtime, could save millions for oil and gas companies.

This makes the manpower very productive and efficient, as cognitive assistants guide and support even the mediocre worker to help him work more efficiently.

Moreover, the machine predictive maintenance would avert bigger mishaps or work getting stalled for hours.

Because of high investments, the number of sensors, the number of instruments, and high-risk exploration in hostile environments, cognitive married with IoT is a best-case solution for oil and gas industry.

Healthcare

There are two primary aspects of healthcare: prevention and cure. Efforts are always being directed by various governments and global healthcare and advisory bodies toward prevention. However, epidemic and endemic diseases still exist. Some diseases are very complicated to treat and even life threatening. Some are widespread: even if we have a cure, it is still necessary to watch out for mass infection.

The data needed for this kind of epidemic monitoring is multidisciplinary and multiple-source. There are various numbers and facts from many organizations which sum up to a complete picture; strategy can only come after that has been obtained. The timely availability of data could still be managed but then in case of a high risk of any epidemic, a smart monitoring and advisory on recommendations to be taken for the next course of action in real time is very much needed. This is where cognitive computing helps.

For treatments, knowledge about the disease is required, and not just from the medical books: a comparative analysis of all recorded cases of the subtypes of the disease and an abstract of all research on that disease published until that time would also help.

If the disease is like cancer, this is very important. A very good example is IBM Watson for cancer (oncology).

This has all the millions of pages of medical books loaded into it and knowledge created out of it. This knowledge could be text, medical videos, and even scans like MRI and CT. It can build knowledge out of this huge corpus of standard medical contents it has ingested. All the historical and more recent cases treated and success path or failure details are fed into it constantly from various sources. This adds up to knowledge, and everything is associated. There is a source bringing in medical comments and treatment methods from consultations with the world's top physicians. This adds yet another dimension of value. The remaining aspect of knowledge (i.e., updated knowledge for all research published to date) has to be ingested as well. Well, that is also taken care of. Thousands of journals and research papers are published with tons of statistics, images, and methods of treatment; all this is also ingested constantly in real time and prepared by Watson as associated valuable knowledge.

The doctor now uploads or keeps on updating all needed aspects of patient and disease (scans, reports, etc.) into Watson, and Watson also runs a diagnosis by referring to all the facts (billions of facts from all the sources available into it up to the very latest); this is done in less than a second, and it comes up with all the knowledge in the world about the disease, even drilled down to be for a specific age, stage of disease, and any other parameter. The results are clear lines of treatment with evidence and in order of recommendation priority. The lines of treatment are not just put out as simple information but are evidence based and could be further narrowed down by adding or removing tags displayed along with them. Say, for instance, that tags with the evidence are shown for a certain line of treatment for a certain patient, and the doctor wants to see the difference in various lines of treatment if he considers some heart weakness diseases alongside previous blood pressure history and age (as there is a chance of weakening heart muscle with some chemotherapy drugs). Watson immediately reconsiders that by looking into all the knowledge within it and then corrects the recommended treatment line based on that new consideration. It updates the tags to add heart ailment types considered. This is simply impossible to be done even by the best doctors in the world. No human can be updated with all knowledge every minute or even hour and cannot even remember all available references. Even if the doctor has a list somewhere, it is not practically possible to go through millions of pages of books for every patient; it would be like researching for 10 years and then coming back to the patient to provide treatment. This is a revolutionary help to medical science in the form of cognitive computing.

Clinical Trials

This is a special area of healthcare, so I've kept it as a separate topic for discussion.

There are terminally ill or critical patients with diseases like cancer, where there is a possibility of benefitting from any relevant clinical research trials that may be available. The challenge here in this case obviously is a huge amount of data from the long treatment of a patient and all those medical reports and scans. To qualify for a certain trial, the patient should meet all necessary criteria.

This is extremely complicated considering the following:

- The patients in this case mostly have high numbers of scans and reports and long medical histories documented with unstructured information.

- The time to interpret all this data from unstructured long history is extremely long, and interpretation is also complicated.

- It is an error-prone manual job and may also deficient, as the doctor doing this may be too busy and might delay or miss some information.

- The information from trials is pretty detailed and the permutation combination of patient stats vs. specific trial match is difficult.

- Considering the large number of trials present, it's very difficult to ascertain the best possible match, and one might even have been missed after an initial finding of a good patient-trial match.

So, this time-consuming and error-prone process could miss some important trials that may be the best case for that patient. The reason is not negligence but the near-impossibility of achieving this in the right span of time. These factors may even cost a life.

The cognitive systems do this automatically and with evidence (i.e., the reason a specific match is recommended). This means that all records from a patient are understood from unstructured pool of data from prescriptions, diagnosis reports, scans, and other laboratory reports from the whole treatment history. This is then almost instantly matched with all of the available trials, and every match is described, with reasons, onscreen.

This could save a lot of lives where the luck and probability factors are replaced with a high confidence level of recommendations.

Summary

When we talk about cognitive computing, we are actually talking about the thinking computer. Such a computer is not limited to doing pattern analysis using a mathematical model. It goes beyond that and follows human cognition patterns and rules as understood from human cognitive science and as re-created in machines.

The human cognitive learning curve goes through various levels of maturity from infancy to adulthood and until we die. The phenomenon of association is key. The experiences registered in the brain should have associations in the brain; this is called associative memory. Any scattered and unassociated details are mostly lost from the brain.

There are various theories of cognitive computing. These are all inspired by human cognitive studies and have been implemented.

The purpose of cognitive systems is to assist the workforce using it. It goes beyond giving yes or no answers or just painting a pattern; it actually recommends solutions for a problem with evidence. This helps in reducing the effects of human error or limitations from important decision-making processes, from top to bottom in an organizational hierarchy.

So, it is not only for operational-level executions but also for overall optimization, synchronization, and making the strategy more effective and applicable uniformly across the organization.

There are benefits in almost every possible industry waiting to be explored and unveiled.

CHAPTER 8

■ ■ ■

Principles for Cognitive Systems

This chapter talks about the principles of designing cognitive systems. The systems to be used as cognitive assistants should be trained and designed in a way that works with maximum output in those areas.

■ **Note**   We have discussed in detail about what cognitive systems are and what kind of benefits we could expect with some examples in Chapter 7. Now let us talk about how to design such a system in principle. These principles are a further base for detailed technical designs and activities. I will mention those steps at a high level at the end of this chapter.

Design Principles

What is meant by design principles? These are the principles or rules to make something. It could be software, a building, a machine, a dress, or anything else in the world, even a process.

There are certain basic steps which are required to design anything. Some steps are mentioned for every type of designing start, as the principle of design. The design then leads to actual creation.

There are certain common steps to design followed by anything on earth, as follows:

- Identify the problem area or need

- High-level scoping

- Identify references to help with the solution

- Feasibility analysis and rescoping

- Identify finer requirements or associations

© Rohit Kumar 2017
R. Kumar, *Machine Learning and Cognition in Enterprises*,
https://doi.org/10.1007/978-1-4842-3069-5_8

- Blueprinting

- Detailed execution plan

- Identify validation checks

- Develop test or pilot or beta version

- Validation

- Fix defects or deviations

- Optimize

- Feedback assessment

This is the path that should be taken for development, whether for an idea or a process or a machine or software.

I believe the design principles may be divided into two categories:

- Overall program to design and optimize. This is the principle covering the technical and the management and quality aspects.

- Overall logic or core setup. This is the technical or logic or core part of it. This is within the scope of overall program management but it has only bare principles related to design or the plan of core development. This is the scope for the real design principle.

So, from the preceding big list, the following should come under a second category:

- Blueprinting

- Detailed execution plan

- Identify validation checks

- Develop test or pilot or beta version

- Validation

- Fix defect or deviations

- Optimize

These are everything needed to develop anything. Anything before is also part of the bigger plan but does not include the actual core of the realization. Instead, it's based more on common sense and awareness. This is the reason these are specific to the plan for the final product.

The others are moreover generic steps and less affected by what the product is to be (e.g., software, machine, process, etc.).

The last one is concerned with gaining deeper insight into the developed product and then taking it to the next level of complexity or enhancement.

Let us discuss all the items in the big list one by one and see what they represent.

Identify Problem Area or Need

This is always the first step always. There should be some need or problem driving it; for example, manual register entry into an office building and punchcard-based entry each have their own difficulties and inefficiencies. This defines the problem area: to get more automated and less prone to unauthorized entry. The result could be a fingerprint- or iris- or RFID-based entry system.

Or, say there's a need to cross a river and bring a lot of things to the other shore; this need could have driven the construction of a boat or a bridge.

The problem, to qualify as a problem, should have to be recurrent or to be a need that must be fulfilled frequently. Very rarely is anything considered a need or problem under this category if it has a singular or brief occurrence and no or minimal probability of any recurrence.

So, such a problem or need should be well understood or even recorded somewhere before proceeding to the next level. The details are recorded by answering the question "What is required?" This loosely defines the problem statement.

Let's try to understand all these points with a simple example of solving the need to find a place of residence in a new city.

So, when there is a requirement or need to have a place to stay together with family in a new city, this should be described by answering the following question:

What is required? A place to stay is required. We will be staying for a long time and could not stay that long in a hotel. So, the problem or need is to find a place to stay.

High-Level Scoping

This is the next step toward design and development. Now, after the problem has been defined, the next step is to see what would be required to solve it.

Once "What is required?" is understood, high-level scoping is required. Now, the reasoning about what needs to be done is developed into a higher-order idea. It proceeds from just being a need or problem definition to becoming a constructive step toward realization. We start to gain a deeper sense of understanding about "What is needed?" So, this could be considered an extension of the previous step with a very fine line of differentiation. But in actuality, this might be done by a specialist or someone with some specialized knowledge. Or, some special knowledge might be required for this individual to reach this point.

Let's extend our example of needing a place to stay. Now we have input from the previous step which highlights the need to have a place for family to stay that's not a hotel due to the length of the visit. So, we have two primary factors: place for family and long term.

These must be used for the scoping exercise. So, now we consider thinking more deeply and trying to answer questions like

- What budget?

- Need to buy or lease?

- Which area of the city?

- What duration?

- What needs to be done? (e.g., agent should be hired or online advertisements should be viewed)

- Who among the family members would take what responsibility?

So, all these goals, features, durations, functions, tasks, and budgets should be followed.

This is the feature of this step. Remember, we have still not gotten into the real design principle formulation here, but part of the bigger principle of program management which will later have steps to allow core design principles to resolve the issue has started by now.

References

This is a wise step of looking at examples or templates that could help resolving the task at hand better by taking calculated risks and better decisions. This is applicable in almost all scenarios either directly or indirectly: directly by using some direct matrices from such an activity done earlier, and indirectly by observation or through some third-party research publications (e.g., Gartner Reports).

In any case, you can avoid risks by learning, planning, and determining where to take your first step before actually doing so.

In our example, this would be asking people around or known contacts in the new city about their experiences in getting a place to stay. What do they suggest or what have they done in this case? For example:

- Would buying or leasing be better?

- Which areas are better?

- Which agents or web sites are good to check out?

- What budget and negotiations should be considered?

- What are the risks and challenges?

- What timeline and process should be followed in all cases?

So, we can say this gives us a much better idea in a real scenario now to recalibrate our scope by considering these inputs. Expectations are also understood. This step helps in understanding the challenges and risks or hurdles that could now be considered inside the plan to ensure a better chance of success.

Feasibility and Rescoping

This is the next step: equipped from learning about the actual implications and experiences in the previous step, we now have a better idea about what the actual scope should be considering the actual experiences in achieving the task.

We now know what was expected, what we planned, and what has happened to people trying to do this in similar conditions and what kind of results they achieved.

This gives us an idea about what could be feasibly achieved for our actual need. It could be all, none, or partial. If all, then that's great; if none, then we need to adjust our needs toward what could be achieved or something that needs to be achieved beforehand. If partial, then we need to decide what could be done better; or if we are fine with partial, then replan and rescope that way. Except in the first case, where all can be achieved, a rescoping is always required. But feasibility must be assessed considering the reference-checking previous step.

So, in our example now we have inputs like the following:

- Buying would be better considering low prices

- The cost is low but still some funding would be required to pay for everything

- The registration of property is complicated paperwork and needs some prerequisite citizenship registrations to be done

So, the feasibility assessment has been done for buying or leasing, and it happens to be feasible to buy (which is generally considered a better choice anyway), but the scope of work has changed and citizenship papers should be considered as prerequisite and then must be added to the existing scope of work.

Feasibility and rescoping are by now using data from the reference step, and this now gives us a more confident scope.

Identify Finer Requirements or Associations

This is one more final check after the previous step to be able to have comprehensive scope availability. This is important, as machine development could come to a complete halt if one needed pin is not planned to be made or bought. So, the finer requirements and associations or dependencies can kill a whole project at times. They are either the finer considerations of the requirement itself or some associated dependencies.

So, continuing with our example, the following finer requirements and dependencies should be considered:

- All payments should be via local check and not cash, so a national bank account needs to be opened

- Recent photographs and a list of education and employment documents should be produced in original during property registration

- House insurance payment and process are musts before registering the property

- State taxes for sanitation and hygiene should be paid before occupying

- Electricity and gas registration must happen before occupancy

- A housewarming party should be organized, including an invitation to send to friends

So, this list shows some finer requirements and dependencies. There might be additional ones that are good to have as well (e.g., the housewarming party might be counted in this category). But now at this stage we have with us things which are completing the requirement with finer details like electricity, gas supply, and so on; some dependencies like a checking account and original documents; and some associated needs like a housewarming party.

This step provides better management of the whole project also and details about all dependencies which might halt things on the ground in their absence.

Blueprinting

By this time, the generic steps of the design principle at program level are done, and now we move toward creation; that's where the first step in actual design principle formulation starts.

We must plan every method, tool, process, and step on paper once to ensure we stick to it and will be able to measure future deviations. This is the blueprinting phase. It has two major dimensions: a sequence of actions (and outcomes after each action), and a timeline running parallel to it. Now equipped with everything from the previous steps, we need to plan things in proper sequence or some in parallel, also giving due consideration to the element of time. So, what comes after what and when is covered in detail on paper.

To continue with our example, now that every required aspect including the dependencies have been ascertained, we can plan things and prepare a blueprint of activities so that we do not miss doing anything at the right time in the sequence.

We must plan in the following sequence:

1. Search for and get details about prospective properties through agents before reaching the new city (now)- Wife can help here

2. Prepare prerequisite document sets (now)- To do together with wife

3. Reach and finalize property via house-finding trips (within first 2 days)- Whole family

4. Open bank account (within first 1 week)- I must do

5. Citizenship-related papers (within first 2 weeks)- With family

6. Finalize property papers (within first 3 weeks)- With agent

7. Pay for property and other utility connections (within first 4 weeks)- With agent

8. Housewarming (within 8 weeks)- With family

For this example, we now have a blueprint of work. Since the blueprinting is in the core design principle area, this is not generic anymore. This is specific to the result, in this case house-finding.

We have the following questions noted:

- What is the sequence of work?

- Who does what?

- What time line is to be followed?

Detailed Execution Plan

By this time, things are in place as a blueprint. Now we need to see all of the minute detailed actions needed to perform every planned activity of this blueprint. The blueprint lists the major activities or activity heads to be performed for completing the final goal, but then there could be other finer-level activities required to complete each such activity in the blueprint.

So, what could be finer-detailed activities here in our example? I will copy our blueprint from the previous section and then try putting the finer execution plan below each point there:

1. Search and get details of prospective properties through agents before reaching the new city (now)- Wife can help here

---

Finer Actions   Find a good agent by talking to and reviewing agencies, setting contract in place with an agent, planning how this happens (such as whether he will send photos and details about properties via e-mail), and determining what the time line is for this activity, what expectations he should follow, and so on.

---

2. Prepare prerequisite document sets (now)- To do together with wife

---

Finer Actions   Find all documents and put them together in one place, obtain any missing documents, take needed photographs, bundle copies in required sets, and so on.

---

3. Reach and finalize property via house-finding trips (within first 2 days)- Whole family

---

Finer Actions   Plan the day for trip with agent, plan a cab service, take a notepad or tab to note details, check required documents, discuss questionnaire with owners, and so on.

---

4.   Open bank account (within first 1 week)- I must do

Finer Actions   Select a bank, meet the banker, select a plan, look for loan, apply for it, follow all the process, get the certificates from bank, and so on.

5.   Citizenship-related papers (within first 2 weeks)- With family

Finer Actions   Plan interview with office, book a cab, appear for interview, do the specific documentations, get the certificates issued, and so on.

6.   Finalize property papers (within first 3 weeks)- With agent

Finer Actions   Get the legal papers ready, read with the owner, make plans if changes required, get it stamped or franked, get it registered, fill out the necessary documents, and so on.

7.   Pay for property and other utility connections (within first 4 weeks)- With agent

Finer Actions   Find out the exact requirements, including costs and documents, fill out forms and submit to respective offices, follow up, and get it done.

8.   Housewarming (within 8 weeks)- With family

Finer Actions   Plan a date, plan what to prepare for, list the guests, plan a caterer, book a decorator, send out invitations, get permission from necessary office to have a party, host it, wrap up after the party, clean up, and so on.

This helps us to plan things in a way such that best results are obtained. This step is also related to method adoptions and process alignment required to do the test better.

Identify Validation Checks

There is always a chance of deviating from the planned path. It cannot be the responsibility of a blueprint to check that we are still on the right track. Every activity has many substeps and even sub-subsets in between, and it is very easy to get carried away or keep deviating toward alternatives. This might make you end up in an entirely different place from what was planned. Therefore, it's extremely important to have a validation plan in place the moment we have a detailed execution plan ready. These timely and milestone-based checks could help in avoiding any deviation.

In our example, we have some checks which we could assume, as follows:

- Contract with agent in designated time, so that we start early with exploration. This must be done with agents that are certified A-grade by government.

- Timely document set readiness before we leave native place, so that we do not need to return to get any missing ones.

- Close finalization of property as quickly as possible to avoid staying in hotels, which gets expensive.

- Ensure within the required number of weeks that all certificates have been obtained.

- Ensure that all bookings are confirmed within the stipulated time to make the party go as planned. This is done only with selected vendors who have good reputations.

The validation checks help us to ensure that we have things done when required and the quality perspective is also checked. So, when we have a check from the time perspective of an agreement with the agent, we have another validation in place to be done with an A-grade agency or vendor.

The validations keep us on track and drive the quality of output too. We expect certain things at certain times and with certain levels of quality, and that is what drives the validation check plan.

Develop Pilot or Test

This is not always applicable in all goal achievement. So, there could be a whole step of planning required as listed for house-finding, but this does not happen for a single individual; in that case, there is no chance of a pilot result but some intermediates would be considered that way, maybe things like practicing the coming interviews with the agent, house owners, or citizenship office.

But for all other areas where we have constant developments with upgrade requirements, this is a very important step. This gives us a first-cut solution and would provide us with an initial version to test how we were able to achieve the goal, and in terms of quality metrics about how effective our efforts were. This shows the effectiveness of process and plan and helps in tweaking it based on this, and it could even help to put in some additional validation checks for further use.

This version is also good in all the scenarios where the developing and using parties are two different parties, and the user could examine the realized things to see if they are meeting his expectations. Even a realized object gives a better understanding at times about the requirements, and some change in scope can happen after trying the first-cut developed objects.

Primarily, however, this step is to check and find all the deviations and defects.

Validation

Continuing on from the identified validation checks: all validation checks planned at that stage are executed at this stage to ensure that what was intended to be realized has been. If any of the tests fail, action and effort in that direction are needed to bring it back to the right path. This is done in the next step.

Fix Defects or Deviations

Continuing from the previous stage, the defects or deviations are fixed in this stage. The strategy for fixing them is already noted at the start and it is implemented now.

This is an effort to realize exactly what was destined to be realized as the goal.

The more that defects or deviations occur, the lower the effectiveness toward development.

But the other side of the coin is that there must be some issues and defects for any project or goal achievement.

Ideally, this ends the cycle of development.

Optimize

When the goal is achieved almost to perfection by eliminating and fixing all defects, there is the scope of additional functionalities to be introduced. This optimization follows recursively everything from step 1: identify need or problem. This will generate the next level of expert objects or goals.

Let's say that a robot was created to carry a glass from one point to another. The next level of optimization could be a robot which not only does the same job, but also avoids any barrier placed in between while doing so. This is a new cycle of events right from the step of identifying the need or problem.

Feedback Assessment

This is a bit like the step of fixing defects and deviations. But there is a difference: the defect-fixing step is intended to fix defects as compared to the original plan and happens immediately after the development is done or the goal is achieved. On the other hand, feedback assessment happens for a long time after the deployment and is intended to find defects which are missing from the assessment of need and scoping. This says what should have been better planned to get to a superior goal, but this takes some time once experience with the goal has been obtained.

This step normally jumps back to the optimization step and then to step 1 (identify need or problem).

Basically, these are the meanings of the items in our list. The actual design principle is executed or created from the blueprint to the defect-fixing step. This covers how to make something in the best way, test it, and after that optimize. The core design or development of the goal occurs only between blueprint and development though. In between validation and defect fixing comes the quality perspective step. Feedback assessment is then done with longer experience at the current level of achievement to move to the next level.

Cognitive Design Principle

Let us now see the same concepts again, but this time in terms of a cognitive design principle. The principle here also will trace to exactly the same steps and have those two categories of higher design principle at program level covering everything and core design principles from blueprinting to development. Quality aspects are from validation to defect fixing.

Before we start, there is one aspect which should be kept in mind: cognitive solutions are not a simple technical skill–driven requirement. This cannot be something which might be an initial design specification requirement and consequently developed beforehand to test. It must be something progressively developed with the best possible design and collaboratively with business or management driving it.

Now let us see the same points in terms of cognitive design. The rule of thumb remains the same: the core cognitive design is only from blueprint to development. Before that is preparation, and afterwards comes quality perspective taking and optimization.

I will be talking about these points in an overview at first, and then in further sections, I'll talk more about the detailed technical steps with their properties and needs.

Identify Problem Area or Need

Obtaining a cognitive system is a strategic decision; if a cognitive system isn't implemented the option for operational activities would be what we always had, namely, enterprise resource planning (ERP), and for business reporting, this would be a data warehouse.

These will still exist in the future; then why cognitive systems in addition? What is the need? This answer would come from strategic analysis of enterprise, industry positioning, and market analysis together with financial analysis.

The details on how to get into cognitive-driven organization are included within the scope of some of the coming chapters. What we will discuss here are only basic guidelines about design principles of program and core cognitive design principles.

So, coming back to identifying problems or needs, the difference between key KPIs and key decisions should be understood. These KPIs should be collected for every distinct business and process area.

Once the key drivers and KPIs are grouped for every such area, the benefits that could be achieved are to be listed as priorities in descending order. So, the highest priority comes at the top. This must be picked up as the first need. The more strategic a need is, the higher-order value it will drive and least precedence it will take for being implemented first. The more operational it is, the higher it goes in the sequence of development. Figure 8-1 shows this.

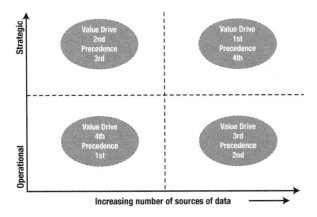

Figure 8-1. Operational vs. strategic value drivers

Once the priority is prepared, you have lists of needs or problems to be solved one by one.

The more sources of data are required and the more strategic they are, the closer it is to a cognitive transformation with the most value.

The less strategic and operational ones have lesser dimensions of truth required and so have lesser scope around them. Also, as per the priority displayed in Figure 8-1, the ones at lower priority are subsets of cognitive processes and get directions from the ones above them or else add up to the higher-order ones. So, the higher-level ones have higher strategic values being generated and the lower ones should have cognitive solutions of taking guidance from the higher ones.

That means that a cognitive system helping to take leadership-level decisions at the top should be providing guidance to the subset of the cognitive solution at the showroom level to guide a salesperson in her language and the activities she's performing at the ground level. The management decision taken by the cognitive system must take data from the ground level to the top of every department, learning the corpus for all department-related business areas and big data for watching the market. The one at store level, in contrast, will have fewer sources of data, ensuring that the strategy is executed at the ground level with less unneeded data.

Now, need should be identified and prioritized.

High-Level Scoping

This is the stage when every department should understand what needs to be within the scope in the first cut for the cognitive molding. Not everything might be visible, but the processes which upon such automation would give the most value should be identified. This again translates into a scoping at a panorganizational level with a wider perspective of what is to be developed overall.

This also includes summary of features, time duration, functionalities, and budget.

Now we have a high-priority process identified with all the functionalities to be implemented.

References

As the cognitive transformation is global in nature and extremely strategic, business references and, if possible, transformation examples should be learned. The nature being global means that even if it must be done for a single department first, or for a handful of priority departments, it would be referring to knowledge required to run it at the global level (e.g., all textbooks for those subjects, all data from related organizations, and relevant live data from the Internet). Even a solution for one small department will be operating at the highest order of possible knowledge. Therefore, references not only related to cognitive solutions but about success related to anything should be read, and an extract of this should be merged with the solution automation. This will create an intelligent system with more and more knowledge and wisdom.

Feasibility and Rescoping

Influenced by the previous step, this would provide the rescoping opportunity, and the feasibility step should be done side by side considering what could be taken inside the scope for the first cut.

Now we are talking about a mature face of an organization scoped with priorities listed out. The whole documentation consists of rescoped solution expectations.

Identify Finer Requirements or Associations

This is important: since now we have all higher-level requirements listed out, we need to finalize the sources we would need and design of data to be brought in. The associations, if any, in operations of related departments should be understood, and data related to it should also be brought into the scope.

This now results in a summary of functionalities listed with priorities and with what data it would need to be realized.

Blueprinting

By this point, we have everything we need to have, and now the actual design principle should initiate. We need first list the activities and priorities against timelines. This also should have responsible people as identified team members.

This becomes the blueprint, which is the first step in the core design principle and helps in its initiation.

Detailed Execution Plan

This is the core cognitive design principle area. What we are trying to create is not any machine learning solution where rules must be created, codes written, or network or deep learning created. We are talking about a solution which is available as ready to learn with all the features required to go through the cognition process of learning.

That is why the execution plan for that specific cognitive solution should start from singular types of issues or need satisfaction. This is best solved via a design thinking approach. Please see Figure 8-2 for the details of the design thinking cycle for cognitive design.

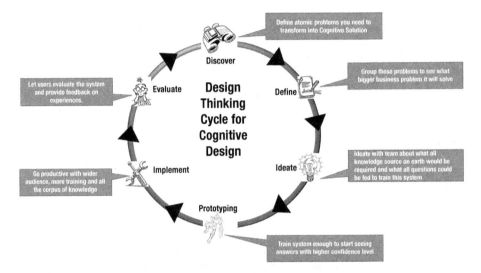

Figure 8-2. *Design thinking approach for cognitive design*

The design thinking process is a nonlinear process, so any step could repeat itself after any other, or the whole process could go back to any previous step.

This is the design principle at core of cognitive systems, a marriage between design thinking and the cognitive system learning process.

The implementation should be started one by one from bottom (least strategic or operational + less data source related) to top (most strategic + most data source related).

The system must learn the process to come up with solution recommendations. So, the simplest and most atomic business process–related learnings should be taught first, and then complexity should go up only after that. This increases the value of recommendations compared to what would be seen for individual business departments or processes.

Let us talk now about one example of execution plan complexity to understand what is meant by the preceding sentence.

Say a company, let's call it ABC, wants to have a cognitive system to make a recommendation for them to decide which supplier from a pool of suppliers would be good enough in case of a revised decision for any order to be redistributed among a new set of suppliers. This means, for example, that planning for realignment must be done for a changed scenario involving another set of suppliers, and ideally, that recommendation should also originate from a cognitive system as an alert to do so.

What could be all the reasons for this?

- Political unrest

- Weather conditions

- Sales driven

- Customer feedback/sentiments

- Supplier performance

There could be any number of reasons. Let us consider only those just listed: what areas of business or knowledge are touched? Let us see:

- Latest relevant news updates

- Weather forecast and analysis

- Sales transaction data

- Concepts of selling (all possible books, journals, rules of this specific organization and learnings)

- Customer Master-data

- Customer feedback (all sources including social media and other web sites)

- Sentiments (text analysis data, voice of customer)

- Supplier Master-data

- Supplier trends

- Supplier feedback and learnings

- Financial data

- Product Master-data

- Product sales data (sales data with respect to products)

- Legal data

- Contract details with suppliers

- Production data

- Plant data

- Order data

And many more.

When all these are available, a cognitive system could understand some high-probability weather issue from a specific supplier region and could raise an alert. Also, based on other details, it could also recommend which should be the alternate supplier and what impact it will have. This is a big strategic and operational recommendation.

All the previously listed department and knowledge areas should be fed as knowledge data from singular areas, namely, the individual operational areas (e.g., sales, finance, or contract data). The number of sources for data is lower here, and data is operational in nature. They all combine together with all other data sources to generate strategic value recommendations in terms of the alert and alternative supplier planning.

The value of recommendation is of higher order as compared to the singular operational department–related recommendations, and it has more capability in terms of the scope of the area being covered for business.

This is what we mean by complexity (operational or strategic level) and multiple sources of data being fed in a particular order increasing the value of recommendations as described earlier. It is not the linear addition of capabilities from individual areas but a joint new capability or value from them together.

So, the execution plans are multidimensional, with time and activity as one dimension that's then associated with connected developments at the next dimension, which further combines with final higher-level solutions using all such associations. See Figure 8-3 for this.

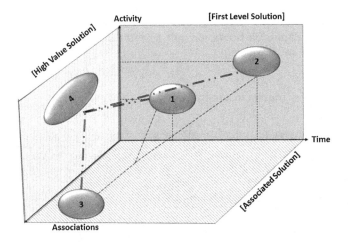

Figure 8-3. *Dimensions of complexity of execution*

In Figure 8-3, the ovals labeled 1 and 2 are two solutions developed for areas in a business over time with various levels of activity. They are individual solutions around individual areas. When we say solution here, we mean a cognitive solution around that business area. These solutions, 1 and 2, belong to one dimension and are the simple individual or atomic solutions.

Now, solution 3 is in another dimensional plane and is associated with solutions 1 and 2. So, it uses some new area knowledge, and all of the knowledge from 1 and 2 is also used. This brings it to the category of associated solutions, those which are more complex then 1 and 2 and are using them as well.

Then we see solution 4 in the figure, which is the combination of all singular/atomic and associated solutions. This is the most complex solution, which is built on top: the highest-order solution.

These are the dimensions of complexity and are planned via an execution plan. So, this is also the complexity of the execution plan.

Now, one thing should be noted here, that for sake of convenience and to be able to easily explain terms like "different levels of basic and associated solutions" (1, 2, and 3 in Figure 8-3) and "higher-order, most complicated solution" (4 in Figure 8-3) that are being used. In reality, the same cognitive solution is extended to the various levels of complexity over time.

So, it could be said that the system is trained initially to recommend simpler solutions and related to multiple singular departments or processes, and then over time the complexity increases with the type of problem (operational to more strategic) and increasing scope of knowledge input to the system. There are no multiple systems created for each and one on top.

It could be shown as in Figure 8-4.

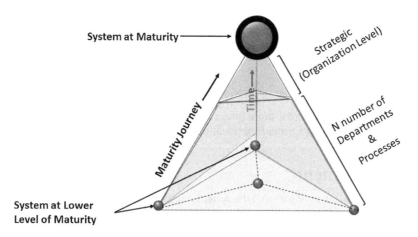

Figure 8-4. *Maturity path of cognitive systems*

These are points needed to be kept into consideration as design principles for cognitive systems as planned in this stage. This must be executed further when development (knowledge corpus building, training, and user interface) starts.

Identify Validation Checks

As usual for any kind of development or goal achievement, it is very important to identify goal checks or validation conditions. It is easier to lose track in terms of cognitive systems. So, very tough and realistic tests should be planned both as positive and as negative tests. The cognitive system may amaze with its capabilities of answering and revealing some interesting facts not known earlier. People could easily get carried away due to this, and any temptation to consider such new data aspects should be left aside to be explored later. Strictly, the validation checks against all planned functionalities desired should be planned and well documented and only tested later.

Develop Pilot or Test

This is when first-cut knowledge corpus is loaded to the system, curation is done, and the cognitive system is ready to create its weighted analysis and make its own learning map out of it. The first set of questions to train the system starts to be added to the system, and the system is now ready to answer. With every new question, the system is further trained. It is good to start collecting questions at early stages when requirements are being gathered. Then, this system is pilot or test level system ready. The knowledge corpus building and related material are explained in some detail at the end of this chapter.

There are other areas of development, like user interface development, which are not the subject of this book.

Fix Defects or Deviations

A quick check with validation parameters decided in the early stage is required to get confidence as to the level of answers.

Optimize

Once the system has been running for some time as per design thinking concepts, it is time to optimize the system with further functionalities or updates in the current ones.

Feedback Assessment

This is a continuous feedback to ensure that the system is organic and new business relations and data points will keep being discovered over time and added to the system. Also, experts should be allowed to keep interacting with the system to be able to learn more in those areas. This will make the cognitive system more and more effective over time.

The design principles for cognitive systems are limited to the detailed execution plan of cognitive systems discussed in Cognitive Design Principle section.

Cognitive Work Analysis

Cognitive work analysis (CWA) is an interesting framework for sociotechnological application development. This term was coined by Vicente (1999); it's a framework which was developed by Rasmussen, Pejtersen, and Goodstein (1994) to analyze cognitive work.

This concept talks about information retrieval by users from systems which are adaptive to the responses as coming in influenced by various internal and external factors. However, the "users" are not considered users but are considered "actors" instead.

What is the difference? "User" is more of a static term to which the purpose is prefixed: superuser, admin user, developer user, business user, and so on. So, the way authorizations and roles are assigned to them, they have a limited relevant list of activities that they can perform in the system. As the actions are finite, the way it must be asked to the system irrespective of real scenarios in hand with the user the input and output remains the same. It does not matter if the user is angry or hungry or sleepy or in the mood to do some other undefined activity. The system won't budge; it will only take designated commands and process the data in steps as relevantly planned into it, because it is limited to serve types of users as defined and limited by rules and configurations in the system.

So, then "context" comes into the picture, and the "actors" act based on current environment and situations they are into and behave accordingly. There could be infinite ways the "actor" can express the same "sentence," but with a different context.

In the real world, the same person could also express the same sentence or line in a different way as influenced by the situation, work environment, and so on. The behavioral changes of expression cannot be the only attributes considered to decide context; other attributes should be considered as well, or else there is no guarantee that "mental instability" could also be considered as valid (Fidel and Pejtersen 2004). So the focus shouldn't be just on behavior.

Scientists (Patricia Katopol et al., 2006-2007 http://collab.infoseeking.org/resources/papers/KatopolUIowa.pdf) have come up with multiple other dimensions like work environment, organizational analysis, work domain analysis, task analysis, decision analysis, strategy analysis, and many more. So, the overall reason for the act by actors should be understood in order to respond intelligently.

Also, it can't be based just on how most people or such actors react in such a situation; it must be smart enough to analyze the situation and the reason behind the interactions.

So, considering all the factors that influence an actor within an organization or subject interacting from outside the organization for specific purpose, a context should be reached out and not only via emotional attributes or plain behavioral signatures.

In a nutshell, it could be said that to be able to design a system for a specific purpose, in-depth understanding of the work should be there. The various influences, whether internal to the job or external, should be understood; this will help to design a system (even cognitive) which could provide expected outputs.

The industrial revolutions brought about first mechanization, then automation, and finally computerization. The computer era has looked for CWA to be able to design systems that would understand context and deviations with respect to work and would fit in to increase productivity. The work space should be analyzed to be able to design a good system.

There were examples across the world during the 80s and 90s in which it was noticed that even while investments into computerization were being done manifold, productivity dipped nevertheless. MIT Press even published a book called *The Trouble with Computers: Usefulness, Usability, and Productivity* (T. K. Landauer, 1995) .

Landauer discussed how mechanical automations were done successfully, but ones related to more human intellectual capabilities, such as reasoning in real time with context and situation, or learning and coming up with a new solution specific to that situation, were not available. This was labeled as the "performance paradox."

A system which is not designed based on work analysis could lead to wasting time due to constraints imposed by the use of specific commands or query language only. So, it should be closer to humans in terms of interaction and responses in varied environments.

So, if the system is not flexible enough, it might be good for one user but not at all for another. The system should be adaptive to human cognitive behavior.

These systems were also marked with a drawback, as loads of data would be needed to be analyzed. The machines were planned from the vision of programmed machines, and so the expectation for a programmer to have more and more knowledge in a specific business area was also mandatory and was a constraint.

CWA is a framework being used for designing complex systems which were socio-technical in nature. This had been used widely in a lot of areas like aviation, training development, team creation, process designs, and so on.

There were constraints mentioned under CWA which could hamper machine-human interactions (e.g., something about the specific situation, lack about skill, etc.).

This was a promising framework and now could be fulfilled in total by new cognitive systems; in other words, the way the framework was designed could be utilized very well to design the cognitive systems. The systems of today could constantly learn from daily experiences and update them live with any information on relevant web sites online.

The reason for putting this small section in between was to see a technology which was close to cognitive computing and could still be used in principle with the methods to be implemented in cognitive systems.

Workspace Design

This is a small part I'm adding just to highlight that even the workspaces where people work are influenced by cognitive systems. The number of people needed to discuss at one point of time for business reduces in physical offices. Collaborations happen over chatbots and people need not be at one place. The cognitive computing machines are mostly working as a virtual person and have their own ID and password for systems.

Instead of having multiple machines for monitoring various raw parameters, we can have single machines communicating in plain human language, thus reducing the number of devices and electricity.

This is an indirect effect of going cognitive, and it simplifies the system interface, usability, and number of applications to be used.

At times, this becomes an additional factor in productivity increase. Not only the systems but also the places go smart and customized for specific work; being cognitive, it becomes converted to design which is more collaborative. People could focus on problem solving instead of spending major time in data preparation and other time-consuming activities. The people who need to collaborate could sit close and have a much more productive collaboration then earlier, as they just stick to the core of business with almost no unproductive activity there.

Cognitive Knowledge Generation and Sources

The key to cognitive solution success is knowledge generation and training. Any cognitive solution starts as an infant. This means it has no knowledge in that area of work. It should be taught and trained to understand and give recommendations. This process is the knowledge generation exercise.

The knowledge-building exercise must be done through a myriad of possible relevant knowledge sources. The products which are targeted for a specific area could come with preloaded knowledge in that area.

But before the knowledge could be brought into the system and training could be done, the system should have some modules in-built to be able to have a structured learning and able to communicate.

Normally, a cognitive system should have the following capabilities native to it:

- Language capabilities (natural language processing [NLP])

- Conversation or communication capabilities (text-to-speech & speech-to-text)

- Connectivity with all sources of data

- Ability to process all types of data (structured & unstructured data)

- Knowledge generation capabilities

- Recommendation capabilities

This is displayed in Figure 8-5.

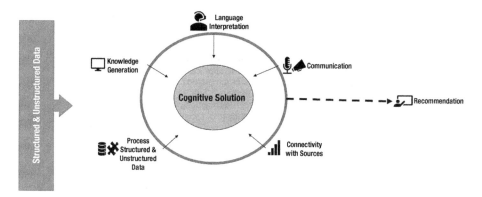

Figure 8-5. *Cognitive system capabilities*

Let us briefly discuss these native capabilities; then we can proceed to knowledge-building steps.

In this book, I have mentioned some cognitive products, primarily the current leader in the market, which is IBM Watson, but the discussions here about the knowledge building and other aspects are generic in nature, although they are influenced by all of them as the most common procedures to achieve things.

Language Capabilities (Natural Language Processing)

We have discussed NLP in detail in Chapter 5.

The cognitive systems should have very-high-order natural language processing capabilities. Systems were considered most usable if they could understand commands in simple natural language like Hindi, English, Chinese, Russian, and so on, verbally or in text format. The output also should be the same way. This makes it more important for cognitive machines, as business department members who are using it day in, day out are not technical people, and the collaborative environment provided by cognitive computing machines would be restricted if a certain computer language would be required with its own grammar and syntax to work with. Figure 8-6 represents such a scenario and users' dilemma.

Figure 8-6. *Cognitive agent NLP expectation*

All the cognitive products are extremely efficient in natural language processing capabilities, as they must be. Normally, system comes trained in certain language capabilities, and over time with training with multiple users, various association models are generated for each of them; with log-in information, it could understand the voice and respond.

Conversation or Communication Capabilities

We have already discussed a lot about this in Chapter 5 and in the preceding section Language Capabilities. This is related to natural language processing in all media including text and speech. For better usability, it should be capable enough to "speak" and "listen" almost like a human. There are microphones to pick up audio signals and then there are speech synthesis capabilities to talk back in a human voice. These capabilities make it an extremely usable and powerful machine. This is called TTS or text-to-speech capability.

See Figure 8-7 for a high-level schematic diagram of TTS.

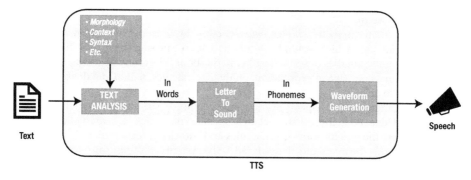

Figure 8-7. *Text to speech (TTS)*

These capabilities are additional supporting functionalities for the cognitive systems, but they play a very important role in usability. The ideal image of a smart system is that the intelligent applications beneath the layers are not exposed to the users; instead, the interactive responses are all they perceive. So, if the system could interact intelligently, it is very well accepted and the usability factor is better, as it's always good to be able to talk with a machine rather than then chatting using keyboard, let alone using commands.

Connectivity with All Sources of Data

This is another important native attribute, to be able to connect with all possible types of sources of data using all possible data adapters or drivers. The cognitive systems claim to be providing wholesome recommendations supported by data from all types of information-relevant sources. It could be any type of source possible and related to the business area for proper recommendation.

So, there should not be any limitations in terms of connectivity with a limited number of specific sources only, because that kills the very purpose.

Ability to Process All Types of Data

Similarly, as mentioned in the previous point, cognitive systems can derive meaning from all types of data, structured or unstructured; these include sources like images, videos, audio, weblogs, and so on.

Cognitive systems have the capability to use a mix of structured and unstructured data and derive a combined meaning out of it. It does not limit it; the recommendation comes out from this data enriched with all possible reliable and standard data in any form for that subject.

Knowledge Generation Capability

All the previously mentioned capabilities are needed to support this ability to get required inputs into the system.

This is the main capability which creates functionality as a cognitive solution. There are various steps which would be required to do so. The steps have built-in all the supercomputing abilities described earlier in this book, like artificial intelligence, machine learning, language interpretation, predictive analytics, neural and deep networks, and so on.

Normally, there are two aspects of knowledge required to be ingested into the system's knowledge. First, there is subject area–specific knowledge (e.g., marketing), and second, there are the organization-specific rules and knowledge/experiences in that area.

Normally, only the latter knowledge is fed to the system for training; the systems come already enriched with the data from the subject area. Otherwise, it would make no sense to start building the knowledge base and training in the subject area. The machine is well-trained in that area with this preloaded and enriched knowledge, and this also helps to create new associations into the existing and new data loaded.

The steps are described in a bit of detail here and then also in the section, "Knowledge Generation - Some Details", further in this chapter.

Recommendation Capabilities

This is the outcome of training the loaded knowledge base with training data, and this then builds the recommendation capabilities into the cognitive system.

The recommendations made by the system should have practical value in any business, and that can happen only if the theoretical knowledge already fed into the system as subject knowledge is mixed with organization-relevant data; if this is the case, then it can come up with recommendations that would be valuable for the organization. Otherwise, it would hardly make any sense.

So, the data is ingested and after that, the knowledge built makes associations with the standard rules of the subject from books, journals, and facts from organizations. This association becomes deeper with training data set in the form of questions and answers by helping system to have better insight into the data.

Knowledge Generation—Some Details

In this section, let us talk in some more detail about how the knowledge is built into a cognitive system.

As mentioned earlier, the system specific to any subject is fed with all available knowledge into it beforehand. This is done by putting into the system all possible basic rules of business in the form of books, journals, and various web-based sources. This knowledge is the basic knowledge base: IBM Watson calls it the corpus. So, if it happens to be a cancer-oriented Watson, it will come at least with all the relevant book and journal/research paper details preloaded; if it is a cognitive system doing marketing-related work, then relevant knowledge is also prefed into the system.

The basic knowledge base is then built into the system by training it. The system using deeper insight through neural technologies would try to segregate the information using tagging and other clustering algorithms. It would create its own learning based on the same and even generate a memory map of the information as associated information, the same way the brain works. So, the questions and answers fed in terms of training data through natural language processing are understood, and various aspects and context of data are derived. All this is then connected as one big complicated memory map. Every point on the map is derived as a distinct node of information based on some training question-and-answer set. This means these become criteria for these nodes. The recommendation then would trace through the same branching of information nodes and come with a recommendation. The more the training or usage, the more complex associations will be created, resulting into smarter cognitive responses.

So, the steps could be listed for knowledge building as follows:

1. Loading knowledge base contents from sources

2. Training it with question-and-answer

3. Loading business area data

4. Training further with business-specific Q&A

5. Segregating of data and associations created between the base and business data to generate groupings inside the knowledge data

6. Mapping information created with all relationships within data

7. Gaining deeper insight from data as recommendations

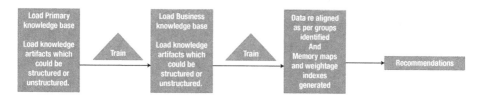

Figure 8-8. *Knowledge to recommendation*

Let us see in brief some details about each of them as shown in Figure 8-8.

Loading Knowledge Base Contents from Sources

This is normally the subject-specific preenriched knowledge provided with the system and is in the form of all basic rule-based knowledge to establish the specialization in that subject. So, if a system has to do a marketing job, the basic knowledge input is all possible good books and journals for marketing ingested into the system. Ingestion means not only that the information is loaded in terms of content but that the system also receives deep training to interpret it. This training is done with the help of experts in that area who feed in the necessary training content as Q&A. The system is a learning and thinking system, so it starts to learn the subject with this.

This is just like associations created in the human or animal mind. The difference in approach is that humans keep getting small pieces of information and instantly make an association and store it, while cognitive machines get the whole A to Z of content first and then get in situations in terms of Q&A and create associations; the overall association with all context is the learning map that's developed.

So, this first step is related to loading such content. The next step is for creating associations.

Training It with Question-and-Answer

As described in the previous section, the training must be done via Q&A. The million-dollar question is "Why so?" Can't it be done in some other way?

Let us see how humans learn. Cognitive learning for machines mimics the same natural process.

To explain, let's take a moment to remember the cigarette story from Chapter 7.

The person who is blind at birth had his first exposure to cigarettes when he never tried but smelled them and knew that some pleasurable burning sticks exist (this is how he was told without knowing the other dimensions like damage to health, etc.).

Now, see what happens inside his head to get this raw information and the associations generated. We cannot cover all aspects but will try to trace the most useful within the topic and scope of the book.

He gets the following raw information:

- Something called cigarette (a new name)

- Should be used for fun

- Needs to be burned to be used

- Need to buy for a certain price

- Made up of tobacco and paper wrapped

Even if this is considered to be raw information, it's ingested in the mind by questions and answers. The same lines could be framed thus as follows:

- What is this called? Something called cigarette (a new name)

- Why it should be used? Should be used for fun

- How is it used? Needs to be burned to be used

- How do you get it? Need to buy for a certain price

- What is it made up of? Made up of tobacco wrapped in paper

So, the brain has an in-built question-and-answer format for learning. Everything we learn goes via this route only and gives it a logical aspect. Even abstract things which are not well-understood go that way (e.g., Bermuda Triangle or extraterrestrials) and are learned about with questions like "Is it really unknown?" or "Does it really exist?"

The other aspect is emotion, feeling, or experience related to any emotion. Feeling or sensations also lie into one bracket of emotion or another.

So, the feeling about cigarettes with all the information by now connects it with pleasurable emotions, and whatever emotions he could assume or hear get associated. This kind of sorts out the location in the brain where it will sit.

Similarly, the cognitive machines also go through all possible Q&A drills with the help of experts to explore and associate information with each other. The sorting happens for the information to be clustered just the way it happens in humans.

The way a human comes up with a "certain feeling" the moment a certain subject is brought up may be his mapping creation with overall knowledge about the same in his brain, and stored in various parts of brain but associated as one map and consequently produces one overall understanding.

Similarly, cognitive systems generate their learning maps out of their subject; that is also dynamic and changes with the experience gained over time.

The very same way, when our subject finally gains a deep understanding of cigarettes and knows about all the negative health impacts, his associations with emotions change, his knowledge examples change, and his overall mapping changes, creating a new "feeling or image" about the product, which is nothing but a map of all associations in the whole brain about the subject.

Similarly, the cognitive system learns and generates maps which might be completely overhauled and re-created based on experiences it gets over time. This cannot be programmed and should not be hard-coded even if possible. The learning should be open ended just as for humans.

Load Business Area Data

By now, the system is ready to perform in a subject area with all the knowledge ingested in the form of maps. The system is ready to think in this direction with its knowledge. But every business is different; for example, empirically the business concepts of marketing or sales could be similar in terms of what is done there, although there could be a great many concepts and approaches mentioned in different books about it.

Again, the same process might have been done in a different slight variation or combination by a specific organization. They might have different experiences and that precious knowledge would enhance the learning of the system with the specific challenges they might have gone through.

For this, the business–related knowledge base must be fed into the system. This is where the real customization of the onboarded cognitive machine starts.

Train Further with Business-Specific Q&A

The system then needs to be trained with its own way of working and interpreting things. Also, business-specific keywords and jargon should be clarified by training it for that.

This makes the system ready with native abilities of the business and tailored to that business, ready to grow further from there.

The three parts that follow have already been covered in the preceding points:

- Segregation of data and associations created between base and business data to generate groupings inside the knowledge data

- Maps for information created with all relationships within data

- Deeper insight from data as recommendations

Interfaces

We talked about interfaces earlier in a previous section is - Cognitive Knowledge Generation & Sources; we discussed why it is very important to be able to get data from all possible interfaces to put knowledge into a cognitive system to enrich its data more and more.

This brings to mind the possible interface groups to be able to bring in data into the cognitive systems.

They could be the following:

Web-Based

These could be sources situated on the World Wide Web or a private corporate web. Or, they could be specific web sites being watched for specific mention of subjects of interest. This will help pick up relevant alerts and sentiments.

For example, an organization's cognitive system could monitor all designated reliable/trusted news web sites. There was a mention of business restrictions for certain pharmaceutical products due to some new sanctions elsewhere. The system immediately understands that for its own organization, since it's in the pharmaceutical industry and doing business in those areas of product and geography, this news might be important. It further tries to understand the news using all other types of business, strategy, financial, and other information already present and then presents to the management an alert with evidence of the expected impact.

There could be weblogs that might be important from web sites or machines from an IoT network that could also provide important information.

Social media is one important area, where already some sentiment analysis options are available. Cognitive machines are also capable of doing this type of analysis; this together with recommendation capabilities would be utilizing this capability in an altogether different way.

There could be research papers and journals coming from trusted sources in large numbers. Cognitive systems could get hold of it the moment they are published; they are acquired from the Web and ingested. The knowledge is created and associated with existing knowledge maps to update one or more such maps.

So, web interfaces are very important and work as windows of knowledge for these machines as they do for us, only with supercomputing capabilities that make them far more potent.

IoT Interfaces

This is where machines sense, respond, and communicate. The sensory devices on board a machine do only one job, that of sensing, whatever kind it is good at and nothing else. The data from the IoT interfaces must be listened to, noted, structured, interpreted, and then associated with all possible associated knowledge of the enterprise to enable a correct recommendation somewhere.

Except the part where we say, "associated with all possible associated knowledge of the enterprise," every capability is mechanical and rule-based.

So, getting volumes of signal data coming every microsecond or less as a single unit set of information, recording it, and creating structured data to interpret it as being below or beyond some threshold are possible by linearly calculating machines that are not cognitive in nature.

But it's almost impossible for a person to consider this huge continuous 24 × 7 and 365-day inflow of data and interpret business value and then associate it with all related business decisions or raise alerts. It is impossible from the perspective of human cognitive limitations and capabilities. A limited area could be matched or related with specific countable areas of business but not with everything. So, a machine giving an alert signal could be interpreted by one department maintaining it and then plan for maintenance. But providing a point of information to a human agent during a financial discussion, taking reference from all machine sensor data a recommendation about how power consumption or machine synchronization would add up to a certain percentage of profit or return on assets, would not be normal but exceptional. Consider just this one association depicted here: in recommending new machine acquisitions, the cognitive agent suggested buying a certain set of machines or accessories based on its understanding and experience of sensors and other business data that these would be the best choice from each aspect towards optimization.

This is where cognitive computing makes the best use of IoT devices, and this becomes a very important data interface.

User Inputs

Cognitive systems are not only thinking and recommending machines but also continuous learning machines. Inputs from users during training or even afterward are important. Also, inputs from experts are required to train it better. The visual or text-based interfaces, which take inputs from users, also bring in valuable learning, taking the system to the next level of maturity and efficiency.

Business Data

Interfaces like scanning, camera, barcode, text scanning (OMR), soft copies of information or data, spreadsheets, pictures, audio, and visuals all contain business information, adding up to knowledge value; therefore, customizing these systems to take advantage of the various interfaces is extremely important.

All related input devices, including text to speech and speech to text, help in this.

The business data is also continuously input, and the training in this area also continues within the systems. So, this also is an important interface.

Standard Data Feeds

These are also like web sources but they provide important single-subject information, mostly scientific or observatory. These could be a weather feed providing weather data or a GPS feed providing traffic details. These are also important interfaces.

Financial and Business Networks

These are designated consulting firms and financial data networks (e.g., Nielsen). These provide updated and live information from a finance and strategy perspective. Normally, this role is done by planners, and they work in large groups on planning operations and advisory operations to top executives on demand or as their routine. Whatever the size of group or expertise, they cannot compete with the capabilities of cognitive machines in this regard. Yes, they still can't replace a seasoned advisor, but they could make them more effective in their advisory role, with event-based recommendations on every piece of information live now. This makes them focus and collaborate more deeply by focusing on things they are good at and not spending tedious hours preparing data.

This makes them a very important interface of data.

Itself

We discussed the maturity of cognitive systems over time earlier and the ability to bring out hidden aspects of data by associating data from many departments, in ways not even thought of earlier: see the earlier example of sensor data helping in machine buying or financial management. This is done progressively and with the increasing maturity of the system. The system itself becomes a good interface for itself over time, making deeper connections and churning out deep meaning of everything with the perspective of including everything else. Multiple learned knowledge maps are combined together to generate one big map to recommend connected things.

Failed Machines

We talked about the cognitive capabilities of machine and their training aspects. But could there be a failure in achieving this? The answer is both yes and no.

Technically, if there is a possibility even with one example of a huge success rate anywhere using the same or same kind of solution, there cannot be a failure possible elsewhere.

But practically it is possible, because of not doing it optimally. But the good news is that unlike the software or ERP applications, it need not to be redone partially or to large extent or completely. Instead of redoing, it needs to be done further. This means a chance of failure, but no looking back; instead, keep going forward to correct it. This also means two things:

- Fixing a failure to achieve a cognitive machine is not failure mostly but underlabored effort

- Fixing is exactly the same as upgrading the system

So, a failed machine means things not running up to the expected ability threshold. There are various areas where a shortcoming could fail it:

- Not planning what needs to come into the cognitive transformation fold and in what priority or sequence

- This is not to replace transactional systems but to optimize them

- Not listing out all the information to be shared with the cognitive system

- Not enough training or incorrect training

- Not setting expectations correctly with the users

To be safe in this regard, the rule of transforming from less data source and more operational areas should start going to the most strategic ones. This is the natural order of knowledge acquisition as well; we go from simple to complex and no other way. This should be evaluated at every level and with satisfaction of having things as expected at these levels; only then should we proceed to the next level of maturity. This also helps to create better learning capabilities or maps and to limit the chances of failure.

Rules of thumb are as follows:

- Plan appropriately based on complexity and business value level (described earlier in chapter)

- Follow the same path

- Validate and ensure expected satisfaction and confidence level is achieved before moving to next level

- Ensure all possible information is ingested

These followed would never lead to a bad failure situation. There might be some issues still in the timeline to catch up from a project management perspective due to unavoidable reasons, but every quality milestone achieved would ensure more effective adoption. These systems, since they're operational systems and not replacing anything, should be able to go with little variance from the pace described here and therefore would not block anything.

Relation with Artificial Intelligence and Machine Learning

We have discussed artificial intelligence and machine learning in previous chapters.

We have already discussed that machine learning is a specialized kind of artificial intelligence which can learn from experiences and alter its functionalities by altering its algorithms.

So, artificial intelligence is about automating things intelligently as if done by a person, whereas machine learning is a step ahead in ensuring these smart machines learn as well.

One of the primary purposes of artificial intelligence is "automation," that is, making machines to do things automatically; in a nutshell, the intelligent implementation of intelligence itself into the machine. But this is not actually intelligence. This is mostly if-else condition implementation to be able to handle things.

However, machine learning took it to the next level and helped it to be more intelligent and to be able to learn. This was the first step toward intelligence or being artificially intelligent in a real sense. Taking the same example mentioned earlier in this book, artificial intelligence made robots capable of moving objects from one point and putting them down at another. Machine learning gave them capability to learn how to overcome frequent hurdles and ensure they overcome that to reach the target point and drop the object there.

Cognitive computing took things a step ahead toward being much more intelligent. It was a much more intelligent machine, though still fighting to be close to a human or even any animal in that sense.

The design of smart machines was inspired by how human cognition works, which still must go a long way, but cognitive computing has taken it far enough along to be called truly intelligent machines.

Some people consider machine learning and artificial intelligence to be subsets of each other and cognitive computing to be a subset of the new specialized artificial intelligence, which can think instead of only learn.

In my opinion, these are journeys toward maturity, and machine learning and cognitive computing are nothing but artificial intelligence. There could be devices/ machines/computers still existing with different levels of maturity, and this might limit them to basic artificial intelligence, with machine learning capabilities or matured to be cognitive computing, but at the end of the day these are all concepts and theories. I believe cognitive computing is the latest form of artificial intelligence.

Some part of the cognitive computing could work as plain artificial intelligence, and some could perform machine learning activities; overall, the machine with capabilities of predictive abilities, knowledge map generation (using weighted analysis and segregation of data as per training information), and talking to IoT devices is cognitive.

Artificial intelligence is generated by being a cognitive-capable machine. The machine is superintelligent in scope of limited subject areas required for business and even surpasses humans in doing so. However, they still cannot be compared with the human cognitive ability to learn new subjects from any subject on earth. Cognitive systems have fixed agendas and they learn inside those scopes only.

Looking at it from this perspective, artificial intelligence is a blanket concept which covers every machine which has any level of intelligent abilities, while machine learning and cognitive computing are distinct differentiating factors. We can call machine learning and cognitive computing to be enabling new capabilities but artificial intelligence is overall intelligent capability and cannot be separately called out in this context.

So, artificial intelligence is the ground on which seeds were sown and reaped for machine learning and cognitive computing.

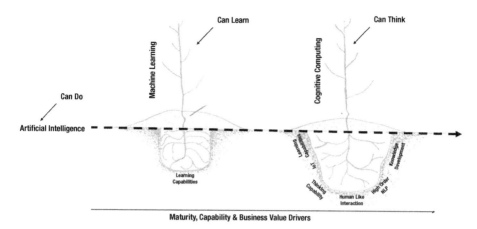

Figure 8-9. *Relation between AI, ML and Cognitive Computing*

Summary

We have discussed cognitive design principles at length in this chapter. The design principles are normally universal with fixed steps. The steps in designing are of two categories: the bigger plan- or program-level principles and application- or engagement-specific core design principles. All these were described in detail with examples for each, and we could see how every point must be taken with care; we also saw the relation with design thinking.

We also discussed the sociotechnological design principle cognitive work analysis to see in comparison how robust work toward designing adapting machines was done. This has similarity to the cognitive thought process, and it has made its own contributions as well.

Then, we discussed the knowledge built up in the cognitive systems. We discussed some basic capabilities expected in a cognitive machine and how that is developed.

We also discussed in detail the knowledge generation process together with examples to see how it traces back to human cognitive capabilities and why this is so.

We also discussed the salient features and important interfaces for cognitive computing. These are much more than a conventional enterprise that software might have looked for to get connected.

A brief discussion on the possibility of having a failed implementation of a cognitive system, its reasons and mitigation, was given as well.

A natural discussion about the relationships among artificial intelligence, machine learning, and cognitive computing was given at the end, and that concluded this chapter.

Further equipped with this knowledge, we will now discuss the self-evolving business intelligence system in the next chapter.

CHAPTER 9

■ ■ ■

Parallel Evolving IT-BI Systems

This is a new concept, and I believe it's the way IT landscapes and business intelligence systems should evolve. I call it "parallel evolving IT-BI systems" (PEIBs).

■ **Note**   We have been taking on concepts which are already there (artificial intelligence, machine learning, cognitive computing, etc.). At times, though, I have dived into capabilities that are expected but not available quite yet. Similarly, in this chapter we will discuss a hypothesis I talk about often: "parallel evolving IT-BI systems."

Where Do We Go from Here?

What is the relationship between IT and business? Which one drives which one: does IT drive business or does business drive technology advancements? It's a chicken-and-egg story.

I will try to discuss certain aspects of this, starting from the historical perspective and reaching up to today and then how it should build up in the future.

So, we will discuss

- How it was

- How it is

- Where it goes after this

We will try to understand all aspects of the story and about the change expected and how complicated it will be. We will discuss the concept of parallel evolving IT systems.

We will talk in terms of the relationship between IT and business throughout this chapter. We know that business engages in activities which are its responsibility and not IT's. But the reason that we've been talking about IT and business together in the whole discussion is to find the best way for them to collaborate. So, in images and dialogue, we

© Rohit Kumar 2017
R. Kumar, *Machine Learning and Cognition in Enterprises*,
https://doi.org/10.1007/978-1-4842-3069-5_9

see business and IT always next to each other; this highlights the dependency and the primary role of IT tools and applications in ensuring that business can engage better in its daily course of action. It should not be taken as a case where business's work is being executed by IT.

IT and Business Relations Today

IT and business have a long-running relationship which needs no introduction. The evolution of IT technologies was always around solving business problems, just like any field of science would have been. But it is also deeply influenced by how businesses need them: consider, for instance, the various eras and concepts of businesses, the need for market situations, and the challenges of globalization. This means that at one point someone (or a lot of groups) thought of creating something to help business solve their problems, and since then they have run in parallel, evolving with each other. IT evolution was limited not only by the scope of business needs of the time, but by technological advancement. There were many technical visionaries thinking into business problems of the future, but they were too far ahead of their time; their hands were tied due to limitations in technological possibilities. Recent developments in processing capabilities, memory chips, and the like have helped realize what was first thought of long ago. In light of all this, we should always note that business is the core to develop IT and so it drives IT and will keep doing so, because it is the use case which IT follows. But with the advancement of IT over time, it's taken a bigger role inside business functioning and has moved from automation to advisory roles.

Let us first take a chronological view of IT-business relationships in brief.

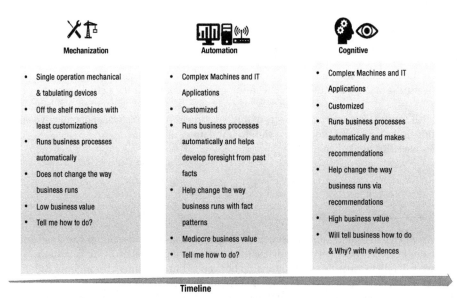

Figure 9-1. *Chronological view of IT capabilities*

The real relationship between IT and business started in the automation ages, around the 1980s. Before that, IT was more of an operator or a giant calculator and not really a specific person or department the way we have now. Rather, IT was mostly related to maintenance and repair.

Business and IT Scopes

Let us first gain some understanding here about what IT and business are traditionally and what the new trend is. We can only discuss the timing and trend of the relationship between them after we understand the scopes.

By legal definitions, any registered or unregistered business organization which is running to make profit is considered "business." But the scope of this book is not legal, so we go with another definition which is relevant and suits the discussion in the book.

Business is everyone in the process of generating revenue for an enterprise, from the top leadership (e.g., CXOs, MD, president) to the ground-level people running actual operations; all are part of business in some way. To IT, these are all known as "business."

The CXO level, being a strategic role, is not considered directly as business if only the people running direct business operations are to be considered. This is the understanding of IT service providers in day-to-day language as far as who their project people interact with to refine, understand, and evaluate any business technical operation. But for our scope and from the perspective of discussing IT systems, we will not differentiate and would consider anyone generating revenue and in any position or role from operational to strategic policy and who in some way is using any IT analytics or business intelligence system to be part of "business." These are the people with understanding of the business areas of enterprise and in one way or another follow the strategic directives of the organization.

So, in this discussion we consider three categories of people in an enterprise: business, IT, and other supporting executors (from a factory worker to a driver). We will discuss only the first two in this book, however.

On the other hand, traditionally, IT is all the people in organization belonging to a specific department called the IT department, taking care of developing or maintaining applications in the form of one tool or another (business intelligence reporting solutions, interface management, system administration, etc.) as and when demanded by business or as routine at their job.

They need not understand the business strategy or even have in-depth knowledge of business processes (generic or specific to the organization). They are the technical geeks, deeply technology-centric. Since the technology is so specific, people in different technology roles could hardly understand what is happening in other system domains. The visibility is limited to their own areas of solution from a technical perspective. Some ERP technologies like SAP needed people to understand functional processes (e.g., SAP functional configuration tasks, SAP sales & distribution, material management, etc.). This is limited to the functional consultants, but for analytics, reporting, and strategic applications the teams working were still more technical than business oriented. The functional configuration teams are more into process molding in systems, and technical IT is the one generating analytics applications, reporting, dashboards, and the like. The way the applications are to be developed is also responsible for that. Also, the end products are fixed in scope and so could be hard-coded with some level of dynamic calculations only.

A famous joke in this regard is as follows: a man was flying in a hot air balloon and realized that he was lost again. He reduces height and spots a man in ground. He asked him, "Excuse me, can you help me with my location? Where am I?"

The man responded, "Yes. You are in a hot air balloon, at about 20 feet from the ground and moving into a direction 30 degrees east to north with about a velocity of 20 m/s."

Balloonist: You must work in IT.

IT: How could you tell?

Balloonist: Everything you have told me is technically perfect, but it still does not solve my question: "Where am I"?

IT: You must be the business guy.

Balloonist: How could you tell?

IT: You do not know where you are or where you are going, and you expect me to be able to help. You are in the same position you were before we met, but now it is my fault.

This is just not a joke. Someone with good experience from IT, business, or both might have written this.

Let us see what we can learn from this joke about the relationship in the next section.

Business & IT Relationship: Boundary

Figure 9-2 in this section, moreover, talks about the same story we discussed earlier in the form of a joke. This is a pictorial depiction of the same.

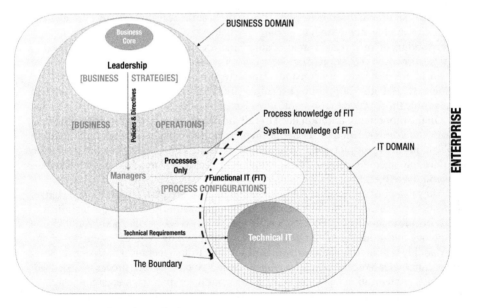

Figure 9-2. IT-Business boundaries

IT has usability in many areas in an enterprise. Some may be

- Network solutions

- Server and other resource maintenance

- Administrative tasks like data backup, user administration

- Software installations on machines

- Fixing hardware like work desktops

- Knowledge and training related to tools used

- Functional configurations of ERP systems

- Development or maintenance of solutions

We are concerned here only with the last two points. There is mostly a gap or boundary (as shown in image as well), between IT technical (mostly) and business. The functional team is 50-50. They are specialized in technical knowledge of software and know processes (both generic and specific). The IT-business relationship maturity is reflected in business intelligence solutions or analytics-based applications, which are game changers as described in previous chapters: the higher the boundary, the less effective the solution and the lower the business value.

But is the connect or disconnect only between so-called technical IT and business? The answer is a big NO. There is also a disconnect between leadership and management all the way down to the bottom. While trickling from top to bottom, the process and directives may become diluted or altered (or at times aggravated), and the big picture and roadmap get lost. There is a disconnect between the functional IT and organization that's due just to the processes being shared by the business managers. Technology IT is a satellite anyway and completely resides inside the technology domain organization of the enterprise. It does not work on processes, it works on objects.

Organizations at times evolve and generate internal IT organizations: this is done for the sake of having closer relationships between IT technical and business. They are in-house IT technical, and they could be groomed in business process understanding, but this also has challenges, costs, big dependencies, and risks. So, this isn't a solution in every case. Also, the internal IT at times tends to lose the competitive factor that an external vendor or multiple vendors might feel and that might lead them to provide better effectiveness and results. Having that feeling of being on the inside might be so much of a comfort zone that it could even pose a risk to profits from such IT investments.

Is this all a case of IT (as discussed until now) being totally dysfunctional? Not so. There are many process methodologies like dev ops and project methodologies like Agile which try to cover this gap. There are process and organization initiatives to achieve this, like a single point of contact for every department working closely with the IT technical and functional architects to inculcate the organizational flavor and increase the business value of solutions.

This was considered extremely successful until 2014 when IBM came out with the concept of cognitive computing. This made people think again about the relationships and collaborations with IT. A new concept was generated and has shaped up well, and by now it's being integrated into business thought processes across the globe. We will discuss that in detail in coming chapters.

Even before that, however, the gap was still being addressed: technologies like planning, predictive analytics, and so forth were all shining. User self-service reporting capability was there to help ad hoc reporting become more effective.

So, there are many thoughts relevant to this problem-solving approach:

- IT-business gap specifics were being addressed already to some extent

- This gap was not only between IT and business; it existed between multiple hierarchies within business also

- The business-level gaps again reflect into the IT-business gap, making it worse

The overall IT-business infrastructure is such that a strategy is identified and a set of operations listed. These specific sets of operations and processes are then molded into IT solutions. These are distributed to managers at the department level in the IT organizations, and then it is a work between these two suborganizations.

It is also not uncommon to hear an IT organization's corporate head tell an IT vendor that "I agree this is needed, but need help in presenting a strong case to business to get them to approve this project."

So, the biggest gap is the presence of two symbiotic organizations with two different core purposes. One gets help to use IT resources with a limited vision, sitting at the end of the tunnel in their departments; and the other, the IT organization, is focused more on adapting the latest in technology and using that to demonstrate their capabilities. They both are not aware of what to achieve at times, and mutual ignorance most of the times leads to failed or poor-quality solutions and delays (about 80% of IT solutions are delayed for one reason or another).

This is the bare fact we are living with; I've seen it personally within almost all the client organizations I have worked with.

There is a sense of unrest, competition, and ego between these two organizations. The reason, simply speaking, is because they have two goals and statuses. The overall goal obviously is the growth and success of the organization to which their bonuses are bound. But at the ground level, the story is different.

This is not because we have two different breeds of people being hired there. No, the reason it is like that is only because of their different goals at the same point in time and their statuses, one being a revenue generator and other being considered a cost only. We can again list some learning about the reasons for issues:

- No consistency and mirroring between the top-level strategy and day-to-day policy amendments for bottom.

- IT technical and functional have their defined solution areas and technological complexities make the technical side focus on technology while business knowledge is irrelevant and time consuming.

- The processes needing to be automated or converted to business intelligence reporting at the department level change frequently, and at times they are not very relevant and are dependent on individual business, which has its own limitations of collaboration. Business needs a reporting solution, but can't be available all the time to help IT translate this into technical solutions. At times, even testing by the user is not in depth; then bugs creep in later, which of course is not acceptable to IT.

- There are so many systems and complex landscapes that despite IT department centralization, it becomes hard to bring all data into sync and derive meaning from it by either IT or business.

- IT departments must go through the complete cycle for any development owing to their responsibility as costs to organizations. So, any solution after all the cycles have been developed must again wait to see the benefits or lack thereof only after some time has passed.

- At times, requirements are too user specific, and that adds extremely less value.

Some of the issues resulting from these factors could be as follows:

- There is often a kind of unclarity when IT developments and business requirements are considered at the departmental level.

- There is an information loss both ways between top and bottom. The picture drawn in the preceding is difficult to understand, as only one part is shared and there's no way to figure out what the whole picture looks like; from the bottom levels, pieces of the jigsaw puzzle may be shared in unforeseen ways, and it becomes difficult for top management to trace back effectiveness.

- There is least the possibility of collaborative work between business departments, which are already trying hard to take information from one hand and pass it on to IT with the other hand (and moreover, that's not their only job). They must be free in between to evaluate what they ordered some time back, and report back to the top.

- The IT (especially technical) is technology-centric, focuses more on technical specializations, and is less interested in business "jargon."

- Technology changes rapidly, and that comes up as overhead for IT to train and retrain people.

- The overall requirements of the organization and departments being out of sync, and also general confusion and longstanding processes of IT delivery, are big hurdles, and they can cause a loss of understanding with regards to what was expected and what created.

- More effort is lost in creating prerequisite IT solutions than in utilizing them for actual business.

- For every new type of problem or requirement, only after going through the complete cycle of a project can the business proceed.

This is the picture of a common IT and business organization. Agile has its challenges as well. At times, it means a lot of rework.

The result could be IT coming up with something very technical, which could make no sense to business at the end of so much genuine technical effort; business usually has limited time to absorb the signature details and high expectations that IT comes up with.

The way out is to find some way to consolidate all the data at a central place and monitor all processes from top to bottom to check how much they're in sync with organizational goals. The challenge is to remove wrinkles from the organization; every departmental level must ensure that they are not going through process overhead. The challenge is better collaboration between departments and among all of them toward leadership at top on demand and in real time. The challenge is for both IT and business to have the same vision and a single path to the goal.

This is hard to achieve, due to the reasons previously mentioned. The solution cannot be only process oriented. It must include technology as well, as that also plays an equal role here. It has a crucial role in terms of capabilities it could build to help and the kind of investment already into it. This has also impacted the way people work, so they cannot be separated out.

IT and Business Relationship: Where Is It Heading?

Until recently, IT used to be the supporting system. It played until now a very important role, but not in the driver's seat; instead, it was in the assistant's seat. Now with changing dimensions of market and increasingly data-driven business, it has started to emerge as navigator for business.

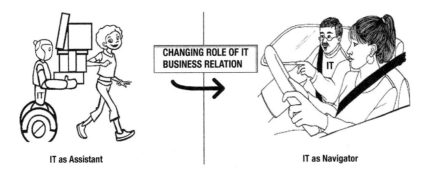

Figure 9-3. *Changing Roles - IT & Business*

At the start of this chapter, we mentioned the chicken-and-egg problem about who is driving who: does IT drive business or vice versa? We concluded that business drives IT's existence but that IT also drives business with its capabilities and has a major role to play (as described in the last section "Parallel Evolving IT-BI Systems").

The businesses of today and of the future have many newer challenges not seen or faced earlier, like some of the following.

Global Economics

Business is at the global level now. And since the competition is also at the global level, the winning factors are not so linear now. Business is done with e-commerce; discussions spread on social media like wildfire.

Businesses cannot run policies at the local level, or even at a country or continent level. It's a global presence and policies that matter. Business needs to be more collaborative than yesterday and today and consider solutions which are futuristic. Decisions should be more robust and timely. Normal is useless and excellent performance is the new average. Vision and energy should not be spent to explore all the possible opportunities, but to reach intelligently selected ones right away and then spend the right energy at the right time to focus there. The global market is more dynamic, with more parameters affecting all locations, and consequently there is potential for overall growth and vision to be changed into degraded performance in no time. Understanding of the rapidly changing market, dynamic pricing, and needed damage controls should be at a global scale.

Organizational geographical differences could cost, not to mention the local department-level differences and lack of collaboration.

All this means more robust IT, because it cannot happen at this scale with only human cognitive capabilities; however good it is, it cannot work with this much information.

This means two things:

- Closer business and IT relationships

- Applications to have a wholesome view of enterprise performances and indexes

Take an example, there are two major players in a similar kind of business might be sitting in two different continents in totally different sets of internal departments. But the competition is there nevertheless.

What is very popular and revolutionary now could be easily overtaken if one is not alert and competing (e.g., Nokia phones or even iPhones). They faced a wave of competition from Android-based Samsung. The new iPhone designs are also a little off-track from how they used to be; this seems to be the effect of global challenge. All that information and those business KPIs should be worked upon quickly, and a closer IT-business integration is required to do this.

I have even noticed in recent times that companies previously without an IT presence at CXO level have started to have that. IT has moved into the boardroom also.

Bountiful Data

Because of the aspects discussed in the preceding section and even due to new technology related to manufacturing or service (e.g., that using IoT sensors), data is abundant.

It started with KBs then went to MBs; when tabulating computers came on the scene, megabytes (MB = 1000000 bytes or 1e+6 bytes) were huge. IBM had developed an MB-level drive that could fit into a truck. In recent years, even terabytes (1e+12 bytes or 1e+6 MB) were considered high. With all the technical advantages, we have already moved to the category of petabytes (1e+15 bytes or 1e+9 MB) and will soon move to zettabytes (1e+21 bytes or 1e+15 MB). There is another dimension to this: the combination of unstructured data. Data lakes have formed which literally cannot work with the current model of IT-business relationships.

Analytics

Analytics-based applications have become common and are now established in the market. This also needs a closer integration of IT and business; without this integration, it won't work at all. This is not about static reports with drill-down and slicing and dicing or with some possibility of dynamic calculations and filters. This is about running mathematical models around the data, and understanding data and business requirements brings IT and business to close quarters. They must work in sync.

Speed to Market

The market is rapid and it responds rapidly in this connected world, with about 50% of the population on the Internet. Product versions are short-lived. They are quickly replaced with other strategies in the market. R&D and marketing must work in sync with sales to ensure they all are together generating and sending out relevant services and products to meet market demand. The variants are to be rapidly made and sent out using potential demand and supply chain estimations. This all will need high-quality IT resources, and that means a more important role for IT and close cooperation between IT and business.

Customer Relations

Gone are the days when businesses would go out and do surveys or engage professional firms, or even better, use internal business data with survey data to come up with major categories or segments of customers and with products and services targeting them. Now, the categories have become finer and have even reached the level of the individual customer. The possibilities now needed are to touch every individual customer and get their feedback. Thanks to the connected world, they can get what they need and the details of their customers (and, no thanks to the same connected world, challenge the wildfire-like spread of a bad name). The channels are many, and so the challenges to monitor all of them are also many. For example, there are billions of posts every day on Facebook or on Twitter; one wrong post there could replicate to millions or billions of users in a matter of a few hours. This also makes the real-time data availability requirement very important.

The need of the time is to understand the benefits achieved by each individual customer and then sell to them what they would accept. A differentiator must be developed in this area.

The customer relations and such data also need IT and business to work together to work around solutions which are more business core–centric and driven by data at the individual customer level. They should work together to realize and keep optimizing solutions doing this.

Look Inside

In Chapter 7, I mentioned that as the saying goes in yoga, "Look inside first rather than looking outside." The same goes for the level of optimization required now. The internal wrinkles and dead processes should be ironed out and removed, respectively. This means that there is an unconventional possibility to gauge the performance of the smaller organization unit compared with the overall enterprise machinery and overall goal. There should be comparisons to remove or improve with the overall picture of the organization; this should be data-driven and not based on gut or personal choice, whether affinity or repulsion.

The organization should be able to adapt dynamically based on the challenges it faces every day. The KPIs should be looked after in changing scenarios to maintain them as per changing scenarios. Financial management becomes much more dynamic in the globally running business world, and all possible parameters should be looked after to keep it stable.

So, dynamic inward-looking capabilities should be created. A value chain should be created inside and kept optimized in changing scenarios. This points toward an iterative approach for designing IT strategic solutions and the need for an in-depth business understanding and IT capabilities working together to create a marvel. An end-to-end solution is required, not disparate solutions incompatible with collaboration. These solutions only happen if

- There is close collaboration between top and bottom and all the departments are connected

- There is close collaboration with these again with IT or using such resources

Collaboration Is Key

More than ever, there is need for collaboration and keeping a watch on KPIs at the global level. This can happen the moment we start to work closely with IT and develop solutions which integrate with others and not run in silos. The collaboration with IT and standardization creates applications which could then collaborate with other systems, and so a collaborative technical framework can be developed.

There are other challenges like marketing, sales, and supply chain, which become a deciding factor for the enterprise running at a bigger platform. All these need a joint effort and solution by both IT and business.

That's where it is heading to.

What Are Parallel Evolving IT-BI Systems?

This should be the new IT for business and business for IT. Let us see how.

What arguments could we make about the issues and relationship gaps between IT and business organizations? Let's see:

- Business considers IT only as a supporting tool, and that is the status of IT in the organization

- Business faces challenges in the global market as listed in the previous section

- Business needs to evolve to face such challenges quickly, but is afraid of the complex process and creation of required IT assets. The process changes or functionalities must be proposed as requirements and should go through the development cycle.

- IT solutions are hard-coded solutions (with some dynamic calculations) requested and designed at some point, which at times is long lost in project delays; when it is ready, there is another need ready in that queue, which by that time has taken priority. But IT also should first finish the first one with all steps to ensure its billing.

- IT is up to date and upgraded with growing technology and running ahead to create new solutions and applications. But within the enterprise, business still finds it as a stone tied to its leg and slowing it down instead of propelling it, where it should have been naturally running together with it hand to hand. Something's wrong here.

- Overall, any enterprise has thousands of processes embedded into business IT solutions, with no way to keep a track of old, useless, and aging solutions eating up resources and time. At times, this brings in irrelevant information.

- The big picture is not seen similarly by all, or even not seen at all, by IT. IT works in silos and that is how it is expected to be, so no offense.

While business success is the goal of all this arrangement, they are blocking each other. Business and IT exist in same organization but in two different time frames and running in two different directions. They need to be running in one direction in a relay race and not in a motor race running ahead each other competing. In this case, their roads might cross at times, but there is too much deviation in between.

The whole situation is depicted in Figure 9-4 in terms of actual effort and value expectations. This clearly shows the increase in timeline and efforts happening and a relative decrease in business value as expected originally, when it goes from top management to business managers and then further for realization by IT.

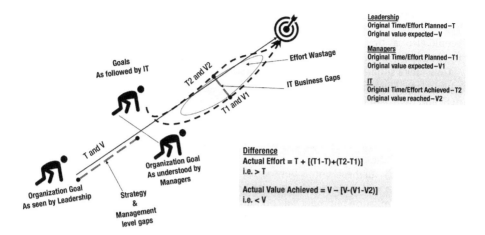

Figure 9-4. *Deviation in value expectations*

The same situation could be seen from a different perspective as well. With respect to the original goal and transformed goals of the various groups shown in Figure 9-4, let us see how it looks when put together in Figure 9-5.

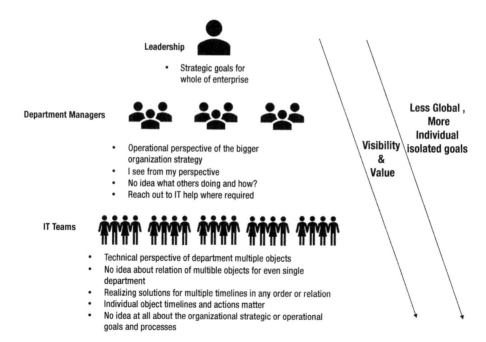

Figure 9-5. *Different agendas*

These two images will become the baseline for discussions further on.

If we summarize the details from these two images, we see the issues more clearly. We could also say that the issues are not because of someone but because of the situation or rather control around the scenario.

Consider a situation regarding where tomatoes should lie on long rollers in a ketchup plant. The harvest ends up in various levels of the rollers, where they are washed, sorted, and then sent for processing. What is important here is small barriers at the sides of the roller which would avoid the tomatoes being lost in between; this is like the control. Similarly, there is control which needs to be provisioned in all the actions from top to bottom and to IT, where the essence and control should be uniformly applied and driving it uniformly until the end.

Very similarly, all these setups between IT and business were started with the advent of IT departments and the increasing role and scope of IT. Over time, they developed into a distinct IT organization but there was not much control development for the same.

So, do we mean that the control would help evolve the IT-business scenarios, and that a better relationship would increase overall effectiveness?

Why did no one think of this earlier? Well, there are already controls in place at the project, program, and revenue management levels; there is also control managed at the IT organization level, a role which requires scope guidance and quality metrics.

But if we look carefully at the two images of problem or solution subject, the value lost and effort inflation still happens. There is still disparity in the vision factor and the connection with business.

The problem is there because of the objective of control. The goals must be achieved together by IT and business due to the need for a close relationship, but quality control and other types of control differ between them and all other parts of the organization. There is no uniformity there. The difference is not only in getting the inputs and passing them on to the next level. It has challenges in measuring return value and quality metrics as well. Even the people responsible and the timelines may be different. So, we can measure results, values, and success factors in multiple different levels and parallel worlds against one goal or against target achievement. If the criteria are difficult in every area and at every level, it means we don't have a truly uniform measurement procedure.

The granularity of details measured may also be different. With all this disparity, we cannot expect this to be even close to perfect. When we say in the global market that "excellent is the new good," this close to perfection would certainly not work.

The overall goal first gets scattered into fractions which then further lose identity and are measured using different mission and value statements and KPIs; how could this be balanced?

We'll explore the answer now. First, consider Figure 9-6, which is a pictorial representation of what we just said. It will help you to remember and summarize our understanding so far.

Leadership Goals	Department Goals	IT Goals
• Enterprise level strategies and goals • Vision (short & long term) to address challenges and growth	• Multiple plans aligned to overall goals of enterprise as per understanding and policy changes • Mission to achieve that with some possible variations	• Multiple objects received and understood from various departments • Targets to achieve for individual object developments

Validations	Validations	Validations
• Summary of results from all departments • Financial summary • Feedback from market reports • Annual, Quarterly • Success index for organization Actual vs Planned	• Success level of multiple plans • Financials for that department • Customer feedback etc. • Monthly, Quarterly, Annual reviews and audits • Success index on agreed plans • Department level validations shared further.	• Time and quality of completion and signoff. • Quality checks for software implementation against best practices and standards • Daily, Weekly, Monthly, Quarterly and Annual – Technical and project reviews & timeline • Bug control and timeline adherence

Figure 9-6. Different agendas and validation points

So, now we see the various goals and validations at each of the three connected areas. This is just a simple example; this could be wider in reality.

What better could be achieved? Keep in mind that until recently, this was the standard organization and not a deficient one. But this setup is no more a norm and should not have been, because if we have more than one goal and ways of working are not similar, validations are not being done using a single control setup: the system might be good but it isn't the one evolving with the needs of today and the future. IT should evolve on the same dotted line with usability and control parallel to business evolution needs. It was not a deficit in reasoning or leadership; it was not possible earlier to do this at all, due to technology being a limitation.

IT should not be just IT, related with business, but there should be a PEIB. It should be business intelligence in a real sense and not limited only to reporting. Business intelligence should be facilitated by IT capabilities and merged with the fabric of management. It should be the thread woven parallel to it, interwoven and not aloof, ahead of it, or behind it.

It should become the navigator, empowering the business not only to do things automatically but also to grow much further ahead in competence and usability to be the essence of the enterprise. It should take the calculator- and robot-type activities from people and help them collaborate freely by taking over tasks best done by them. It should be naturally part of the system.

The parallel evolving IT-BI system should prevail to make IT and business a single entity. In practice, the IT and business organizations should still exist, but the relationship and work orchestration should change. It should become mutual and complimentary.

What are the properties of how this works? How should we achieve this PEIB?

This will be answered in detail in the next chapter; we will talk about the first question in this chapter now.

PEIB can be defined as follows: "The IT system which naturally takes course with the desired needs of business, controls itself, and brings in auto and on-demand validations to measure business success KPIs with a complete coverage of policy and strategies from top to bottom as integral and natural parts of business processes and action. It gets driven by business needs, which are generated by its own actions and procedures at times." We could see the difference by depicting the same scenario in Figure 9-7. The difference is obvious if we compare with a similar example in this chapter.

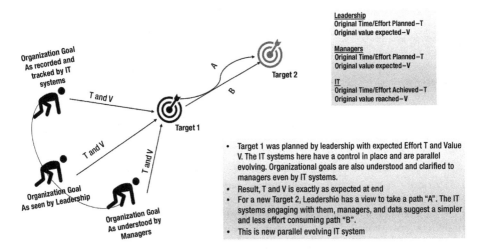

Figure 9-7. Meeting paths and values with cognitive

IT has a control system which not only helps to record goals, but also helps business to understand and clarify the big picture. It provides the combined puzzle as a single result to leadership. It helps in achieving the desired and expected result. It also helps in telling how the next target should be achieved, at least in an advisory role. This is possible because it has a view of all the results from each department and all possible knowledge and resources.

This is the correct use of the artificial intelligence, machine learning, and cognitive computing capabilities. This is the new business intelligence.

Where Is This Placed?

This is placed inside the existing IT system; it does not require shutting down existing IT systems and tools. It sits on top of them as a controlling and governing body. This has cognitive abilities.

The existing systems are all there to do the operational tasks and reporting. This new way of doing it optimizes them.

Business focuses on business activities and not how data has to be prepared. IT people work to set up data loads, label them, and train and maintain the system; they're not into business jargon. The system works to help business dedicate itself to do the task it's best at.

IT systems for reporting are complicated, and business intelligence is time-consuming to establish. This current way of development is no longer required. The PEIB system is a live system, and supported by cognitive abilities, it keeps learning.

Is there any difference between cognitive computing and PEIB?

Technically no, but functionally yes. The PEIB will use a basic cognitive framework to achieve the results, but the PEIB framework will help determine how to use these cognitive abilities and what the organization setup should be around it to help PEIB capability systems. PEIB is a way of doing it within an organization; it is not a tool but a process and a framework. So, PEIB is a concept to be adopted to be able to use the cognitive computing and all resources (people, process, and technology) to the max, thus minimizing the issues we face with the IT-business–related challenges now.

Having learned about cognitive computing and related concepts, we are familiar with their capabilities. But this concept of PEIB will give us a practical way to use them in terms of a live organization which would use it as a business intelligence system of a higher order to be able to grow better.

Before we see how this PEIB should be placed and how it should be part of the orchestration, let us see how we are doing it now.

We have multiple levels of decision-making; at the top, decision-making is driven by the vision. The vision drives missions and strategies. Most of the time, these are driven by one or more people having a vision based on personal ambitions or facts as perceived by them. They do consider some facts before reinforcing it as a vision, and this is where the decision-making starts. The vision is the first step toward all the actions then being initiated as a chain reaction. This is the riskiest part of the whole arrangement. If the vision isn't the right one, everything below is at risk. The personal attributes of emotion and influences of cognition might play a role here too, making it diluted or defective.

Then the vision is converted to missions based on the facts pertinent to the organizations and the organizational structure. This then is passed on to the departments to be followed, and they translate it into their own operational language and then execute it. In all of this, IT works to provide tools to consolidate data, find patterns, enable communication, and so on.

There is a need to place cognitive capabilities strategically in the system landscape and process to control these lapses or biases. This would also control how and why IT should work.

So, let us see in another image how PEIB should be placed in a system and process. Figure 9-8 roughly describes the concept of PEIB.

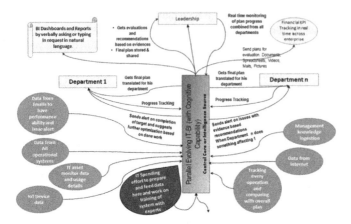

- All Data end up into this system e.g. Business Transaction, System Monitor, IT asset usage, IoT, Internet, Weblog, Email, Chat etc.
- All required knowledge built up into system e.g. Sales, Marketing, Management, People Management, Psychology etc.
- All vision, plan statements evaluated against this system
- All final plans finalized and then monitored with this
- All department levels released with this plan theme and translated to there specificities
- All departments and connected dependencies and departments monitored and alerted for any issue
- All kinds of data could be use as input for plan, structured or unstructured, even speech
- No Business Intelligence dashboard needed to be developed. All required reports generated ad hoc on demand

Figure 9-8. *PEIB system concept*

Business, IT, and a new member—a supercomputing capability cognitive system—are the three parties now.

The third party in the team is the one which works as central control, as mentioned earlier.

Business still belongs to the business domain and the IT people to the IT organization. But the relationship has changed now. Instead of connecting to each other directly, both interact with this central resource now. This becomes the new central business intelligence running the show. The scope of the term business intelligence is not limited to the BI reports and dashboards, but to a whole new bigger scope which encapsulates the whole of the enterprise's business.

IT primarily works to feed and train this system. IT's responsibility is to ensure that all knowledge required is being ingested into this system. The knowledge maps are being generated with sufficient training data, and different experts inside and outside collaborate to train the system. Ideally, such a system should come equipped with all the required knowledge areas. The organization data is fed too and trained with the help of business. The required user interfaces are created by IT, and operations like networking, server backup and maintenance (enterprise-wide), access management, and software installations remain primary areas where IT and business interaction happens now. But requirement gathering for reports, analytic tools, other dashboard development, and so on are not required any longer. The functional arm of IT which is related to configuration of IT systems with business rules could stay for some time and slowly could be handed over to this central supercomputing core. This supercomputing core also has one or more user IDs of its own. The IT has more and more generic activities related to data preparation, tagging, and interface management. These are core technical requirements. Training the system after data upload would be the only point where business would need to be helped in doing the monitoring.

Business now interacts for all its requirements with this system and not with the IT group.

Working Through a Plan

Let us see the difference from the start of a vision or plan and then estimate the expected time/effort and value generation against expectations.

The leadership thinks of some new vision and directive as per the global scenarios and business drivers. They plan it over a Word document template with images and graphs. They have certain website blog examples and business data in spreadsheets which they are putting together to see how they could finalize and shape up this new vision statement and various new missions under this umbrella.

They have a board of ten people sitting in a discussion panel, some locally and some remotely connected.

The discussion starts and they come up with a certain vision about the new variant of product they should make and a new sector they should plan to jump in within six months; based on discussion, they plan to start it from certain European countries. They think this is going to be the next big thing for their business, and they conclude. Now rewind: before they conclude, they pose the same question to the cognitive central system and provide all the details like document, picture, graphs, videos, blogs, and so on; also, they provide their arguments verbally as the system listens. They have also mentioned certain business data used for calculations.

The cognitive system comes up with a certain possible supplier issue that might creep in if location A is selected as the new product's manufacturing place and evidence based on facts like weather issues, earthquake risks, and political issues that might come up as per latest news, and overall experience earlier with the raw material suppliers in that area. It suggests based on the details to go for product manufacturing from location B instead of A and presents evidence. Also, it suggests starting the launch in phases and from a certain region, which has more probability of consuming such a product. It has also come up with writings and feedback from the Web that are similar to the weblogs shared and provides a detailed analysis of all. Considering the suggestion, the board plans to go with the plan as recommended by this cognitive agent. This plan even has a clear picture of prediction of which supplies should come from which of their suppliers, which distribution channel finished goods should travel to, and in what proportion based on current sales from the showroom. This also has clear details about the plan as affecting revenue and costs per department and effects predicted as profit in three, six, and twelve months.

The related promotion channels are also weighted, and proper analysis of existing and future customers is also provided. This plan has everything. The leadership is satisfied with the evidence-based solution and asks the system to set it in action.

The moment it is set in action, the plan is communicated to relevant departments and translated or segregated for the part they take care of, with dependencies (if any) from other departments. The system keeps a watch on the progress of every department and keeps generating the big picture from total result sets in real time from all departments. This now provides the leadership a real-time monitor on the status of the plan rollout and execution overall at every department level and at the organization level.

The departments are alerted on time, and for any functional step they know that if they are stuck, they could always request the system to guide them toward the best options to choose from.

The plan is being constantly monitored by the system, and this is being checked from a performance perspective against milestone and quality validation checkpoints. If somehow the plan is not working well overall and some things need to be changed in the plan at the department level or overall, the system raises an alert and lets the leaders or managers know what has gone wrong and what should be done to resolve the situation.

Another aspect is reporting. Reporting was considered a boon when it was invented and products like business objects started to come on the market. Today, after so many years into it, one thing which is obvious is their development complications. The product is good, but it needs to be developed with a certain requirement before they could be used and that means a lot of money and time. Other complications are there like delays, lengthy stages of backend, ETL, and so on. So, the reporting being requirement driven and complete development cycle dependent is a limitation. You need to come up with a certain report and then you have a bunch of certain reports in your arsenal to be used. Tomorrow will show a new kind of information; make something new. There is one another aspect to it: there are reports created over time which are never even used after some time. It's not uncommon to see a long-running system with 20,000 reports and with statistics showing that only 150 were used in the last two years. This also indicates how short-lived reporting requirements can be at times.

All that effort goes down the drain very quickly and then another one is required. Ad hoc reporting is a good option available nowadays, where users could dirty their hands to be able to create their own reports. But this has limitations, like the back end needing to be ready with data and that it could be achieved only within a scope defined for that report.

This is also taken care by the PEIB concept systems: no need to create dashboards or reports. Reports could be created on the fly using these systems and data, with no restriction of what combination is required to be displayed. This also happens in simple natural language.

So, if a manager sitting in the room discussing some aspects of data wanted to see how it looks from a certain perspective, no need to get a report created or data pulled out and loaded in spreadsheets to convert it. Just ask the system in simple English using the term used in organization or business area.

This is also one of the most important characteristics of such a PEIB system concept.

So, the systems are business intelligence with the aid of cognitive capabilities at the core: these evolve around the needs of the business, and the business in turn grows around the cognitive capabilities.

These IT business intelligence systems then self-evolve with time and need, and this is the ultimate destination of parallel evolving IT-BI systems.

Properties of PEIB Framework

As mentioned earlier in this chapter, the PEIB system has at its core cognitive capabilities.

But just putting a cognitive capability machine at the center and without any structure would not help. There should be a way to use resources to maximize benefits and control the conflicts and loss of productivity the organizations are fighting to manage now.

The PEIB should be essentially placed properly, or else the system itself might become a white elephant on top of so many already there. We will discuss these things in the next chapter. Before that, let us familiarize ourselves with what exactly the PEIB would look like and what properties are expected from such a system.

Figure 9-9 shows some of the key properties to be kept in mind while following this framework.

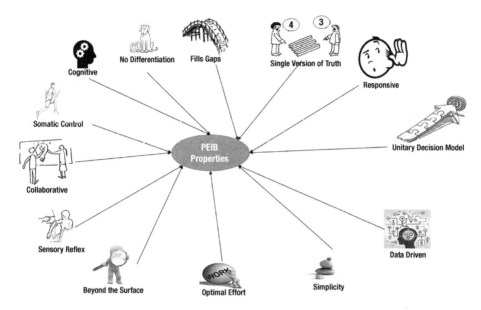

Figure 9-9. PEIB properties

Cognitive Capabilities

As mentioned at the very start of the section, the core of the PEIB is run by cognitive capabilities, which merge all the capabilities into one. The cognitive capability is just one part of the overall system landscape, and the old operational/transactional systems are not replaced with it. It is there only to unify the efforts and capabilities of the existing systems and put controls on all possible ways to maximize the utilization of people, processes, and technology, which are considered the three areas of resources under one roof.

The cognitive capabilities include all types of knowledge inside: they could be people-centric, like human resources, psychology, sentiment analysis, and so on; process-centric, like marketing, sales, and so on; or technology-centric, like system and network knowledge.

No Differentiation

The PEIB framework and the system driving it do not differentiate between people, process, and technology resources. They help to manage all three equally, and this includes the decision makers at the topmost part of the hierarchy as well. So, this framework views everything with a single eye and with just one objective, that of maximizing benefits and sustainability of the enterprise.

183

If it helps to monitor performance of results achieved from bottom and summarized to top, it also puts a validation on what the top management is proposing by validating and putting pros and cons of the decision they are about to make and makes it more data driven than by gut feeling or experience-based assumptions only. Decisions based on experience are not bad or useless. It quickly takes the decision to a bracket of right choices for the situation and on top of that the system then makes it sharper with data-driven facts.

Filling the Gaps

There are various levels from top to bottom and also various horizontal levels. The information flows through these channels. It is very much possible that some vital information is perceived differently even if it is sent completely and received at the other end. So, a mission statement might reach to departments and in case of no validation control continuously monitoring the resultant plans and actions, departments might deviate from it to a large extent. This could happen at all levels. The PEIB framework would help to prevent this, because it is validating resultant department-level plans up to every level and keeps validating the result outcomes it sees, including any deviations. This avoids any gaps. This is one of the important properties this framework can achieve.

Single Version of Truth

The goal for success is having a single version of truth to monitor and implement successful executions. But the version changes at every level because of the way it is perceived and the part of the overall action plan that part of the organization executes. So, for sales, it is achieving high sales numbers, and for the technical development team, it is having the fewest bugs in a new sales operation and following timelines of development, while for the billing team, it is ensuring that billing and recovery are on time. So, the KPIs vary and at times they are out of sync. The overall picture is lost where the strategy was to go for a higher profit with a new line of product. At the end, even if all the departments were doing the maximum to achieve, it may happen that they miss a key ingredient of strategy that was expected relative to a new product line. In all this chaos, targets were achieved using sales of an older product line and not focusing on the new product line, because the purpose was to stop making the old one.

This happens well if a single version of truth, even for strategy, is monitored using the PEIB framework; every department could see the achievement tracking using planned KPIs, and the overall management also sees the same. Any deviation sends alerts to everyone to get on track again. If the marketing department plans for a new advertisement and displays elements not proposing the new product line and sticks with the old one, the system provides feedback that this is deviating from the plan.

Overall, all decisions and plans are made keeping the single version of core truth in sight, and they're even monitored that way.

Somatic Control

Biological sciences use the terms soma (body) and mind. Things related to the body are somatic. Very similarly, the PEIB also shows articulated somatic control over the complete enterprise and the plans/missions running inside it. It works as one body of enterprise and not as multiple bodies or suborganizations operating in sync or trying to do so. This creates an abstraction of a single enterprise body which has complete control over all situations and activities.

Once the enterprise has a set of missions and operational or strategic plans, it is distributed and monitored across the organization to take a leap toward the planned target as if a person or robot is moving its limbs together to reach a target. This looks a little abstract but this is how the PEIB system represents with the level of work distribution and control, with the various components being people, processes, and technology working in sync.

Sensory Reflexes

The PEIB systems have the very distinctive features of sensory reflexes and control. The body and mind together with the reflexes send alerts to the mind to be able to take automatic preplanned actions to save the body from much damage. This is the way reflexes work.

The same is demonstrated by the PEIB systems. They could send sensory alerts in case of emergency threshold breaches. An example could be the system-level alert automatically interpreted by the PEIB framework, which using a user ID and password does a system backup and restart. This could save the system from damage. There could be a scenario in which one of the department's actions could be damaging to another by creating performance issues. The system could raise an alert with recommendations on possible paths to be taken. This alert monitoring system, intended to control damage before it happens or once the risk level is at a threshold limit, is just like sensory reflexes. This is one very important property.

Unitary Decision Model

We've discussed the decision-making process polluted with biases in Chapter 7 and likewise some in this chapter as well. We know how important it is for there to be a provision to regulate decision making in the ambit of the overall vision and critical missions of an enterprise.

The decisions made at every level (vertical or horizontal) should echo the policies or missions set from top to bottom. They could be composite or singular (i.e., motivated by a single mission or a group of them).

The PEIB framework helps in taking care of this. The system closely monitors every department and subdepartment level to ensure that every decision made at the most finely detailed and atomic operational levels is an echo of the higher mission(s). This is nothing but ensuring operational effectiveness.

For example, cross-selling and loyalty were two foci for an enterprise for any given year. This was echoed in every policy at every level coming out of that mission, and this was monitored by the PEIB framework. Some examples could be as follows:

- The finance department ensures that the budget for producing and procuring goods is such that we will be able to have products which could be cross-sold. The moment a budget is allocated in a way that it is inclined not to be able to allocate a budget mix to enable this, the PEIB framework immediately shows this in red and as a deviation. This, once tweaked or recommended by the system, is shown as green.

- The vendor and customer departments also see a red flag for the proposed plan once validated by this system if they do not enable plans following this. In fact, the vendor team gets recommendations of vendors who could supply raw material together for all or the majority of the objects to be made for cross-selling, to reduce cost that way. The customer management gets data of such customers recommended who could buy connected things.

- The production planning across the plants would only generate plans to ensure the soon-to-be cross-sold products are made in the right mix and no other way. The recommendation would flow from or be validated by the PEIB.

- The logistics and supply would ensure a correct mix of cross-selling products to be sent to the right store destinations.

These are just some of the examples of how decisions at every level should echo the mission or missions, and how this unitary decision model should be managed by the PEIB framework.

Responsive

This is one of the most important and long-desired properties for any organization, and is therefore also a very important property of the PEIB framework.

Businesses have always wanted to have a very responsive environment in an enterprise to quickly align around changing needs or timeframes. Setting this up is a time-consuming and daunting task.

There have been challenges in achieving this, as responsiveness is related to collaboration and timely upgrade. This is easier said than done. We have talked about these challenges earlier in this chapter.

This is where a win or loss in the market may happen. The enterprise sinks or sails. Nokia is an example. The response to the changing market was not carefully heard by all the internal organizations. The R&D was being done toward new age smartphones. They even made prototypes of Internet-based smartphones; in fact, Nokia was one of the first companies thinking about that. But due to poor cooperation among all the business arms, they failed to put focus on software. Apple and Android uprooted it.

The responsiveness of an organization should be well evaluated by all possible possibilities for an organization, and that's where the right level of responsiveness for change comes. Moreover, that's where the PEIB framework helps. Had Nokia had PEIB that point of time, the framework would have picked up news about the new operating systems and done a rational evidence-based study on that option as well, which might be overlooked by some powerful decision makers as of no importance.

This is thus not only a primary property but also the reason why the PEIB framework should be there.

Collaborative to Core

Think of an enterprise where management makes decisions which are data driven and evidence based, backed with state-of-the-art predictive analytics. The overall recommendation also is an aware decision comparing all relevant news and research papers, whether marketing, sales, business in general, or related scientific and political/geographical. All relevant business facts are already on the table and up to date to help in decision-making. The management is doing only what it is good at: mission definition, goal setting, and mission statements.

The managers, on the other hand, are busy making decisions based on experiences and backed by validations in this regard by the PEIB framework.

All the managers are free from planning what they want to be presented to them as reports, dashboards, and writeups before they could collaborate at all levels within the organization. This is a feature of the PEIB framework.

So, people are free of prerequisite build-up and report consolidation. This all being taken care of, they have their desks put next to each other and try various flavors of planning and collaboration. This collaboration to the core is a very important feature of the PEIB framework, increasing the overall effectiveness of the enterprise.

Optimal Effort

All the benefits and control also help prevent effort drain in the wrong direction or even less effort being spent at the right place. This level of monitoring and continually comparing with the bigger picture also could help the PEIB framework to understand what processes are not required, absent, or overly complicated.

This means a lean and highly effective organization. All the unnecessary flab and deficiencies are picked up and fixed.

This is an important property and good side effect of the PEIB framework.

Simplicity

Leonardo da Vinci said, "Simplicity is the ultimate sophistication."

No doubt about the saying of the genius. Assume a machine to be run through dozens of levers that need to be pulled or pushed or rotated every minute. The machine makes something. Compare this to a machine which runs with a single touch of a button, and any maneuvering required is through a simple interactive touch screen. Also, add in the possibility of having your own workflow or functionality programmed if needed. Which one would you buy?

Obviously the second one. You could focus more on business rather than on operating the machine and learning about all the levers. This is exactly the difference that comes from using the PEIB framework.

This system is simple: the processes are planned so that by spending less time in handling and interpreting multiple technology interfaces, people could spend more time in doing business. The rest is taken care of by the framework and its cognitive abilities.

Simplicity is a huge benefit and great property, which keeps all the complexities under wraps and keeps things simple to work with. It could be operated by verbal instructions as well. The complexity is not even exposed to the IT managing it, which needs to run only through the basic tasks of loading data and helping the system train.

Data Driven

A myriad of data from different channels and walks of life would be required to come up with a decision or conclusion. But this is not always possible due to time and human abilities and biases.

This is not the limitation in the PEIB framework. The system never gets tired and the enterprise derives benefits of a completely evidence-based data-driven culture, getting required details even from nonconventional sources like news, blogs, and social media platforms in any format (audio, video, or images).

On top of that, it is evidence based. So, this is more realistic. Instead of saying I believe from my previous experience this might happen and I have seen 50% of chances happen, which is reconfirmed by the data, if we could be able to say the confidence level of this decision is based on the strong evidence pulled out from all sources, we know what we are saying; people do trust this more and there is a higher chance for success.

This also safeguards from emotional decisions which might be influenced by bias (Chapter 7).

Beyond the Surface

The PEIB framework once implemented goes 30,000 feet in depth to a situation, even at times when it looks like it's very hidden. So, a mail trail interpretation may help organization to detect fraud, bad behavior, or even harassment without going and reading every mail going and coming.

This also helps in finding the right people and grooming them with right people skills even before an issue surfaces, making things more complicated.

The framework has these capabilities on top of normal cognitive capabilities to read mails coming into a mail box being monitored by some machine and responding in a relevant way or forwarding to a human operator if required.

This also helps HR to ensure that the most capable people in an organization are retained.

These capabilities integrated into the system are a very new dimension of demonstrated capability.

This framework combines knowledge of codified learnings, specific business rules, and a way to align the enterprise in a way to get maximum benefits. The system learns from the experts the best of the skills, and it also runs from the examples business has already gone through and it grows beyond it. PEIB is a complete way of doing things using a proper combination of people, process, and technology. We will discuss in the next chapter about details to implement or set this up. As of now, just three dimensions are there for implementing the PEIB: methods, cognitive core, and the knowledge dimension (see Figure 9-10).

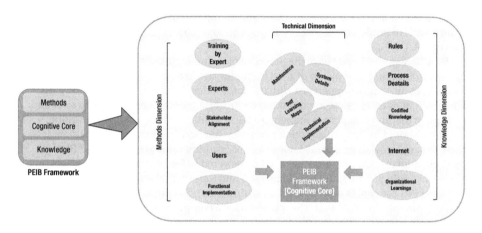

Figure 9-10. *PEIB framework basics*

Is It Complicated?

Whatever we have discussed in the previous section about the properties of the PEIB framework with cognitive capabilities, at core it has a lot of information and aspects attached to it.

So, is it so complicated to achieve?

The answer is no. It is not at all complicated, but should be done in the right way or else there are chances of losing time with few benefits coming out; that might be a difficult situation.

This is a framework and a combination of technology and process. The stakeholders are also defined for every area of the framework, and the path to reach this is specific.

This makes it a little complicated and time-consuming, but in today's world of fast results, the framework implementation is suggested in some way, the system build-up happens incrementally, and the value out of it starts to be visible in little time.

There is no one type of organization which should use it; rather, it should be used by all. There might be cost constraints for some, but then someone will come up with a cloud-based SaaS to fix that tomorrow.

Why Is This a Game Changer?

Looking back in this section, we have talked at a high level about the concept of PEIB and its characteristics. Although we will discuss it in more detail in the next chapter, we will discuss here why PEIB will be a game changer.

We have had ample discussions by now about the concepts of machine learning and cognitive computing. I have tried to put forward various technical, business, and use case–based details, scenarios, and arguments about how these are game changers for business.

PEIB would also use these at the core, and on top of that is a framework targeted for organizations to implement its other components and parts (i.e., methods and knowledge dimension).

So, whereas we already have the presence of technologies like machine learning and cognitive computing, and plenty of good examples and use cases, implementing them in an organization cannot happen just with this knowledge; however, in-depth knowledge about them does exist. These are moreover technical subjects. There should be a vector or adoption method and plan to implement these solutions in a specific organization.

There should be defined adoption processes, methods, and guidelines to do so. Where to start? How to go ahead? Loopholes? Measurements and estimations? Best practices? A lot of such questions need to be answered before the right mix and elements of these technologies are induced and merged into the enterprise at the right time.

This PEIB concept is the answer to all of this. This way of doing things lets the knowledge in this area build up. The framework is a complete solution targeted to be there to help gain a deep understanding about it to use these technologies properly and appropriately.

There cannot be single rule of thumb or the same prescription for all. The PEIB has adoption methods and details also as part of the framework.

PEIB, being a framework in the form of a concept, has all the necessary guidelines clearly stated. This will help organizations to get over the first problem they have the moment they hear about these technologies; the problem may be said like, "OK, sounds excellent; but how should I take my first step? What do I need to do? Is there any test for me to ensure that my organization is suitable to go for adoption of such a technology? What would be the best time for me to get into this or at least start? If this must be developed as a progressive capability, what is my first level and how is that decided? There are problems and challenges I may hit on the way; what are the blockers and false positives which I might come across?"

So, a lot of questions come to mind the moment these fascinating technologies come to be implemented for one's own organization. All these have an answer in the PEIB implementation roadmap in Chapter 10.

This roadmap or recipe is PEIB. This is a game changer because for the first time a book has opened an avenue for discussing this, first providing all necessary technical know-how with business use cases (all chapters before this one), and then presenting a framework for their adoption. When there is something new, there are arguments to take it forward; maybe these will be shared with me and addressed in later versions of this book or someone else might take this forward. But this book is intended to help in business language to understand the technology base of a framework and the associated challenges. I will also cover in the last chapter how the organizations, IT service providers, and consultants working there should collaborate to address this. This all addresses one important aspect of why cognitive and machine learning is a game changer.

The framework is PEIB, and this is the essence of the discussion about adoption and is the game changer. This leads to the thought process for achieving the game changer technologies like machine learning and cognitive computing.

We will discuss a small case study now and then will proceed to Chapter 10 for discussion on the transformation roadmap, which is nothing but the PEIB framework as coined and described by this author.

Case Study

This case study is to demonstrate what differences will be present by comparing a PEIB framework–using organization and a normal one.

Organization ABC (a hypothetical organization) is a manufacturer. They are doing well in the market in terms of sales and planning to explore new segments of manufacturing.

They have many manufacturing units across the globe and they all are running a centralized ERP system and sensor IoT-based applications to monitor their manufacturing process and tools. They even have a good business intelligence system and want to go beyond these. Management went to a consulting firm and looked ahead to have a four-phase PEIB transformation applied for their organization to be more efficient in the globally challenging market. They were earning well now; the target was to cut the costs further without discomfort and sustainability with time.

There had been plenty of operational and some strategic decision slips. This had cost them, but this was the most possible with the current system, ERP, and automation maturity level, which again was considered world class. ABC had been focusing on optimizing reporting capabilities as much as possible to real time. The option of having good ad hoc reporting (user self-service) and data playgrounds for business decision makers were made available as workspaces. They could play around with data in a safe sanitized environment and were able to do some level of data modeling for any urgent ad hoc reporting need. The mobile-based personas were developed recently with the latest UI technologies to enable them to have a faster mobile-based workflow. They had some of the latest memory-based databases running as back-end databases and had increased their computational capabilities many times over. The lean data models were giving the benefits of faster developments and lower costs. The long-running organization had established processes both overall and for individual departments with local processes as required. The financial management was also a central database with near-real-time reporting capabilities.

This was the face of an organization swanky and well equipped with the latest technology to help business at all levels and operations on the ground to run intelligently. The IoT-based tool monitoring and other inputs were monitored by a dedicated department to have alert-based maintenance and the least need for scheduled and disruptive maintenance. Parameters getting red somewhere would help to send an alert to the technician, and he would schedule a visit to that area to fix it and respond back with status, which was again rechecked and confirmed by the base monitoring station. This caused some impressive benefits in terms of lower maintenance and less disruption of work.

Management had heard about the cognitive abilities and machine learning and other products available, and this drove a willingness to bring them into the organization. So, many demonstrations were visited, and industry workshops were attended. All showed the technological marvels and use cases for benefits in the specialization of products. From chatbots to the cognitive supply chain, everything is available.

The question was how to go ahead with this: Where to start?

Management went ahead and bought some products related to factory automation using cognitive capabilities that were intended to be run on top of existing applications.

The expectation was as seen in various product demos, but the reality was very different. The tool was bought and implemented with guidance from the product seller and a vendor. The project plan and budget were signed off by business on requirements they considered to be fine now to start. They let the vendor apply the software as is, and with training of the software to reach the initial working level, they signed off on them and then took care of the support and maintenance internally. Bob and his team, who were looking over the earlier IoT infrastructure, were trained along with the vendor team, and they took over the support further. They were of course certified by that time in the product's features.

The ABC Corporation mentioned the automation capabilities and, based on product and solution expectations, predicted benefits coming ahead and even announced it to some extent at investor meetings.

But the reality was tough. The solution did not come up with the kind of capabilities it had shown in the demonstration. Every time, there was one new project running to add some more capabilities to it. But somehow it would not reach the level of satisfaction. This had already inhibited them to further pick it up for wider coverage in the organization. It was not returning on investments the way it was planned and had by now been considered another white elephant.

Finance was not very happy about this, and it was considered as overhead by the business as well. They could not see much direct benefit. Of course, the cognitive model had given a capability increase to the maintenance team, where they could speak with the system, and predictions were good for maintenance, but this limited scope was questionable with such heavy investment, where again and again projects were running to explore it more and connect with something else as well.

This removed the immediate focus from the widespread use of the cognitive solution as a unitary application. It was supposed to be an option maybe wherever surplus was available to be invested and then taken over.

With the current challenges in the market, they found it better to focus and were happy with the 3 to 5% benefits returning from the maintenance area; increasing the scope of the application at the enterprise level seemed difficult.

The actual experience was demotivating. The reason was not of course the fault of the product. Cognitive solutions are elastic and moldable, provided that they are implemented properly.

They had missed gauging the need for and charting a path toward the proper use case. This miss caused them to lose track of the reason for the investment and undermined the case for further investment, which looks for validation of returns over time with proper metrics. Without proper metrics, it is harder over time to keep bringing in more investment. The flow of investment should have a roadmap printed on paper, and that too with proper validation, expectations, and sequence. The setbacks and challenges expected should be known alongside best practices. There should be a plan for evaluation of the enterprise to see what should be taken first to see returns and easy integration capabilities. The sustainability of the application should be considered, and that happens with good knowledge capability handling it and with a vision of taking it to the next level. Cognitive solutions could be increased into value over time, but only provided that there is a plan and identified paths and priorities for it.

This was missing for ABC Corporation and resulted not just in missing the boat, but also in further spreading discouraging words for the technological marvel possible now with so much good work behind it.

This is where the PEIB system comes in the picture. We will discuss this in detail in the next chapter, describing how it unfurls to provide all the needed support for corporations to start right and keep going that way. This is important not only for the corporations themselves but also for the sake of these technologies to be able to help the most.

Summary

This chapter was an introduction about the parallel evolving IT-BI system, a term coined by this author and abbreviated as PEIB.

The discussion in this chapter started with understanding the scope of IT and business in organizations. We discussed their roles and scopes. It was mentioned that the purpose of putting IT and business side by side was not to say that at the end of the day all activities to be performed by business will be executed by IT. But it does hint at the deep relation of IT-enabled applications and services needed for tasks. The purpose of this book is to help revolutionize thought processes, with proper understanding in simple knowledge, about technologies like cognitive computing and machine learning in being game changers. Those businesses which can enable this should be able to sustain further; otherwise, implementation of these tools will be extremely difficult.

We discussed further the challenges and an unseen boundary that happens between IT and business and the negative consequences of this.

The discussion further headed toward how IT-business relationships are moving in a different direction. We discussed the global challenges and need for this change. We understood why collaboration between IT and business, between top and bottom, and among the various departments is needed.

We discussed the concept of PEIB and about its placement with other existing solutions in this chapter. The properties of PEIB framework were discussed further. We understand that this is not complicated to achieve if done with proper planning and methods as suggested in the PEIB framework (to be discussed in detail in the next chapter).

We discussed further about why this will be a game changer and tried to understand further using a hypothetical case study which is inspired by real business examples I've seen.

With this I conclude this chapter; let us discuss the PEIB framework in detail in Chapter 10.

CHAPTER 10

■ ■ ■

Transformation Roadmap

This chapter talks about "transformation roadmaps" using the PEIB-based framework.

■ **Note**   We have discussed some benefits of PEIB framework–based adoption of the cognitive core in an organization in previous chapters. Also, the basic definition and details of the framework have been described. This chapter will dive deep into the adoption of the cognitive core using the PEIB framework.

Before we get head-on into it, let us see how to go about all the things discussed in this chapter.

This chapter is all about the PEIB framework and talks about the adoption of the cognitive core in enterprises. This chapter will have many estimation templates and go-no-go guide templates to help in deciding on various aspects.

Before we jump into that area, we will first have some basic facts collected here, which will help us determine the various frameworks, guides, and data flows.

These facts will give us some idea about IT expenses, their categories, priorities, and the various sizes of enterprises/businesses making investments toward these.

We will have details for every step of PEIB, which will include several test and estimation templates for use.

Some Facts

This section will list out some relevant facts from research groups like Gartner, Spiceworks, and Tech Pro Research. These are needed to understand the contents further.

IT Expense Priorities

This data was published by Tech Pro research (http://www.zdnet.com/article/it-budgets-2016-surveys-software-and-services/) and it is as follows for IT budget priorities for 2016.

© Rohit Kumar 2017
R. Kumar, *Machine Learning and Cognition in Enterprises*,
https://doi.org/10.1007/978-1-4842-3069-5_10

There are 16 priority headings mentioned for expenditure. Out of these, big data–and analytics-related investments are a major priority for only 15% of enterprises. Some other cost-saving priorities as major + medium + minor priorities, respectively, are as follows:

- Improving efficiency & business process is 43% + 37% + 14%

- Increasing productivity using technology is 42% + 42% + 11%

- Managing risk is 30% + 40% + 22%

- Ensuring compliance is 28% + 35% + 26%

- Simplifying IT management is 22% + 33% + 33%

- Business process automation is 30% + 30% + 25%

- Customer-facing applications are 17% + 30% + 25%

Now if I remove all "not-a-priority" ones throughout and just consider the comparative line graph between the previously listed together with big data analytics (major, medium, and minor) investments plotted against all other expenses (major, medium, and minor), we see Figure 10-1 (let us call the first one group A and the second one group B).

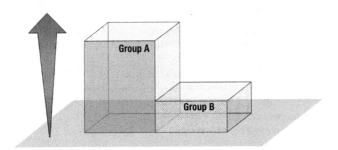

Comparative Investment

Figure 10-1. *Group A vs. B comparison*

The comparative analysis with the same numbers gives us group A as much larger than group B.

The graph is drawn by considering 100 point areas for each of the 16 expenditure priorities, then removing those points (equal to the mentioned percentages) for the cost-saving expenditures as mentioned in major, medium, and minor. These become the non-cost-saving area values and then are kept against the cost-saving total as mentioned before to derive the values.

This means that for the preceding list and big data, the total proportion of investment possibility is much higher than those of all the other purposes.

These group A–related areas are all that could be addressed by the cognitive core. Cognitive could do all these functions:

- Improving efficiency and business process

- Increasing productivity using technology

- Managing risk

- Ensuring compliance

- Simplifying IT management

- Business process automation

- Customer-facing applications

Cognitive could do the majority of this, if not 100%. So, we could say that in a way, we already have existing IT investment funds which could be progressively merged into the PEIB framework plan. These costs are recursive costs and used every year, but with cognitive core these costs will see a downward trend individually under each heading, pushing the profit margin up and overall IT-related costs lower.

The expense growth year to year from 2017 further up to 2020 is not considered more than between a range of 0.3% to 2.5% max. But considering the savings I mentioned in group A–related costs, this would get an additional percentage coming from there, and a negative expenditure in IT would be promoted with increasing value.

Latest Trends

This is about the latest trend that is going on toward adoption of cutting-edge technologies, which has sent a positive graph growth from 2014 onward and is predicted to go up further.

The graphs have clearly shown a growing trend in AI and IoT from 2014 onward. (See Tech talk: the latest trends in IT - https://www.spiceworks.com/marketing/state-of-it/report/.)

This means that there has been an industry trend already for three years now, which is still increasing.

Enterprise or Business Size

There is no hard-and-fast rule in categorizing the size of an enterprise as small, medium, or large. But we have taken an average approach and tried to describe them with some parameters listed, which we will be using further in this chapter (Table 10-1).

Table 10-1. *Small, Medium, and Large Businesses*

	Small Business	Medium Enterprise	Large Enterprise
Employee Base	0-100	100-999	1000+
Revenues	$5 to $10 million	$10 million to $1 billion	over $1 billion
CapEx(IT)	Limited	Some extent	Large
IT Models Prevalent	Pay per use	Capability, function based	Advanced
% Share of Revenue for IT	Highest	Medium	Least
Expenditure Amount	Least	Medium	Highest

The smaller organizations end up paying a higher share of their revenue toward IT costs as compared to their medium and large counterparts.

While smaller players mostly adopt a pay-per-use model, the greater the size, the more advanced this becomes.

PEIB Framework

Before we get into the nitty-gritty of the PEIB framework, which is a framework I propose for cognitive digital core transformation, we will first look at two things: the overall high-level details of the framework PEIB with its flow detailed and the costs included in cognitive core establishment. These two things will allow us then to get into the details of PEIB framework (Figure 10-2). This is a framework I came up with to simplify adoption of the digital core for organizations. We will discuss each of the sections of PEIB in detail with short examples and alternatives. Also, wherever required, I will provide relevant checklists.

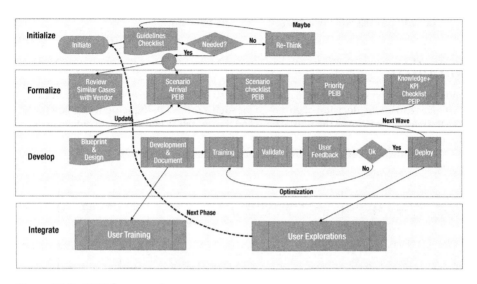

Figure 10-2. *PEIB framework*

The flow shown is the PEIB framework with methods (e.g., scenario arrival), cognitive core, and knowledge process (both occur later in the development of the cognitive core).

We further see horizontal swim lines i.e. initialize, formalize, develop and integrate in next section.

There are some costs which are required additionally for preparing and adopting the cognitive core, and they are required at different phases of the PEIB framework.

These are some of the prices required at various designated phases (swim lines) of PEIB (Figure 10-3).

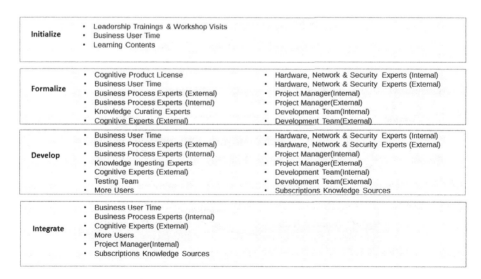

Figure 10-3. *Costs at various PEIB levels*

The PEIB process will be discussed further in detail now.

Initialize

Initialize is the first swim line in Figure 10-2 and so the first phase of the PEIB framework. This takes care of the decision of go-no-go for such a project to implement cognitive core. The PEIB framework gives the partial flow and the guideline checklist to decide to go for this or not.

This guideline checklist is a simple checklist as follows (Figure 10-4).

Size Factors	Small Business	1
	Medium Enterprise	5
	Large Enterprise	15
Application Factors	ERP Implemented	5
	ERP + Analytics (Excluding Big Data)	8
	ERP+Analytics+Big Data	12
	Analytics (No ERP)	2
	Big Data + Analytics	5
	Cloud Based SaaS without ERP	2
	Cloud Based SaaS with some ERP	2
Focus Industry	Healthcare Banking & Finance Oil & Natural Gas Telecommunication Government Hi-Tech Manufacture	15
	Retail Pharmaceuticals Utilities	8

Result Interpretation

Score	Level of Transformation
1 to 4	No need. Maybe some Cognitive SaaS could be used as prepackaged solution
5 to 7	Might Live without it
8 to 15	Some core business to be transformed e.g. CRM, Finance, Supply chain
16 to 20	Good Scope
20+	Must

Result has to be calculated from all the three categories & not less than that

Figure 10-4. *PEIB guideline checklist*

What does it mean and what is the thought behind these calculations? Let us see some examples for each of the result interpretation categories.

- 1 to 4 result category: A small business (1) with cloud-based software without ERP or with some small ERP and belonging to none of the focus industries in there (score 0 for focus industry as not in list). The total is 3. They could still go with some small cognitive solution (open source or SaaS in pay-per-use model). But this would not require any transformation roadmap as such.

- 5 to 7 result category: It could be a small business with ERP and still not in any of the focus industries or medium with some small ERP and SaaS applications and not in any of the focus industries. They could go for it or not. But it's not a strong use case in general; they could go through on an individual case basis.

- 8 to 15 result category: These are medium-sized enterprises with good ERP and analytics backbone but not in focus industries. Considering existing IT maturity, they could have some core processes brought under the ambit of cognitive computing capabilities.

- 16 to 20 result category: These are large enterprises with ERP or medium with focus industry and ERP. They have good scope and should go for it.

- 20+ result category: These are medium with higher-value focus industries and good ERP analytics maturity and everything beyond that. They should go into cognitive core and try to have extensive developments to optimize to the max.

These are the innovative types which would be industry benchmarks for this adoption.

So, the initialize phase is a test for the organization to get into the next level of engagement using cognitive core. This would help in answering the very first question: Am I a good case for this?

This could be iteratively discussed and might need some more repetitions to come to the correct result category.

The PEIB guideline checklist gives the first concrete answer to categorize the enterprise and set the right tone and expectation from the start.

So, if you are into a category of "Might live without it," your expectations and investments should get the right focus. This is the scenario as of now; with time this might get changed as more cognitive solutions become common over time. So, today something in the "no or might be" list might upgrade to good scope or beyond, as there will be many open source– and/or cloud-based SaaS applications available over time regarding this.

The role of the PEIB checklist is the first step to give confidence in the decision and standardization of response.

Formalize

This is the most complicated process stream or swim line in the image. This has many guideline methods defined and is a long process. The success of the whole implementation lies on the shoulders of this one. This one is so important that it makes or breaks a project like this.

There is a fair amount of planning that goes on here to be executed in the next swim line process.

If not done properly, this could make the whole project leave an impact that no one would want to address or take to next level. Instead of a profit-supporting project, this becomes a white elephant with limited value, and as everything implemented needs a maintenance cost, the values seem insignificant as compared to this.

This process swim line is divided into five different subprocess or methods, all of which I mentioned in a nutshell in Chapter 9. This is also inclusive of four checklist evaluation templates to ensure we come out properly ordered with proper tickets to fly and with the right dates and destinations. The importance of this step is that it also helps to set proper metrics to measure and estimate the implementation at various phases and at the end to see that projects are not deviating.

So, this PEIB step makes the process

- Ordered

- Aligned with what is needed

- Aligned with what comes after

- Detailed down to the nuts and bolts

- With all knowledge drivers listed and aligned

But aligning knowledge drivers at this stage helps to ensure not only that all that is needed is already listed, but also that proper expert support is planned and ordered on time.

This step of PEIB thus formalizes the requirement neatly to ensure everything is documented like

- What needs to be achieved clearly and down to the finest details?

- When does this all need to be achieved?

- Are the KPI metrics set to ensure we have a proper measurement scale in place both for how deep we went into different dimensions and for how to keep tabs on this over time to avoid any deviation?

This PEIB swim line process ensures a measurable and achievable goal setting with clear goals.

Let us discuss each of the five processes/methods under the swim line of formalize one by one.

Scenario Arrival Matrix

This is the first process in the swim line, although it's actually mentioned second. The first process of "review similar cases" is a supplementary process to this one (Figure 10-5).

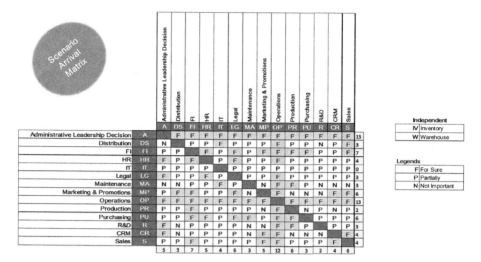

		A	DS	FI	HR	IT	LG	MA	MP	OP	PR	PU	R	CR	S	
Administrative Leadership Decision	A		F	F	F	F	F	F	F	F	F	F	F	F	F	13
Distribution	DS	N		P	P	F	P	P	P	F	P	P	N	P	F	13
FI	FI	P	P		F	P	F	P	F	F	F	F	P	P	F	7
HR	HR	F	P	F		P	F	P	P	P	P	P	P	P	P	4
IT	IT	P	P	P	P		P	P	P	P	P	P	P	P	P	0
Legal	LG	F	P	P	F	P		P	P	F	F	F	F	F	P	3
Maintenance	MA	N	N	P	P	F	P		N	F	F	P	N	N	N	3
Marketing & Promotions	MP	P	F	F	P	P	F	N		F	N	N	N	F	F	6
Operations	OP	F	F	F	F	F	P	F	F		F	F	F	F	F	13
Production	PR	P	P	F	P	P	P	P	N	F		N	P	N	P	2
Purchasing	PU	P	P	F	P	F	F	F	P	F	F		P	P	P	6
R&D	R	F	N	P	P	P	P	N	N	F	F	P		P	P	3
CRM	CR	F	N	P	P	P	P	N	F	N	N	N	N		F	4
Sales	S	P	P	F	P	P	P	P	F	F	P	P	P	F		4
		5	3	7	5	4	6	3	5	12	6	3	2	4	6		

Independent

IV	Inventory
W	Warehouse

Legends

F	For Sure
P	Partially
N	Not Important

Figure 10-5. *Scenario arrival matrix*

This is the second checklist and is a major proposed checklist. It helps in decision making. The preceding checklist keeps in mind a general manufacturing organization, which procures raw materials and then processes it to sell it in the market (e.g., a beauty soap manufacturer). They have dependency on inward processes like procurement, production, maintenance, HR, and so on, and on outward processes like CRM, sales, and marketing as well.

So, the focus here is not about the composition of the proposed grid in the scenario arrival matrix (Figure 10-5) but how it is done and the purpose of assigning legends F, P, and N (which mean required "for sure," "partially," and "not important," respectively).

This is a techno-process framework and not a technical framework only. It has the flexibility to align itself around any permutational combination of business requirements and not just to have one single hard-and-fast composition step. "How this is done" is important here rather than just adopting it as it is.

So, the scenario arrival matrix shown in Figure 10-5 is an example checklist for the mentioned type of business; now I will discuss how it was arrived at to explain the philosophy and concept behind this. This is required to achieve this swim line's step of formalizing the requirement.

The important departments are listed twice in the figure, on the x and y axes. These are the departments that should or could be considered for cognitive capabilities. One thing should be kept in mind before we proceed further in the discussion: the departments mentioned here are candidates for cognitive capabilities and not just automation. These departments are already existing and functional. The cognitive layer must be enabled for these and not created from scratch. Also, the big data and IoT framework is already there.

For the sake of understanding, we go from left to right in the grid and from top to bottom. I will try to explain from the second item in the list, "Distribution," as this has all the legends present (F, P, and N).

Department names mentioned on the left side are checked against department names mentioned on top and crossing them. For distribution, the second cell is grayed out: an analysis of distribution vs. distribution cannot be done.

The comparison should be done using a single question: "Would I need this department to ensure the basic running capability of the department I am comparing against?" There might be scenarios where it makes sense to connect one department with another department's data for the cognitive application to work well, but we will consider here only the most important ones, in the absence of which it will not be possible to have basic cognitive capabilities for that department. We are doing this to look for a most basic cognitive capability first, working across.

Also, before starting the comparison, make sure you are listing the basic capability expected.

Let us now do this exercise for the "Distribution" row and see how it is done in this example.

For the basic capability scope for distribution, I will need a cognitive capability to ensure the sales information, operations information, and all connected logistics systems (connected via IT) are able to orchestrate using these data as a minimum requirement. I should be able to ensure intelligently what is sold to ensure what to deliver and use operations data and logistics data (through IT solutions) to do it most efficiently. An additional example would be using weather forecasting big data capability for this. I will mention once again that these are not standard statements for any specific department that I am making here; these could change differently for actual organizations, based on what they need. Just focus on how it should be done.

Keeping in mind the preceding discussion, let us do comparisons:

- Distribution vs. administrative leadership: We will mark it N here as no direct flow of data is required from this department. Once we can establish a full-fledged cognitive capability, information needed from this department would be trickled to distribution. But for most basic capabilities, we do not need this.

- Distribution vs. distribution: Same department so not required to be done. Grayed out.

- Distribution vs. finance (FI): FI is the lifeblood for any organization, but I am looking here for the most basic functionality now and would keep it as P. This means it's partially required to do in-depth profit/loss-based analysis with financial evidence-based recommendation, but this could be overlooked for the first-cut cognitive solution. Had we expected in basic functionality that a financial impact analysis is also required with a first-cut solution, we would have marked this as F.

- Distribution vs. HR: Same as FI; it is of course needed to manage resources, but basic functionality can overlook this now and we can put it as P.

- Distribution vs. maintenance: This is required at a higher maturity stage of a cognitive solution to add maintenance status perspective of carriers and production machine to calculate possible delays. But we can live without it for now, and so a P is marked.

- Distribution vs. marketing & promotion: This is a very high-end niche data for marketing to establish details about the analysis from dimensions of customer satisfaction, supply effectiveness, and distribution readiness of recommendations for newly selected markets for campaign. But it could be marked as P for now.

- Distribution vs. operations: This is a very important and key data for distribution-related cognitive ability to be developed. Operations will help this to operate in the first place and, in parallel, the logistics will be managed through this as well. So, an F for this.

- Distribution vs. production: The data from production may help optimize the distribution solution to even have an eye on batches coming out from the factory and matching them with sales and delivery data. But that is the next level; let us skip this for now and call it a P.

- Distribution vs. purchasing: The purchasing department could be involved with all the other departments for doing shopping for them. But this cannot drive the basic capabilities of distribution and so a P.

- Distribution vs. CRM: This relation is similar to that described for marketing. So, a P for now.

- Distribution vs. sales: This is a key department in relation to distribution and so an F.

All Ns are mostly not required anytime, all Ps are not required for basic capability but may be added later, and all Fs are very much required.

The scenario and judgement to arrive at an F, P, or N is based on a hypothetical manufacturing company and could be different combinations of F, N, and P for different actual scenarios, purely depending upon their own understanding. But keep in mind only two things:

- Would I need this department to ensure basic running capability of the department I am comparing against?

- What is the most basic cognitive capability I have planned for this department?

The horizontal number is the number of Fs in that row and shows how many data sources or points at a high level would be entering the scenario to create a basic cognitive capability for that department: we call it IN, and for the preceding distribution example it is 3.

There are some numbers at the bottom of the grid as well. They are the number of Fs for that column, read from top to bottom. These are OUT and show how many basic cognitive scenarios in the grid would need data from that department (e.g., the second column for distribution shows a number 3 again, meaning it will be providing data to that many cognitive scenarios planned).

All the preceding logic and concepts give us an overall table with the following IN and OUT numbers (Figure 10-6).

Abr	Process	IN	OUT
PR	Production	2	6
MA	Maintenance	3	3
DS	Distribution	3	3
S	Sales	4	6
CR	CRM	4	4
MP	Marketing & Promotions	6	5
FI	FI	7	7
OP	Operations	13	12
A	Administrative Leadership Decision	13	5
IT	IT	0	4
LG	Legal	3	6
R	R&D	3	2
HR	HR	4	5
PU	Purchasing	6	3

Figure 10-6. *Raw input from scenario arrival matrix*

With this, we will move to the next level in this swim line: the scenario checklist.

This process could be fine-tuned with the process mentioned in Figure 10-2 as *"Review similar cases with vendor."*

This means that engagement of vendors' and external experts' involvement should be early and at the level of scope formalization. This helps in arriving at a finer matrix at the end of the creation of raw input from the scenario arrival matrix (Figure 10-6).

Scenario Checklist

We will be refining the formalized scope with this step. The input for this one is the table received from the previous step in Figure 10-6.

Thus, table is first sorted by IN (low to high value) and then by OUT (high to low value).

This brings in the correct sequence in terms of areas on top to bottom which would need more IN. The ones needing the least would go on top and the ones with the most go to the bottom. The areas at the top level in the hierarchy for cognitive capabilities would need the most basic and singular area-related cognitive capabilities.

The table now looks like the one in Figure 10-7.

Abr	Process	IN	OUT
IT	IT	0	4
PR	Production	2	6
LG	Legal	3	6
MA	Maintenance	3	3
DS	Distribution	3	3
R	R&D	3	2
S	Sales	4	6
HR	HR	4	5
CR	CRM	4	4
MP	Marketing & Promotions	6	5
PU	Purchasing	6	3
FI	FI	7	7
OP	Operations	13	12
A	Administrative Leadership Decision	13	5

Figure 10-7. *Sorted data from scenario arrival matrix*

Now what we have here is an overall list of priorities which seems to be followed to be used as a sequence of cognitive solution development. But this needs to be further broken into areas which are "bread and butter" on one hand and additional "value add" on the other. The distinction would be different for individual organizations based on how and where they operate, their market scenarios and challenges, and their primary organization directives. But for our scenario, we are taking it as shown in Figure 10-8. We call this the scenario checklist. This gives us clarity on how to organize departments/areas with clarity and reason.

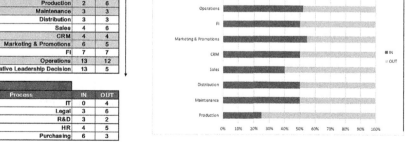

Figure 10-8. *Scenario checklist*

This also needs some business understanding along with a thorough discussion to arrive at the following:

- What goes in the bread and butter area and what goes in the additional value add section?

- The gray bands and consecutive white ones in the bread and butter table is a suggestion for line items to be considered together, as they are the most closely associated processes.

The value adds and the other items represented in the bread and butter table are shown graphically again in the next graph to clearly elaborate visually how this looks in terms of IN and OUT. This graph should be read bottom to top.

This again is purely specific to the organization in question and needs a thorough discussion with the involvement of all department heads together for best outcomes. Also, the cognitive manager and experts from the vendor doing this should be involved at a later stage to get their input to ensure this list is fine-tuned. This list is the next important milestone in formalizing the scope.

Now let us describe in detail the thought process in arriving at a list like the one in Figure 10-8.

The Bread and Butter List

The first table lists in the same order only the bread and butter departments for my manufacturing organization. I need these to be definitely transformed. The remaining ones are moved to the additional "value add" table.

There are certain important-looking departments like IT and R&D also in the value add table. We will talk about that further in this section.

Also, there are grouped departments in the bread and butter table. Let us see how this data received from the previous step and sorted here is helping us and how application of business know-how adds value in arriving at this scenario checklist for this business example.

The following is the order and grouping (order from sorting and grouping from business know-how):

- Group 1 and Sequence 1: Production and Maintenance

- Group 2 and Sequence 2: Distribution and Sales

- Group 3 and Sequence 3: CRM and Marketing

- Group 4 and Sequence 4: FI

- Group 5 and Sequence 5: Operations

- Group 6 and Sequence 6: Administrative Leadership Decisions

First, let us validate the order and then the grouping for each level in order.

Validating Order in Example

I mentioned in previous chapters that capability should be looked up from inside for improvement in current business scenarios. We need to have robust processes as always but more streamlining and process optimizations than earlier. Instead of just looking out for opportunities, we should be inward looking to cut the flab out of the system and ensure a solid base for cognitive capabilities.

This thought process drives and justifies the preceding order. Of course, to arrive to such an order, we need to be working properly as per the PEIB guidelines to arrive to a proper scenario arrival matrix.

Let us see what this order means here by following Figure 10-9.

Abr	Process	IN	OUT	
PR	Production	2	6	Building up a solid manufacturing capability and reinforcing it with first in class maintenance capabilities to ensure better up time and least fault rate.
MA	Maintenance	3	3	Now let us optimize our distribution and sales area and align it mutually. We already have cognitive capabilities in production, which gets clubbed into it. We have by now a robust cognitive recommendation capability for core production, maintenance, sell and distribute capability. A spine framework capability.
DS	Distribution	3	3	
S	Sales	4	6	
CR	CRM	4	4	Now with things streamlined internally, let us look out side. Let us build a robust recommendation capability for CRM and Marketing. Both are interrelated. This gives us by now a robust internal develop and delivery framework and marketing capabilities to sell more. These areas together provide a recommendation capability in any direction.
MP	Marketing & Promotions	6	5	
FI	FI	7	7	Now cognitive capability should be finalized for FI and this would provide recommendations for core of business i.e. develop, market and sell. With this operations as a whole could be developed adding everything together. This follows the administrative leadership decision recommendation system sitting at top.
OP	Operations	13	12	
A	Administrative Leadership Decision	13	5	

Figure 10-9. *Sorting order meaning (high level)*

The image shows at a high level why this sorting order is justified and aligned as developed from the first input steps in the scenario arrival matrix. That is what is reflected here into the sorting order we have at this level.

Let me describe this sorting order from the list and as described at a high level in Figure 10-9.

This order is for our choice of hypothetical manufacturing industry; based on our inputs and then the created sorting order, we see that this order is also bringing forth two essential things:

- Quick-to-engage-with areas of business are being considered first, using the required number of inputs. The quick-to-engage-with areas in my case are the ones giving quick cognitive solutions with the least data input.

- This provides a quick insight, example, and experience of the cognitive solution.

We considered here the manufacturing example, and the best way to start could be suggested by the departments; it could be anything (i.e., which process they want to bring in first and what should happen overall).

It could be a highly expressive MBA-represented marketing group quickly listing benefits they could churn out if they get this ability, and it could be sales and distribution team afterwards, but what is the real order? This is set up automatically by the sorted list shown here and arrived at in this stage using PEIB guidelines.

The shown sequence is good for this specific business. Assume we had decided to start in a different order:

- Marketing & Promotions

- Operations

- Production

- Maintenance

Now what we are saying here is that we will be having the cognitive system for marketing applications at first before anything else is developed. Keep in mind one thing: the cognitive system is developed with knowledge in all the areas and training imparted to it.

If we need to get recommendations for marketing and promotions, we need to analyze sales first to understand buying patterns. This means at the time of development of marketing & promotion cognitive solutions, we need to bring in a knowledge corpus for sales as well, and training should also be done from that perspective. We do need to understand the distribution pattern to see occasional recommendations for marketing and see where we could reach quickly in terms of the new product services we are going to create campaigns for. We might also like to have an optimized production to support these money-saving and market-grabbing cognitive solutions for marketing.

Thus, at the time of the development of this system, we need to bring in all the data from these areas, along with all the knowledge content for these, and then train the system with all of this material.

Also, in previous chapters I mentioned that these are not separate cognitive solutions but one solution getting matured with time because of additional data, knowledge added, and training (initial and by use).

Note that it will always be difficult to add knowledge and training to the system in parallel but progressively. This would be better if the system is ready with knowledge and training from every layer before and then goes to the next layer, which is built over this.

This is automatically taken care in the exercise done under the PEIB framework.

So, our example and sequence indicate that we should evolve the internal production capability and then evolve how we are selling and distributing it. This will bring in a lot of values already. Go ahead and optimize how you reach out to clients and serve them. Next, start transforming the FI systems to ensure that the FI KPIs are also speaking the same language. Then, optimize operations to bring everything under this umbrella. People might come with an argument that FI is the lifeblood for any organization; why not start with it? But just to remind you, the FI system is already in place and reaping benefits from previous levels of cognitive transformation. This is FI cognitive transformation, and it will get details and cognitive capabilities from all the layers developed before it in the organization. So, FI comes later here. After these operations, we are OK to start with the final administrative cognitive transformation.

This explains that the sequence we arrived from previous steps—scenario arrival matrix and scenario checklist—is good.

Let us discuss the other aspect of grouping.

Validating Grouping in Example

For the sake of convenience, I will once again list the levels and groups taken in our example:

- Group 1 and Sequence 1: Production and Maintenance

- Group 2 and Sequence 2: Distribution and Sales

- Group 3 and Sequence 3: CRM and Marketing

- Group 4 and Sequence 4: FI

- Group 5 and Sequence 5: Operations

- Group 6 and Sequence 6: Administrative Leadership Decisions

We know this is coming from the business understanding we have. This will have a lot of impact on the overall project timeline and blueprint.

What we say here is to group the most closely orchestrated departments/processes together. This will need deep standard process and actual experience of the organization.

Group 1 and Sequence 1: Production and Maintenance

Production and maintenance belong to same group for developing and manufacturing. They have a close-knit relationship and would overall help in achieving the most important goals, like

- Quicker manufacturing

- Least wastage

- Fewest errors

- Avoidance of routine maintenance downtime

- Use of a cognitive maintenance timeline, which saves a lot of time

- Better production planning

These are some benefits which we get, and they are interwoven between these two processes together. Besides, this gives a quick result in terms of measurable benefits. The KPI indicators could be identified to measure the status, progress, and benefit after implementing this transformation.

This should reduce costs by around 11 to 40% further in recurring IT investments and boost productivity by around 30%.

This core cognitive setup will already have knowledge related to manufacturing, smart maintenance, and smart manufacturing process.

Group 2 and Sequence 2: Distribution and Sales

Sales and distribution are part of the same area of business: selling and making arrangements to distribute to customers. This may also include internal distributions to different manufacturing units. This includes the logistic component.

These would definitely be needed to be worked on together, as they orchestrate together. Also, they might need production-related information to be able to recommend for internal distribution–related recommendation.

This may also leverage data from the maintenance arm of cognitive models to be aware of maintenance or downtime impact of objects being planned for manufacture, giving a more 360-degree view of situations in distribution.

When we reach this part of the transformation, we are working only on it and not on anything else. The training does happen for other previously implemented areas but from a current subject perspective, further creating associations with previous training in those areas. So, it enriches both the previous one and the current one through this approach.

Group 3 and Sequence 3: CRM and Marketing & Promotions

Now we are ready with basic and core manufacturing, maintenance, sales, and distribution transformation. We have an efficient core running and getting trained day by day. This level now will extend it toward a better CRM and marketing & promotions capability. Just having a lean, smart, intuitive core for manufacturing to deliver the organization already starts to reap benefits. With this fast returning of value areas, it would be possible to go ahead with the next levels, which do not immediately show value returns as compared.

Now the CRM and marketing & promotions do need data from sales and distribution. This is already ready. On top of this data, they would also need the system to be trained in these beforehand, and that is already done by now. The confidence in the system is already available by this time, and the organization is ready with resources further in this direction. Clear recommendations are given based on production and maintenance about each and every such unit, and this helps in planning marketing based on what could be possible to make and deliver at a given time after promotions. Geographically relevant campaigns would be possible, and benefits could be achieved.

This will have the already present back end transformed and enabled to focus only in this area.

Group 4 and Sequence 4: FI

The FI department will already see benefits in the accounts due to the previous transformations. Now it is time to transform the FI department itself. This transformation would run on top of the previous steps to further optimize and record the money aspects and planning at every level and area transformed by this time.

Group 5 and Sequence 5: Operations

The whole groundwork is done for everything connected to operations, which is connected to all the departments and processes below it in level of the hierarchy of cognitive complexity required. This analysis and assessment could be done for this department as well. This will take the organization to a level up and closer to an industry 4.0-level upgrade, which needs the overall operational framework to be thinking on its own and assisting users to make relevant and smart decisions every time.

Thus, the IoT- and big data–driven operational organization is achieved.

Group 6 and Sequence 6: Administrative Leadership Decisions

Results achieved in the previous level are automatically helpful to the leadership as well. These become the eyes and ears of the organization to them. A further level of maturity, built by integrating various operational divisions to be unified under a single decision system, is done at this level.

We can see with this example that the choice of sequence achieved by a proper scenario arrival matrix helped us to determine a proper sequence, and the example justifies the same for our example of a hypothetical manufacturing organization.

The Additional Value Add List

This is the additional value list segregated in the scenario checklist in Figure 10-9. Considering the distance from that image, I will again put forth a different version of the figure highlighting the value add list, so that it is easier for us to discuss (Figure 10-10).

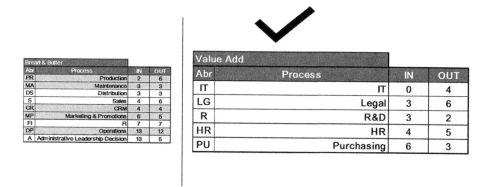

Figure 10-10. Highlighting value add list

We had removed certain departments/processes from the main table of the sorted data from the scenario arrival matrix (Figure 10-7).

These are separated in a similar fashion: we have done grouping in our example using the business know-how and understanding. This could be different for different organizations. For our example of manufacturing business, we have taken the following out as additional value adds:

- IT

- Legal

- R&D

- HR

- Purchasing

For my hypothetical company, I had taken them out. This is a process in PEIB where the organizations should list out separately from the main list what they see as additional value adds and not as the main bread and butter.

There must be some solid reasoning behind doing this. This is a very important strategic activity and helps gain focus in the desired areas. The listed additional value add areas should be those which would take the cognitively derived value of the organization to the next level of effectiveness, but not including them would help build a first-cut cognitive organization and develop confidence in the transformation. Also, these are the areas which would need a fully transformed organization to start to reach a further level of effectiveness.

IT cognitive abilities will help a live IT environment where the IT workforce would only be working in the areas they are experts in: maintenance of system, networks, firewall, data upload, interface development, UI development, and so on. They need not utilize their energies much in understanding a process and then work. They would be, however, helping in training the systems, but they would be only working from the technical perspective. So, it makes sense first to have everything "alive and thinking" before declaring the complete IT as cognitive. Some future knowledge and training required further to optimize it would be in order to have the system self-repair and self-maintain. There's no need to plan it separately and earlier. Also, this a non-revenue-generating department and so should not be planned with bread and butter scenarios, as those are revenue-generating areas and give returns and confidence in the usability of the cognitive transformation.

Legal cognitive abilities will help in all areas of the business, but then no one would benefit by starting with it. This should be created on top of a full-grown cognitive organization. This does not generate any revenue of itself either, and so should come later.

R&D cognitive abilities could be argued to be something separate and need not wait for long in the additional value add list. In a way, this is right but not from a thinking perspective of a cognitive organization. In conventional organization planning, this is valid, but not for cognitive. The cognitive applications do not work in silos. The R&D would work on core research data and inputs sent by production and other relevant departments (e.g., marketing department sending market feedback about functionality changes to develop more user-friendly products or designs). This is where cognitive transformations make a difference. The cognitive systems assisting in R&D don't need any specific input to be shared but could automatically provide recommendations based on everything required. In addition to this, of course, the required research and other data are connected via relevant and trusted Internet sources.

HR cognitive abilities are the new smart generation of resource management, skilling and tracking the resource capabilities for various needs. But this also not a direct revenue-generating department, and as it needs data from all areas with cognitive transformation, it should be kept on the second list.

Purchasing cognitive abilities are required for good purchasing recommendations, but these do need to be integrated with all the other revenue-generating operational organizations, and so they should go on the second list.

So, the list contains all the areas which would contribute toward a wholesome cognitive organization but they should not all be taken up in the first shot.

Some reasons are as follows:

- Not being revenue generating so not able to provide a good measurement of return on such investments

- Not directly related to any process but shared among many

- Needing a wider cognitive background to start

- More regulatory then operational in nature

So, the purpose of this list build-up is to remove essential from added value things, and so this list has a very important role to play.

We will now move to the third component, called the scenario priority list.

Scenario Priority List

This is the part where we should reach out for a high-level flow chart for the scenarios and then put them as a flow chart to have a visual map and flow for what we need to consider as the scope. The same could be used further in the knowledge checklist and blueprint & project plan (Figure 10-11).

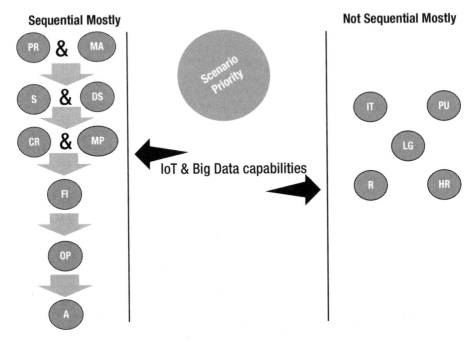

Figure 10-11. *Scenario priority list*

This is a simple activity and is more technical; it is nothing but clearly putting across the result of discussions and validations as one final list of achievable objectives in a time sequence. The bread and butter list is put in the decided proper sequence. The value add list is free of any sequence. They could be put into any convenient order. The big data and IoT are also mentioned as a prerequisite setup.

This list will be the input for the next level of PEIB process, hich is called knowledge checklist.

These priorities should be fully evaluated and, with engagement of internal business experts and external cognitive and business experts, ironed out and published. The previous two lists should also be validated to ensure confidence in this final list. This will almost close the confusion, dilemma, and chaos in scoping by this time. Further ahead, it would be business as usual in project planning with some specific changes related to cognitive transformation.

Knowledge and KPI Checklist

The next process, which is very important, is the final step in this swim line of the formalization process. Two main areas are there for this step:

- Knowledge checklist preparation
- KPI identification

A lot of cognitive process could fail if proper knowledge management is not planned. How this is important?

Well, cognitive means thinking machines, but what is the capability which makes cognitive computing most important? That capability is knowledge ingestion in an area and being able to recommend solutions or guidance based on the learnings. This is done though using the training with data, which helps the system to understand the context of each bit of knowledge accumulated under its hood and to create its own learning indexes and maps as knowledge. This is like associative learning in humans, with the exception that we get knowledge bytes with data bytes. But these machines get knowledge in bulk and then generate further knowledge out of it later.

It comes out that the learning capabilities act as thinking capabilities in action in these machines. Knowledge becomes primary and thus itself a source of further knowledge.

This makes it very important that

- Good knowledge sources for the first-time core knowledge build is ensured (generic and internal)

- Good training is planned

- Continuing sources of relevant and trusted information of various types are identified

These factors should all be planned for. PEIB says that these should be planned the moment we have the final priority checklist available. The planning will help execute the function of cognitive enablement and result in a good cognitive build.

A knowledge checklist should be made carefully at this stage of scope finalization and under many headings, as shown in Table 10-2.

Table 10-2. *Knowledge Checklist—PR and MA (Indicative)*

Codified Knowledge

Machine Manuals

Product Details

Quality Methods & Process

Quality Measurements

Product Manufacturing Process

Power Efficiency Measures and Standards

Repair Machines

Model Part Details

Knowledge of Process Challenges

Operator Manuals

Issues in Operations

(continued)

Table 10-2. (*continued*)

Others

Specialist Knowledge Base

Specialist Question and Answers for Training

Standard Research Papers

Standard Journals

Related News Websites

Internal Knowledge

Internal Specialists Knowledge Base

Internal Specialist Question and Answers for Training

IoT Feeds

Historical Logs

Historical Failure Details

Other Historical Issues

Machine Repair Logs

Machine Modifications

Customized Machine Manuals

Product Details and Specifications

Internal Codes

Internal Quality Control Historical Data

Internal Quality Control Process

Internal Quality Control Metrics

Power Consumption and Issues Data

Internal Process Flow

Internal Manuals

Historical Production Data

Continuing Knowledge

News Feeds

Free Web Sources

Subscription-Based Web Sources (Other)

Subscription-Based Technical Information

Machine Manufacturer Feeds for Software and Hardware Details

Software Upgrade Feeds

(*continued*)

Table10-2. (*continued*)

Human Resources

Expert Operator

Engineer

External Process Expert

Internal Process Expert

Product Expert

Product R&D Specialist

Cognitive Expert to Ingest Data

Enterprise IT Counterpart Learners

IT Expert Internal

IoT Data Expert: Internal

Following people continue for knowledge continuity

Enterprise IT Counterpart Learners

IT Expert Internal

IoT Data Expert

Every department and process area listed in the priority list from the previous step should be processed here further. Each item there should have accompanying knowledge resources listed next to it. PEIB recommends the knowledge list should be under the following five headings:

- Codified Knowledge

- Other

- Internal Knowledge

- Continuing Knowledge

- Human Resources

The details in Table 10-2 are indicative, and the real list might be more exhaustive. Apart from that, the "codified knowledge" heading is mostly preloaded as an enriched knowledge base in that specific area by the cognitive product provider. Any gaps should be understood and taken care of.

Let us see in a bit of detail all these areas of knowledge and their properties as recommended by PEIB.

Codified Knowledge

This is mostly the standard diverse knowledge in that area of the functioning of the cognitive service. So, in this case of production and maintenance it is something like creating an engineer and product expert by feeding all standard engineering and product content. Also, the repairing and maintenance aspect is fed. There is a need for IoT integration as well, so related engineering knowledge is also fed. This knowledge is mostly prefed and ingested in the industry solution and is present as already enriched data (i.e., pretrained in that area as well). This provides all the conceptual knowledge efficiency and rule detail to the cognitive solution. This is the biggest part of the knowledge built up and may take much longer to load and train. But as this comes as product feature, this should only be checked with the vendor for any gaps.

Other

This is also knowledge that's expected to be prefed and ingested in the system, but based on journals, videos, audio webcasts, and other material that's relevant in any way. The knowledge in this area is not only straightforward learning content but also research and news related to this. This is also normally the responsibility of the vendor, but gaps should be checked for expectations. There could be questions, then a build by the specialists working from the vendor to put some more knowledge dimensions for specific business needs for production. This will tune up and update the system.

Internal Knowledge

This starts to bring in major value to the system. All relevant knowledge, documents, logs, and historical relevancy data like repair logs, repair tickets, resolution logs, and so on are to be loaded. Also, the internal expert also works with the external expert to frame questions and answers to ensure data is enriched too. Web-based sources like weather, news, machine hardware and software upgrades, and so on also need to be integrated. The product details, the codes used in production, the process details to the finest possible level, and quality data like process, metrics, and historical data for quality assessment all should be fed. In parallel, the data is being enriched with the help of internal and external experts. Since this makes the installation specific to the organization, it is the biggest knowledge-building exercise and should be planned down to the finest details. Two things are very important in this planning:

1. Expert advice from the functional and technical experts from the vendor

2. Involvement of actual operating and managing people and not only the managers in the data resource listing exercise

The internal IT plays a good role here by helping the vendor to get integrated with data sources by helping with the technical aspects.

IoT experts from the organization should also work with the external vendor IoT data experts to help integrate this valuable source of data properly.

Continuing Knowledge

The cognitive system is a continuously learning system; it learns not only from operations and daily data coming into it but also from external knowledge sources to keep itself updated from the perspective of awareness of anything new happening in those areas. This could also be the machine providers' feed for news, alerts, hardware, and software information details. This could also connect to software update feeds and could help autoupgrade also using a user ID as another employee would have done. This connectivity helps by keeping the system updated and progressively enriched with new data. The question/answer–based learning should also be continued.

Human Resources

This is also something to be planned with the knowledge source listing. Proper training and orientation of selected people via internal and vendor workshops should be done to make them more cognitive implementation oriented. There should be people identified, aligned, and assigned. These should be people performing those operations and not only managing or supervising these processes. There should be a list of people designated to work further to keep enriching and loading data once the vendor moves out. There might be a possibility to have hyper-care and support contracts with the vendor to help in the process of settling down.

KPI/Feature

Now the list finally needs to be updated with the KPIs or features expected: there could be many for every department. The ones selected should be measurable or identifiable. For example, the "application should work better at the end" is a vague statement; instead "the system should be able to present alerts on sensor input and should suggest the right parts and methods to fix such problems within 3 to 10 seconds" is a quantifiable and identifiable statement. See Table 10-3.

Table 10-3. *Final Knowledge Checklist for PR & MA (Indicative)*

Codified Knowledge
Machine Manuals
Product Details
Quality Methods & Process
Quality Measurements
Product Manufacturing Process
Power Efficiency Measures and Standards
Repair Machines

(*continued*)

Table10-3. (*continued*)

Codified Knowledge

Model Part Details

Knowledge of Process Challenges

Operator Manuals

Issues in Operations

Others

Specialist Knowledge Base

Specialist Question and Answers for Training

Standard Research Papers

Standard Journals

News Websites (Related)

Internal Knowledge

Internal Specialist Knowledge Base

Internal Specialist Question and Answers for Training

IoT Feeds

Historical Logs

Historical Failure Details

Other Historical Issues

Machine Repair Logs

Machine Modifications

Customized Machine Manuals

Product Details and Specifications

Internal Codes

Internal Quality Control Historical Data

Internal Quality Control Process

Internal Quality Control Metrics

Power Consumption and Issues Data

Internal Process Flow

Internal Manuals

Historical Production Data

(*continued*)

Table10-3. (*continued*)

Continuing Knowledge

News Feeds

Free Web Sources

Subscription-Based Web Sources (Other)

Subscription-Based Technical information

Machine Manufacturer Feeds for Software and Hardware Details

Software Upgrade Feeds

Human Resources

Expert Operator

Engineer

External Process Expert

Internal Process Expert

Product Expert

Product R&D Specialist

Cognitive Expert to Ingest Data

Enterprise IT Counterpart Learners

IT Expert Internal

IoT Data Expert – Internal

Following people continue for knowledge continuity

Enterprise IT Counterpart Learners

IT Expert Internal

IoT Data Expert

KPIs/Features

Alert with details of issue, history, way to fix, and correct parts on the sensor input of the IoT device

Should be able to generate a new production plan based on new priority order by verbal input alone

In case of a jam in a machine, should be able to stop the factory line toward that unit and alert with details

These features could be also the ones recommended by the vendor in addition to the expectation of the organization.

So, by this time, starting from scenario arrival matrix we are done with the formalization step, which is the second swim line in Figure 10-2. We are ready with the following by now:

- List of bread and butter (priority) departments or processes

- List of secondary or additional value add areas

- Scenario priority list to have everything connected and visualized in a flow

- Knowledge checklist with five PEIB headings aligned next to every process/department in the priority list

- Needed human resources planned, identified, oriented, and ready to work

- KPI/features checklists for expected features

In a nutshell, scope is finalized at this level. Everything that needs to be done is listed, along with the timeframe. Additionally, the KPIs/features put against the complete priority list are ready. This will reinforce that a check or control could be established to ensure no or minimum deviation with proper resource management required.

We will now move to next swim line of the PEIB framework: develop.

Develop

This is the third swim line in the PEIB framework. For the sake of convenience, I will put the PEIB framework here once again with the current swim line marked in Figure 10-12.

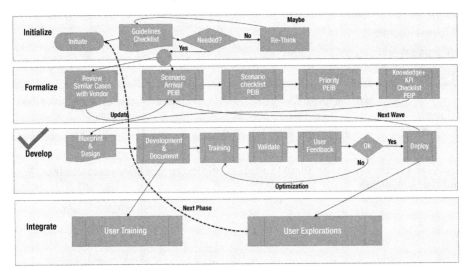

Figure 10-12. *PEIB framework*

This area has six processes and one decision condition. The processes are a little different here than in conventional software implementations, as this has a recursive path triggered by the decision condition and which may take it back to previous steps based on the satisfaction condition.

We will discuss each of the steps in further detail.

Blueprint and Design

These are two distinct areas. Normally, the blueprint is a joint effort together with the vendor doing cognitive transformation, and the design is done completely by the vendor. But for cognitive transformation, PEIB recommends a joint effort or exercise throughout the blueprint and design.

The cognitive transformation project, being unlike any other software development, needs a collaborative effort throughout the processes between the vendor and the client. This is more of a strategic engagement and needs every step to be monitored instead of milestone or weekly reviews. There is effort involved, which could be managed by separating the core working team and the management team. But all this effort will pay off with a very strongly enriched system with less dependability on any vendor over the long term.

Blueprint

This is the usual blueprint stage. The system is designed further from the finalization stage. The finalization stage was also done together with the vendor experts. There is not much maturity and experience with such implementation/transformation currently in the market; since the nature of this is extremely strategic, vendor support is required even during requirement gathering.

The input for the blueprint phase comes from the final version of the locked knowledge checklist from the previous stage. The knowledge checklist is a very detail-oriented requirement; it must have complete details on every step and resource required from the organization.

The only part remaining is now with the vendor, which needs to finalize the system/product details, server size, network adapter, and interface details, along with its own resource plan. The blueprint is a sum of these. All these details are captured together with the implementation strategy of the vendor; any impact on running system availability and their testing strategy is done around the predefined KPI and features from the knowledge checklist. They could additionally add some test cases. The chances of the same are little because the previous checklist was also created using the vendor only.

The PEIB framework recommends PEIB control (Figure 10-13). This must be achieved using a finer alignment, again around the expected features and validation KPIs, to ensure that there is no gap in understanding between the vendor implementing team and the organization's expectations. This must be double-checked. PEIB recommends having a stepwise review of the blueprint document with the vendor, strictly around the goals and expectations. Wherever required, the vendor should be able to show some small models or prototypes of the solution as demos to provide more clarity of the blueprint vs. knowledge checklist, which contains the final flow of transformation, knowledge association, and KPI/feature checklist.

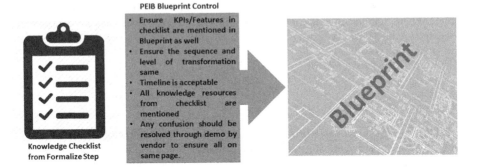

Figure 10-13. *PEIB blueprint control*

This will ensure that there is no deviation at this stage of the project. It is highly recommended to follow this process of blueprint control, because such is the nature of cognitive transformation and so many features come up which are far more exciting to see and adventurous that losing track and going away from reality is very possible. Sticking to reality becomes difficult. Normally, software has a definite look and feel and data output expected. We know by which button created in the software what will be achieved. But for cognitive transformations, this is extremely difficult. Since the technology is so new and powerful, there are many new features which might mesmerize both the developers/configurators and the people from the enterprise. Therefore, it is extremely important to have a quick reality check against the KPIs and features expected in the knowledge checklist.

The knowledge checklist should be transferred completely into the blueprint for the vendor's further operations. PEIB adds a new control called "PEIB blueprint control in process."

Design

This follows the blueprint, and consists of detailed plans and timelines for every step to be taken. It is driven by the vendor expert teams on the ground and takes some detailed analysis in understanding the requirements to the finest level. This is inclusive of exact databases, interfaces, applications, and so on, and their interrelationships. The steps are mentioned with fine granularity and are inclusive of the data inclusion and enrichment (training) steps. The blueprint is completely transferred into design. There is milestone-based validation marked for the development to execute knowledge checklist KPIs and features. This must be mutually agreed to.

Development and Training

In the case of cognitive transformation, this is a little different from normal software development. It includes the user's involvement right from the development stage, which means that even the development should be different. PEIB suggests the following subareas:

- Technical base development

- Project design guided development

Technical base development is installing the technical hardware, connecting to the network, adding required interfaces with source data servers, and starting the core capabilities of the cognitive system. This is the time when the basic capability check is also done to ensure all codified knowledge from the knowledge checklist is available to be used. These are the generic business capabilities and should be demoed to the users. So, users from different business areas have already started to interact with the system from this phase. Over time, the "Other" area should also be enabled.

Project design guided development is then the part of development which will transform the system to give it shape to start working for the department.

This would include the interface design and knowledge upload. The knowledge upload will be followed by the training operation.

So, the fourth swim line, integrate, has already has started and user training starts to happen in parallel. The users have already started to participate in the first and second phases of development tests.

The development includes all the columns mentioned in the knowledge checklist, and all agreed and planned data must be loaded or made available. The data enrichment via training is the most important part of the transformation. The better it is done, the better the consequent results.

When it is done substantially and in view of the cognitive experts and the closely working business user, it looks mature enough. The validation milestone is triggered.

Validation and User Feedback

This is the execution of validation KPs and features identified in the formalize stage and mentioned in the knowledge checklist. This was transferred further to the blueprint and the design.

This is done by a bigger audience and at different levels. The target expectation list is shared. Also, a provision of adding issues encountered and suggestions is provided to such users. PEIB recommends that it is necessary to involve people who never participated in any of the transformation engagements and kept aloof. They work as a control group and could be of value in validation. The resulting feedback then should be verified. If the threshold of validation is not reached and some crucial new suggestion comes, it goes back to the training or even data-loading phase and then to training. Normally, there would be a training requirement for further enriching the system performance and experience. Once found, good to go. Then comes the next step: deployment.

Deployment

The deployment of the cognitive system is a little different from normal software deployment. Normally, databases of the productive system have more data than any other server in the landscape. This is the same for the cognitive system as for the development system. The only difference is that more users are allowed to get into the system. Higher cores of servers may be switched on to enable more traffic. At this stage, the second wave, the additional value add, could be started to be implemented too. The system is now opened to use by a bigger base of users and rolled out to all slowly. The various interfaces are enabled for various users, based on what they need to do. This automatically takes it to next stage, the integrate phase, also called the user exploration.

Integrate

This is the final swim line. The first process of user training already started from the time first phase of development had finished. The second phase of user exploration started after deployment.

Why do we call it integrate and not go live here? The reason is that this is a phase in the development of cognitive capability that has been newly enabled. These users have received capabilities which are not completely mature. These must become more and more mature and capable over time with further training, usage, data input, and so on. It will get more and more integrated into the organization and would help to make it more deep-seated in giving deeper potential recommendations. Therefore, this is called the integrate phase and not just a go-live to users.

Organizations may want to go for the next level of transformation if they want to go from this stage onward and follow the complete cycle of events again.

This completes the description of the PEIB framework of cognitive implementation.

About the Costs

We had a short discussion about the costs earlier, and they were shown via Figure 10-3. The costs listed there were not an exhaustive item-based list for the same but indicative. The real cost case could be ascertained only through the real scenario in front.

But the costs become less as compared to the realized benefits. The system cost and license price may go up over time like any other software, but then the optimization it brings in lessens the overall cost of operation and increases the effectiveness in decision making at every level many times, further providing benefits. So, compared to current expenses, the overall future cost might be in a negative direction as well.

This not only brings in effectiveness but also optimizes the IT resources being used earlier by

- More optimized use of the data from them

- Making the use more effective and user driven

The enterprises of now hardly use even 2-3% of all data acquired for any decision making. This might go ahead to reverse this fraction with cognitive applications.

The PEIB is a guiding light framework for the organizations to make their first step in this direction with confidence and to keep walking ahead with the lowest chances of deviation.

Digital Transformation

The PEIB framework proposed here would lead to a cognitively enabled business, but what it would be doing in principle is making a very-high-order digital transformation for the organization.

The organization would be able to disrupt every single process and digitalize it to its core by fully implementing the cognitive solution.

The three key elements for digital transformation could be

1. Leadership the Vision Driver

2. Customer Experience Enhancement

3. Operations and Employees

What is stopping us now? There is not a single big- or medium-level enterprise not talking about this now. The digital transformation is already a need and an essential element of survival in the future. Organizations not following this might fail.

The business model used to be far more stable earlier for a longer period. With the changing face of business and sustainability in the world of the global market and social media, it must constantly adapt even on a daily basis now.

This is where human limitations become a barrier and a digital core is required. This helps people do what they are supposed to do best and not spend more time in preparing what they need to do quickly.

The cognitive core brings those much-needed digital transformation abilities for organizations. It disrupts all three of the elements mentioned at the start of this section. Let us see how in short.

1. Leadership the Vision: This is supported by an elastic supply of information, insights, and recommendations from the cognitive system. This also works as a control to ensure that human limitations (e.g., biases) do not affect the decisions. The vision statement is also justified with evidences, so that is also supported. This increases the overall effectiveness of decisions and plans. The same goes down to the executors in the language they understand and in a way that is applicable to them. Again, the same is converted from the bottom up, coming back as one picture to enable constant and consistent monitoring.

2. Customer Experience: The customer is king as much now or even more than earlier. The customer, even if she is one in a billion, is heard today with the powerful tools and technologies available. The products and services receive feedback in minutes and must be responded to rapidly. This is the power of customer experience now. The customer is now an omnichannel customer, with the same user experience enjoyed from every channel, be it website, mobile app, or brick and mortar shops.

3. Operations and Employees: The cognitive capabilities give the digital core for operational consistency and effectiveness as well. The employees at each level are empowered more and made more productive by means of these transformations. This increases job satisfaction too. The operational functions and processes could be made more and more effective over time, cutting away deficiencies and also nonessential processes.

So, the digital transformation is enabled to the core by the cognitive capabilities and adapting to the same is facilitated by the PEIB framework.

A Holistic Transformation

A holistic transformation would be one which has following properties:

- It has happened in all the areas equally: people, process, and technology

- It has transformed in a way that it has spanned through each level from top to bottom, connecting the processes along the way

- It truly drives a data-driven and evidence-based culture and not an assumption- or bias-based culture

- It is flexible, smart, and capable enough to rapidly adapt to the changing requirements with the needs of business and not become a roadblock

- It is simple but extremely effective, and usability is high across the organization

- It provides visible benefits by using it

If these properties are there, it could be considered as a holistic digital transformation. This is all present when we have cognitive capabilities implemented across the organization.

So, a cognitive organization is the future and this leads to a holistic transformation. PEIB helps is achieving the same. The framework is designed in a way that it helps organizations to get into the holistic transformation easily and in a standard calibrated flow of methods/processes.

In the absence of such a framework, there is a very good chance that the organization might not start properly in the right direction or lose track midway, and that itself is a big challenge toward digital core achievement.

Cognitive in Manufacturing

There are plenty of organizations now using cognitive capabilities. I will mention one here. Who does not remember the smartness of IBM Watson in winning the game of Jeopardy? But these kinds of cognitive capabilities are by now even helping businesses to make smart decisions.

The cognitively enabled businesses of now are far more effective than those of yesterday. The manufacturing industry is a good example.

The manufacturing industry has cognitive computing capabilities helping from factory line superautomation to supply chain everything. The factory machines could talk to the cognitive core using sensors, and in turn the cognitive core keeps an eye on the tool parameters. These tools could be monitored for any defect which might come. For example, the temperature of a drill going extremely high may let the cognitive system quickly check if the cooling oil tank is empty, or if it's running too rapidly, or if there is some damage to the drill tip itself causing more friction. Even the drill tip may be change to another type if it is sensed that the material is difficult. The production plan is another crucial area on the factory floor. The plan must be changed at times when there is a change in product volume or output mix. This takes lot of effort and mathematics to be done by the planning team and this becomes automated via these capabilities. If there is need of a software update, the cognitive system takes care and plans it when there is no use or least use of that tool, keeping the uptime more and more. Any failures and issues are managed effectively by informing the right person, providing detailed data as evidence-based support. Details of previous occurrences are also provided. The technician could also take help from the system about the required technical know-how. The marketing and supply chains are all managed by one core cognitive system and could provide deeper insight into data. It could monitor the entire supply chain and the vendor performance.

The real-time web data access like news also helps the organization to plan about certain things. If it sees a chance of weather disturbances in a certain part of the world where it might affect the raw material supply or create chances of damage to a production unit, it raises alerts and provides alternatives at times where possible. It might help to replan the freight path for the safe passage of supply chain trucks.

So, it increases the overall uptime and effectiveness of the manufacturing organization, also taking care of vendors and customers by monitoring their data.

Summary

This chapter is based around the transformation framework PEIB helping in the cognitive transformation of enterprises.

Most of the IT costs we have now are recurring and need to be done every year. The value proposition of such investments done every year is zero or extremely low in terms of bringing out value. Data also is becoming vast day by day. Unfortunately, with the way we use tools of IT now, we hardly even use 2 to 5% of the data in decision making. Even organizations using big data capabilities are hardly using it in decision processes.

Organizations are aware of the capabilities of cognitive computing, but only a small fraction of them are extending hands to implement it in the true sense. There are some very good case studies available of organizations which have implemented it, but this number is still very low.

The challenge currently and mostly faced by organizations is that they need to figure out how to take the first steps ahead toward the right path toward implementing cognitive capability.

We discussed in detail about the PEIB framework with lots of examples and images. These framework-based evaluations, checklists, and methods provide an easier, quantifiable, and trackable path to cognitive implementation. This is a game changer.

The PEIB framework is explained well in detail and with relevant examples. The cost incurred especially in the cognitive implementation is also highlighted.

The four swim line phases of the PEIB (initialize, formalize, develop, and integrate) are described in detail. These phases have many checklists and methods. All this is explained in detail. As mentioned, this is a process framework; it has capability to be shaped for different types of industries. The example given here was of a hypothetical manufacturing organization.

Also discussed was the final knowledge checklist and then arriving to create blueprint and design through it. The blueprint has a control mechanism especially defined in the PEIB for the cognitive project.

We talked then briefly about the costs involved, return possibilities, digital transformation, and holistic transformation properties.

We then concluded with a short example.

We will proceed in the next chapter by discussing the road blockers for this transformation.

CHAPTER 11

■ ■ ■

Transformation Road Blockers

This chapter talks about the road blockers in transformation.

■ **Note** We have discussed transformation roadmaps in detail, using the PEIB framework to obtain confident roadmaps which are highly measurable and help avoid deviations along the way. In this chapter, I will discuss the transformation road blockers in detail and will cover some important risks and causatives.

Chapter 10 was dedicated to discussing the various aspects of formulating and planning the transformation.

We discussed the proposed PEIB framework, which has predefined set of activities and checklists to help decide the scope and priorities for the cognitive transformation. It also helps further to ensure how it should be managed and adapted.

With these details and steps mentioned in this framework, there should be clarity on one grand question: "How should I go ahead to take my organization toward cognitive transformation?"

Still, there are some road blockers which I will mention here. These should be known and understood to avoid any further issues or challenges in the cognitive transformation.

The challenges listed further in all the sections in this chapter are any of the following:

- Method or Scope Related

- Planning Related

- Implementation Related

- Adoption Related

Besides this, the very fact that this concept is so new makes adoption difficult at times.

© Rohit Kumar 2017
R. Kumar, *Machine Learning and Cognition in Enterprises*,
https://doi.org/10.1007/978-1-4842-3069-5_11

Figure 11-1 lists all the categories and challenges listed under them.

Method or Scope Related	Planning Related	Implementation Related	Adoption Related
• Use Case Relevance • Assorted Demos • Traditional Methods	• Strategy • Top Down • Wrong Initiation • Vendor Entry • Milestone Tracking • Right Involvement • Knowledge Resource • Resource Alignment	• Scope & Blueprint Alignment • Anchor Points • System Training	• Ignorance • Cost Factor • Industry Core Absence • Cultural Shock • Maturity & Enrichment Plan • Limited Release

Figure 11-1. *Various challenge categories*

Method or Scope Related

Challenges in this group are related either to irrelevant methods being adopted or to things intervening in scope finalization. The scope at the initial stage also depends upon the possibilities: if there is no possibility which is identified for ascertaining use case, scope is impaired. If scope is not identified, going ahead is not possible.

Let us see in some detail the three challenges falling under this:

- Use Case Relevance

- Assorted Demos

- Traditional Methods

Use Case Relevance

This has been a challenge for many new technology adoptions. They are launched with a big list of possibilities and capabilities mentioned on the wrapper, but fail to pick up in the market, as not enough in the way of practical use cases has been identified or picked up by the prospective customers or users.

Cognitive is no different than this. It is good to hear about, get amazed, and see wonderful example videos and presentations about it.

There are some organizations which have clear cases for cognitive: for instance, heavily IoT-driven organizations like oil and natural gas, manufacturing (complex), digital products, retail, supply chain, and so on. These could easily correlate. But some industries like building industry, simple manufacturing industries (e.g., cement), finance industries, and internal organizations (HR, accounting, etc.) fail to present a strong use case.

The use case for one's own enterprise and its different parts and activities is at times difficult to identify. For a small use case, it would be an additional burden on already large IT infrastructure investments and capabilities.

This absence of identification of use case at times is also credited to the very low information about it in the market and the absence of similar examples coming up around, which at times is common at early stages of new technology.

With time, when a lot of organizations use any technology, it becomes easier to see and compare. But at the beginning, with limited examples, it is difficult.

For example, leadership from an organization went to a recent trade and technology show. The organization belonged to the banking and finance domain. The trade show gave them an idea about the technology at a high level via some presentations and demos. But this was not all they saw in the show. With all that they knew already, this new unknown would not capture significant space in their memory. The demos had to do mostly with nonbanking and nonfinance organizations. They could also not figure out a bigger use case and benefit because of this.

They could not even think of a possible use case using this technology which would not have been possible with the currently available technology.

These and many other such scenarios might exist, and they become some of the road blockers. They prevent prospective users from using this solution.

It is a joint effort from the industry supplying the solution and the organization which might use it to overcome this challenge. But mostly it falls to the suppliers to target the correct domains with correct use case examples. Also, the existing business areas should be explored with new capabilities in mind to propose brand new types of use cases in existing industries to disrupt the current execution strategy, leveraging this new capability. This might be a completely new way of doing something never done earlier.

At times, this seems a very simple issue or challenge, but it really pays off if realistic scenarios are already projected for the possible use cases rather than just talking about general properties or limited industry examples. These could create an illusion around the product and could show a very different personality of the product.

Thus, the inability to find relevant use cases applicable to specific organizations is a challenge.

Assorted Demos

The company making or implementing the new technology often concentrates on just one use case. Even demos relevant for an industry often fail to demonstrate the other capabilities. They might go for a demo or two showing the factory line automation or cognitive-assisted maintenance but nothing further. An internal argument runs about why to invest only for these two bread-and-butter earning areas and risk money by adding one more gizmo which might become a white elephant. We are investing a lot already in the optimized running of the business and tuning things up; this becomes an additional burden. This is a good use case, but overall what is the growing benefit over time? Do we have any such possibilities? These thoughts and many like it would cross minds, and this brings down the probability of investment and thus adoption of the technology by organizations.

To get into the fine print, let's say we get a document describing the in-depth diffusion of the cognitive system organization-wide and the benefits affecting every organ of it. This is what is often missed by both parties–implementing organizations and implementation partners– and it is a good plan to help them understand its inception both gradually and with immediate results. The PEIB framework is designed that way, and these kinds of approaches would help further tackle this challenge.

This all adds up to a situation where at times the assorted demonstration exposure becomes a blocker for adoption.

Traditional Methods

Traditional software development methods as they are currently applied might become a road blocker in transformation.

The cognitive transformation should not be planned and treated with traditional implementation methods.

The reason is that this is mostly a training exercise for the application, which is preenriched in a specific group of business domains. The technical development is limited only to the interface developments and UI development. This is not even a functional configuration exercise, where the predefined business process must be configured and the focus is on doing it appropriately. Nor is it application development or report creation. Instead, this is primarily training the system in the most appropriate way with the collection of all required data and knowledge and loading it into the system.

There are two groups of participants in the training: the vendor team and the enterprise team. They play their own roles (as in the PEIB steps) in achieving good training.

Thus, the process cannot use software development methods involving role segregations. The development phase needs the involvement of users as well as the developers from the cognitive team. The scope definition would also need inputs from the vendor team.

In a nutshell, it is a collaborative job from start to end. A phase needing a certain skill or role more will have more involvement from the corresponding team, but all teams go through hand in hand. So, while scoping of the project is driven by business and people from enterprise, the vendor team shares relevant knowledge in helping them achieve it optimally. The development team drives the development, but the users go right along with them.

So, planning to have this and other irrelevant methods might slow down or completely derail the transformation exercise and could instead end up being a hurdle for the right kind of transformation.

Planning Related

Just like any game, the cognitive transformation also needs to be played according to the right set of rules at each stage. These are very critical because the technology is very strong and a little deviation in planning could very soon end up at a very unsatisfactory result.

The planning starts from the thought of going for this and ends when every step planned is executed to get the final solution in hand.

So, planning at every point should be as close to perfect as possible. The following sections discuss some of the planning factors.

Strategy

The cognitive transformation is the core digital transformation and is a strategic plan covering the whole organization.

This should not be treated like any other tool-building exercise or reporting exercise, which exists at one place in the organization and not necessarily in another.

The whole core of the digital transformation is to make the organization data-centric. The data-centric decision to take advantage of the learning and recommending capabilities of cognitive brings the whole organization to a different level of maturity and excellence. The organization becomes a single digital entity, and a response from one organ of the organization is felt at every end. For example, a machine overheating at a production unit also drives purchasing recommendations via internal historical data analysis. This may become a driver to purchase only certain brands of parts in certain regions; the cognitive system could drive some distribution data by understanding that the part has a high probability of breaking down, and by considering the part's availability in service stations the or availability of the right technicians, it might drive some decisions in distribution by reporting that a delay is possible in supply. Then, another production unit could be immediately invoked to produce additional numbers to fulfill the order in time.

This is all connected, but not naturally. It is built with incremental knowledge and connects all organs together slowly. Otherwise, it makes no sense to have a cognitive capability limited to just one suborganization permanently or for the long term. This kills the purpose of its existence.

By all these arguments, it's obvious that the strategic nature of the transformation should be considered before taking any first step. Then, a plan to unfurl it to the whole organization as the digital core over time and in the right direction should be created. The PEIB formalization stage is a well-defined way of doing this initially and then maintaining it. This kind of formalization step is required because every organization is different, but the ground rules remain the same. So, a proper framework like PEIB would ensure that it is following the path that an organization like it should follow, and that this is being done correctly and uniformly over every organization.

Top Down

This is also connected to the previous point about the strategic nature of this transformation. The strategic nature of the transformation is understood, but at times organizations think about the big solution first (i.e., leadership decision enablement using cognitive capabilities to be brought in first). This would work technically. So, if you remember the previous chapter 10 and how and why we decide to go from bottom to top, we see it's the overall knowledge of business coming from each arm slowly summing up into a cognitive capability for the organization as a whole. This enables building the next level of maturity and capability.

If the previous capability is built properly, when it goes to the next level it already has tuned up and polished its ability to learn at that new level. So, when you go from grade 10 to 11, for example, the physics you learn is built from the previous level of detail and information is enriched progressively at every level. Cognitive works very similarly. It may be possible to teach someone in college the concepts of fission and fusion directly, without prior physics. But all prior knowledge must also be passed to complete the meaning and thus the understanding. So, if starting from the top, the system would need every bit of information to be loaded and trained at once. This is not going to be optimally successful in the example of our student, because at every stage of learning physics, she was building a concept or a mental picture one year that optimally was refined and upgraded the following year. But if this is all attempted at one time, quality goes down and it becomes more superficial.

Something similar happens in case of a top-down approach of setting up cognitive capabilities. A better alternative is to follow a progressive and relevant path (formalization phase of PEIB) good for the specific needs and composition of that organization. Doing it all at once may make it superficially trained and maybe too complex with so many dimensions to be trained at once.

So, if planning is done top down, it becomes a blocker in the transformation roadmap.

Wrong Initiation

It should be planned so that it keeps building the knowledge required at the next level of abstraction for the organization. This means that good planning must be in place to ensure that the proper sequence is being followed.

This is how we did in our PEIB framework formalization phase in the checklist creation, which provides rules to decide about this.

"We cannot do this" is not the problem; rather, "we should not do it" is the correct statement here. It's best to reach out and pick the low-hanging fruit first to start getting gains out of it and then progressively upgrade to the next level. This ensures that the knowledge is well polished and enriched at every level and already giving results at previous levels.

This is the right way of doing it. If not done properly, a wrong step will be selected first. This could result in financial blockers at the next phase, and so this should be avoided if possible.

Vendor Entry

The vendor is the party doing the cognitive implementation for the enterprise. They are considered the experts in this. Now this has two dimensions:

- They are not only technical experts but cognitive computing capability experts

- They are experts for cognitive and maybe industry but not for the specific enterprise

Every enterprise in the same business area also differs in many ways. So, no one rule of thumb could work exactly in another, no matter how close they are in terms of business type. So, the vendor and the enterprise should collaborate to complete this loop of knowledge.

A successful cognitive transformation is a joint venture of vendor and enterprise end to end, and end to end is meant literally in this case. So, the vendor should be a part of the game from conceptualizing the scope or before. Normally, vendors are brought in after this stage. They do scope refinement only from the perspective of technical/functional blueprinting and translating it into a form that could help implement it.

But in this case, it's a joint venture throughout. It would be a wrong decision not to do so.

So, the vendor entry has a significant impact on the success or failure of a transformation. This becomes a blocker in obtaining a successful scope if not managed, damaging the whole result at the end. Vendor collaboration should always be in place early.

Milestone Tracking

I do not mean here that milestone-based tracking is not good. It must happen. But doing this just by itself could be dangerous. The PEIB framework is designed for the collaboration thing, and all our discussions until now have been about this as well. So, the leadership at various levels should also participate frequently to ensure that things are on track. The people on the ground in the enterprise, namely, the managers and users, could very easily deviate in the long run bit by bit and end up facing the opposite way after some time. Regular presentations on acquired capabilities as they relate to the team's focus subjects provide a good control mechanism. Leadership should also take pains to see what is being cooked and how much is done with the right set of priority KPI and features listed already in the formalization phase of the PEIB framework. This could be a double check on the transformation roadmap to help keep it on track.

Using only milestone-based formal reviews and appraisals might become a blocker in transformation.

Right Involvement

The involvement of the right people is always required for any project to be successful, and this is true for cognitive transformation as well. But it goes beyond this for cognitive transformation projects.

Normally, the right stakeholders are required at the top levels of departments, which means the people who act as SPOCs (single points of contact) for such departments. They were required along with business representatives during scope decisions. Then, some of these businesspeople would play the role of SPOCs to keep testing first-hand the solutions developed. The ground-level people would interact mostly with these SPOCs and rarely with the development team.

The result is tested and released for all; then, the feedback and requests would go to these stakeholders and again a new little or big requirement would be ready for the next cycle. We mostly needed SPOCs to act as summary knowledge holders in the department and help the development team by testing the quality and features as representatives.

But the cognitive transformation would need involvement of people at every level in every department. Not 100% of the population, to be sure, but all kinds of users. This is required almost all through and thus adds costs as well. But over time, this will go down significantly, as with knowledge enrichment the direct effort curve for training and contributing by these people would keep going down steeply while the usability of the system would keep going up with the natural usage of its capabilities, apart from any formal training.

At the department level, the SPOCs are required to keep an eye on KPI and feature tracking to check on deviations, but then they are not the only active participants. They help in keeping the control on direction of transformation.

Failing to be able to meet this requirement may result into a system that is not optimally trained and effective, and this is a major blocker for the transformation to be on the right path.

Knowledge Resource

The cognitive system is at core a system that can learn and generate knowledge. For humans, learning means building basic maps in the mind; these are connected by various experiences over time and stored as associations. These associations keep modifying with new experiences and events; this changes the perception and response for the same event. Now to have an expert learning in one area, say "treating cancer," one needs to keep enriching knowledge by studying various courses in medical school. These learnings, together with lectures, practical internship, and experiments, keep getting enriched. The questions asked during the courses provoke ever-deeper thoughts and further enrich knowledge. The questions become more and more inward over time. Something may have started in class from questions posed by the professor to help thinking in the particular direction in which the skill needs to be developed; however, after education and years of practice in hospital, these questions become internalized. So, the person with all learning and experience now asks questions to himself; for example, "if this certain condition were treated in a certain patient this way, and this previous patient became ill with this combination of drugs, what should I do in this case, which seems to be similar except that the patient is double the age of those earlier patients, and is also female?" So, the difference is that the questions initially were aimed at training and now are used for problem solving. The earlier ones originated from the outside and the later were inward. Training plays a major role, but without proper input of ample knowledge resource it becomes limited in effectiveness.

So, what does this mean if we translate it into the current blocker scenario? It means the knowledge resources required (core, other, internal business, and continuing learning) should be planned extensively, without any compromise, and very much in advance; and stationed next to every stage of the transformation.

This could all be missed if the transforming organization has inadequate knowledge about how cognitive systems work best. That is why external experts are required here too.

No matter how good the training, if the overall resources of knowledge are not good and ample, the association between knowledge corpus will happen with a limited scope of information and consequently with limited effect.

There could also be blockers in terms of getting things in the right format or when needed, cost considerations, or even knowing about the cognitive option in the first place or knowing how to find it.

Laziness or perhaps overly high expectations for quick results could also be a reason.

This could become a major blocker in achieving the successful transformation. This might bring in a very diluted and less intelligent solution at the end.

Resource Alignment

We discussed in "Right Involvement" that the right people should be assigned to the transformation roadmap of the organization, and that this is different from what is seen for conventional projects like, say, ERP projects. Just before this, we also discussed the high value of having a good variety and amount of knowledge resources fed into the system to get the desired depth in the recommendation capabilities of the cognitive machine.

Now this section talks about an interesting blocker, which is a combination of both. Let's say that a project has planned every material (learning content) and the role of every human participant to the finest possible detail. Everything is listed out; all people are identified and we have a solid plan of action ready with details on which resource goes where.

But the time dimension (i.e., availability at appropriate times) is equally important. So, another road blocker is not planning the availability timeframe for each resource (any type). Cognitive transformations should be built progressively for all the reasons explained earlier in this chapter.

The top-down approach works technically but not practically in giving desired results. So, the time of availability may be missed, and for a previous level of knowledge development this means that the efforts at this level should have been done already. If time must be held strictly to what was decided for every stage of the project, efforts will be low in quality and/or the timeline will be too long.

Either way, not good. So, it becomes a major blocker to the success of the transformation not to have an availability plan with respect to realistic timelines or a backup plan in place throughout.

Resources should be aligned on time and with planned quantity and quality for the success of the transformation. Otherwise, this could be a major quality issue and may completely derail the whole transformation, because with every failure due to this at a previous level, the next level becomes even more prone to planning failure, because now overall complexity has increased.

Figure 11-2 depicts the difference between the normal software development (e.g., typical report development) and cognitive transformation.

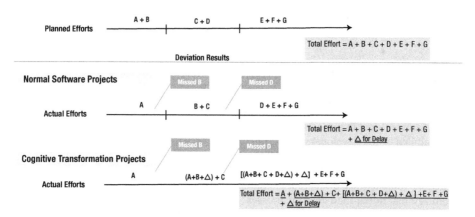

Figure 11-2. *Comparative effort scores*

In normal software development, any missing steps are passed on to the next step, but the quantity of effort stays about the same from one part to the next. So, with missing steps at every stage of the project, the overall efforts remain about the same with some delta (Δ) for delays.

But for the cognitive transformation, every missing step also needs delta effort together with its own effort to compensate for reaching the combined maturity with more missed inputs at every level. So, if B is missed, then at the next stage its effort is added as

A + B + Δ instead of just B. The reason is that at this new level, the C + D process should have matured together with already enriched data from the A and B enrichment. As this did not happen in the previous stage, this must happen together with C here, and if D is missed as well, the total effort thus becomes (A + B + Δ) + C instead of just B + C.

Further, in the next stage C + D matured together with A + B should have carried forward to be then enriched with E, F, and G. But this has not happened. D was missed. So, now C and D getting enriched or trained with A and B and then with E, F, and G should happen, with additional Δ effort added even with D as it has moved to a higher complexity level and would need more effort to realize the result.

The result, with additional Δ for delay as in the previous example, is much more complex in terms of effort consumed.

This can be a very difficult blocker in a cognitive transformation roadmap. It might even completely overturn the project. Figure 11-2 is a linear example; considering the multiple processes and relations being transformed, it becomes many times more complicated and takes a great deal of effort.

If Δ is not consumed at every stage, then the quality is correspondingly reduced by same factor and this has its an unpredictable result.

Implementation Related

There are also challenges or issues which might come up as road blockers during implementation. I am not listing out the generic ones here, like network failure, human resource procurement, hardware procurement, and so on. Instead, I will mention three major issues which might become road blockers for a successful transformation in any organization; this will be from the cognitive transformation perspective only.

Scope and Blueprint Alignment

The scope comes about as the result of great efforts and is primarily driven by the organization. I am using the word "organization" here instead of just "business" for a reason. Conventional IT projects are driven by the needs, tests, and results of business users, fulfilled by the developers and configurators. So, when we talk about them, we talk from the perspective of business and IT.

For cognitive capability transformations, it is the sum of everything being done and the people doing it and a direct representation of every type and role. So, referring to "organizations" rather than just "businesses" is appropriate. A scaled-down version of the whole organization must contribute.

Again, the organization drives the scope formalization with the help of experienced vendor consultants. The formal scope comes out after all the exercises mentioned in the formalization phase in the PEIB framework in Chapter 10.

This must be the translated "as is" by development or other project teams in the blueprint. This is extremely important in cognitive transformation projects considering the possibilities of deviation and of the time and effort growing out of bounds, as shown in Figure 11-2.

This could become a risk or road blocker if not thoroughly discussed, validated, and approved.

The cognitive transformation is different from other projects in many ways. The blueprint in cognitive must be a collaborative effort, and the technical development team drives it.

But if the transformation is not done according to the blueprint, there is a very good chance that the requirements will not be converted into the final results properly, and this might spoil the whole transformation cycle. The result might be a lot of deviation from expectations and even missing capabilities from what was planned originally.

Anchor Points

It is difficult to perceive actual velocity and direction in an open sea. The same is true for the cognitive transformation, which is like a sea itself; the possibilities for enriching learning in any specific direction or process area are actually unlimited.

Consider this situation from our previous example of cancer treatment and medical treatment in the "Knowledge Resource" section. The person started with a graduate-level study of medicine. She goes further to the next level and specializes in one area of treatment; then maybe she could go for a super-specialization. This means she is an expert in only one area of medical science and does not focus on specialized treatment of other ailments like those of the heart, abdomen, liver, kidney, et cetera. Although she has a fair idea of these, being a doctor of medicine, her main focus is in just one area. She keeps learning in that area of specialization and over time might go ahead into one focused type of cancer only or one specific type of treatment procedure.

Similarly, let's say there is an enterprise that has planned certain areas to be cognitively transformed in a certain sequence. But the fact also is that the system has practically unlimited capability to learn in all areas, depending on the amount of knowledge resources, training, and time invested in that particular area. So, there is a very good chance to get a shift in focus during any phase of project execution and get carried away. This may result in major time spent in a few departments or areas instead of striking a balance, as planned for a specific timeline investment.

Therefore, we talked about putting "measurable" and "clearly distinguishable" KPI or features as anchor points at the formalization step of transformation. This helps to avoid deviation. As a matter of fact, it is always feasible to enrich the system in any one area to higher specialization, but then in practical situations with limited time and expected benefits this might come with disadvantages to the initially selected scenario.

Failing to create anchor points in plan can become a blocker, and the overall result may become distorted and unpredictable.

System Training

The knowledge-building exercise in cognitive computing is the core. Planning to have everything included and provided in time is important, as we discussed earlier in this chapter. These things ensure proper inflow of codified and uncodified data into the system. This is very important to ensure that all the aspects upon which recommendations could depend are covered.

But this job is not even halfway done. It's necessary to ensure that all these resources are utilized to build the desired level of intelligence into the system.

This is done via a good training of the system; as mentioned earlier in this chapter, there are questions which are pointed inward and outward. The outward questions are needed (remember the "Knowledge Resource" section) to build knowledge. The inward questions, which are considered for this part of the discussion, are needed to solve problems and further develop and enrich the knowledge based on its new outcome (desired, undesired, or anything in between).

If a cognitive system is loaded with all the data and not trained with extensive sets of questions, it will make no sense when it used for recommendations. This is not a search application to find relevant texts from a database and push to the user onscreen. It must understand the texts, and that requires training to gain deep understanding of the core subject area and business-specific knowledge. Until the trainer himself is an expert and knows the questions that could be asked in a multitude of ways for a related subtopic, he cannot do it well. This becomes a blocker in a successful transformation roadmap.

There is another aspect as well. As mentioned in the PEIB framework details in Chapter 10, there is a certain sequence followed for every organization for transformation: the transformation path. Every level should be enriched as much as possible before moving to the next level. Skipping a level may result in exponentially more energy and effort needed to fill in the gaps at later stages. The training quality at every level will affect the quality level of every subsequent level.

This makes it one of the important road blockers to the success of the transformation.

Adoption Related

A dictionary definition of "adopt" is "choose to take up or follow an idea, method, or course of action."

The adoption-related issues are of two types.

- Those that occur when we think of adopting something or not

- Those that occur after we have it in place but need to follow some action plan to be able to continually use it properly

So, one happens before adopting it and the other afterward, when it's necessary to follow procedures to keep using it properly. The second one could be adaptation as well (i.e., to adopt it properly).

Let us now discuss some such challenges which could become road blockers for the transformation.

Ignorance

Ignorance is not always bliss. There are cases I have seen when there is not much awareness about the latest developments in the industry and even ignorance about the consequences.

Many research firms have already mentioned that top-listers in the industry could fade away if they don't follow the trend of industry 4.0.

This is a definite trend coming; in fact, it has already started, with a lot of organizations deep into it or at least taking the first steps.

This ignorance is also at times considered a big risk and blocker in cases where the latest trends in technology, industry, or both are not understood.

Cost Factor

Whenever I speak with a top executive about the cognitive solutions and benefits, I see a series of expressions. They are amused, impressed, and then quickly put a hand in their pocket and say with raised eyebrows, "seems expensive." The next thing that crosses their minds might be "How would I be able to convince business to take on this new cost, when even the current budget had to come out of such insane negotiations?"

This reality can be a major blocker in this category. It can stop the path before the portal to exploring the solution or the transformation roadmap is even reached.

The point is that there is a big expense with a good internal resource involvement as well, further adding up costs, complexity, and efforts.

But do you remember the discussion at the start of Chapter 10? The savings incurred would over time negate the recurring cost happening in terms of major investments in the IT budget year after year. The investment in cognitive is different. The system is self-evolving over time. Although it's an autonomous system, the maintenance perspective remains for sure, but the value perspective goes up year after year with use. The training becomes ingrained in the organization and further external costs are not seen anymore.

There are many such arguments which could be brought forward but then the costs are there and some new kind of costs (including subscription costs) are added up, which becomes a blocker.

Industry Core Absence

We talked about the resources required in Chapter 10. For the sake of convenience of discussion, I will again put that information here as Table 11-1.

Codified Knowledge
Machine Manuals
Product Details
Quality Methods and Process
Quality Measurements
Product Manufacturing Process
Power Efficiency Measures and Standards
Repair Machines
Model Part Details
Know Process Challenges
Operator Manuals
Issues in Operations

(continued)

Others
Specialist Knowledge Base
Specialist Question and Answers for Training
Standard Research Papers
Standard Journals
News Websites (Related)

Internal Knowledge
Internal Specialist Knowledge Base
Internal Specialist Question and Answers for Training
IoT Feeds
Historical Logs
Historical Failure Details
Other Historical Issues
Machine Repair Logs
Machine Modifications
Customized Machine Manuals
Product Details and Specifications
Internal Codes
Internal Quality Control Historical Data
Internal Quality Control Process
Internal Quality Control Metrics
Power Consumption and Issues Data
Internal Process Flow
Internal Manuals
Historical Production Data

Continuing Knowledge
News Feeds
Free Web Sources
Subscription-Based Web Sources (Other)
Subscription-Based Technical Information
Machine Manufacturer Feeds for Software and Hardware Details
Software Upgrade Feeds

(continued)

Human Resources

Expert Operator

Engineer

External Process Expert

Internal Process Expert

Product Expert

Product R&D Specialist

Cognitive Expert to Ingest Data

Enterprise IT Counterpart Learners

IT Expert Internal

IoT Data Expert—Internal

Following people continue for knowledge continuity

Enterprise IT Counterpart Learners

IT Expert Internal

IoT Data Expert

In the context of Chapter 10, this table provided an indicative list of detailed knowledge items. But for our discussion here in this section, we just need to focus on the headings. The headings are as follows:

- Codified Knowledge: The knowledge giving the basic flavor of the cognitive system. So, if for cancer research, it should have all codified detailed knowledge from this area.

- Others: This is also related to the previous option. This has Q&A to train and enrich data from the previous category. Additionally, all research papers, journals, videos, and so on are provided here.

- Internal Knowledge: This is the area where organization-specific knowledge contents are loaded and training is done for this.

- Continuing Knowledge: This is comprised of knowledge sources beyond what was given at the commissioning of the system.

- Human Resources: This is the temporary (project phase) and future human resources plan.

We are concerned here about the first and second points. The core knowledge capability is imparted to the cognitive system to work in a specific area. This is specific to a certain task, process, or industry. This could be known as the industry core.

The presence of industry core will always give more confidence to organizations to go for a certain solution. The more relevant it can be in this regard, the higher the chances that its adoption will happen.

There had been examples of software which were very nice industry-specific fits (e.g., utility, electronic, manufacturing, retail, banking and finance, etc.) or process-specific fits (like finance, material management, sales & distribution, etc.). This is a genuine attracting feature which ensures a close fit of application with the least number of customizations.

So, for cognitive solution it could mean the following:

- Industry-specific codified knowledge (all) in rigorous training based on enriched form

- Added value by adding all research contents to it and enriching

- New age use cases which might come about because of this also gaining additional capabilities

- Knowledge update until the date of installation

If these are not there, it's very obvious that this could be a first-level blocker, assuming the mammoth task of converting base metal into knowledge gold.

Culture Shock

The definition of culture shock in terms of business transformation could be defined as follows: "A feeling of uncertainty, confusion, or anxiety that people tend to experience when a change happens in the way of doing their daily business and tasks." This is more prevalent if the transformation is very different from the current state. This can arise because of unfamiliarity with the new tool and personal assumptions about the complexity and fear of losing the comfort zone of using previous means.

The cognitive solutions are sometimes also demonstrated as high-end gizmo applications, and fear of being incapable of using them might be in the back of the mind. Also, fear of the cognitive solutions outperforming and thus replacing human resources is a very important cause.

Consideration of terms like "high end" and "complex" could also result a perception of high cost.

People even might find it too intrusive into their personal department-level nuclear families, since it's almost an all-pervading culture. Cognitive computing capabilities relate to all and have an enterprise-wise span, utilizing all data from every corner at any point of time, so local curtaining of information/data and the like could not happen. This much transparency could be difficult at times, when you'd have no time to work on damage control. All these thoughts also are related to the culture shock phenomenon, and that may work as a blocker.

Fears of more complex IT-related knowledge being necessary for users in the business department and of IT people of getting thrown out or made redundant by this are also some blockers.

Maturity and Enrichment Plan

Even when "ready to be used for the first time," the cognitive system is not truly ready. It keeps gaining experience and learning with time and with new data. There is certainly the need for training it as well. This is known as the future maturity and enrichment plan.

If this is not done, the system might only keep getting data and perceiving the meaning out of it based on its preexisting knowledge in that area. Without training, this will be not of much use if it belongs to some new area of business or new process.

This might become a blocker going further, as expected growth of maturity is not possible if the system is not trained more over time and used with the addition of new data also.

If this is not done, the system might not grow to the fullest bloom, and this may become a blocker.

Limited Release

Limited release is also a defect in planning to understand how the cognitive system will evolve and work better over time if used by many people. The cognitive system requires everything from the smallest activity data to the biggest financial and production planning data. This means it should be planned from the start to serve every level of the organization as low in the hierarchy as possible.

The more widely it is used, the more it gets an understanding about the organization. So, keeping it to an elite group or a group composed along similar lines could hamper the overall usability and maturity over time.

This becomes a huge blocker as no good use cases are planned with that vision; even down to the ground level, not using it largely keeps it from getting to understand and becoming able to analyze areas of business. This is a blocker for sure.

Some of the challenges that have been discussed in this part of the chapter could be overridden just by following the PEIB framework. But some should be counted and kept in view to ensure that they don't become blockers. Some are even related to awareness and willingness issues, which could happen without any control, but the needed control could be built over time.

So, change the way of transformation to avoid major challenge and blockers.

Risks

With any activity, there are always certain risks involved. Even while cycling, risks are there, and considering all the dangers in the world, the risks could multiply. So, falling from a cycle might at maximum result in a fracture or dislocation if on a slope with high speed. But there may be serious injuries or even a fatality if the cyclist is rammed with a vehicle. So, risks are not only relative to what the actual tool or vector could create; they are a sum of the environmental factors interacting with it as well.

The same goes for cognitive transformations. The risks are not only because of any probable failure of the system in question but it could be due to surrounding parties, situations, and influenced scenarios.

I consider the risks here into four major categories:

- People related

- Process related

- Technology related

- Management related

Figure 11-3 shows the four categories with some more individual risks listed.

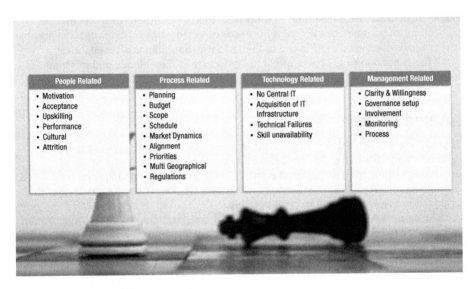

Figure 11-3. *Major risks*

People-Related Risks

These risks are with respect to the various human resources working on different projects. This includes all levels of people working in the organization except for some top chairs.

There are also further risks listed in this category.

Motivation

There are certain risks related to personal motivation. It is impossible to have perfect motivation for all % people for 100% of the time of the project.

There is always a chance of motivation loss in the team. This could be infectious as well. A crisp process-driven organization is a solution.

The risk could be mitigated by frequent contact among multiple layers of the team and finding and ironing out small issues and concerns very early.

This becomes a risk, so it's important to ensure that a certain level of enthusiasm and motivation builds up in the team; if not, transformation might take a hit due to low motivation. The team should see the big picture and have a sense of understanding and responsibility over the whole process.

Acceptance

This is a very important factor; it's notorious for impacting many transformations over the years.

The current state of things is always taken as a baseline, and people develop their expertise all along depending on the fact that the baseline won't move from its place any time soon. Any change like this, even if it's small, is noticed as a challenge. But bigger changes, such as the cognitive transformation, can become critical in this regard. The change in the whole baseline upon which my expertise is based means that I need to build up an altogether new competency. This might cost me my reputation, my work, or even my career.

The fear and the probable discomfort could be a risk which might lead to rejection. The cognitive system is not the operational system, and users might tend to use it less or overlook it, taking it as just a technology gizmo. But the less it is used the worse it is, because it needs to be used as much as possible to be able to provide further value.

This is a common risk for most technologies or process transformations. Cognitive transformation, being a combination of both, is more prone to be affected by this risk.

Upskilling

Cognitive transformation needs three levels of skill enhancement:

- Technical know-how (at least) about the way this is

- How to use it (although simple)

- How to maximize benefits out of the current process by doing it differently and by doing it the cognitive way

This aspect should be kept in mind when a cognitive transformation happens. A rollout of upskilling and awareness is necessary to make people aware of all three aspects.

This also helps in improving acceptance and acts as a motivating force, because when people have interest in something they tend to own it in a way, and results are always better. The assumed challenge and risk in their mind are eased, and they can participate in all the exercises; so upskilling mitigates all the risks discussed before.

This helps in mitigating these risks before they become a big bubble of failure.

If not done, this might lead to a big risk, because at the end of the day the workforce must use it to make it successful.

Performance

This is always a key KPI in workforce management and business project management. The performance hit because of change is at times a ripple effect caused by many unmanaged risks like upskilling, acceptance challenges, and lack of motivation.

This creates a dilemma for the workforce, and their productive hours at work may decrease substantially. This might be also because of two exactly opposite reasons as well:

- Technology and process changes are considered very challenging to adopt

- The transformation process is so interesting that a lot of time goes into playing with it

This could be compared with the same scenario in the 1980s, when computers started to become more popular at workplace; the technology was so amazing that half of the time people were doing unnecessary and unproductive work.

So, if impact possibilities on the performance of the workforce are not considered, this could become a grave risk to the success of the transformation.

Cultural

Like any culture, work culture has also a prominent effect on any organization. No two organizations will ever have identical work cultures. I will not mention any names, but there was a prominent example of this in the IT industry itself. One successfully running IT company was taken over by another manufacturing giant. They had put their very good managers, who had developed their careers with manufacturing industry exposure primarily, into this newly acquired company. Their purpose was to homogenize their culture with that of the mother organization. These were handpicked successful senior-level managers who were brought in. But the result was the opposite of what was intended. The new IT organization had a hard time working in this setup. The reason was not only two organizational cultures but two industry cultures. Had it been an IT-to-IT culture homogenization, it would have been easier, because the basic framework usually remains the same in most of the management aspects.

The cognitive transformation doesn't just change the IT setup or bring to hand some high-end solutions. It is a strategic change. Also, the industry is moving in the market toward consumer experience enhancement. Similarly, they are moving in their offices toward a more employee-centric and employee experience–based organization. The cognitive digital core disrupts the current work culture and brings about a much more productive and collaborative way of working. This must be infused slowly and long before the actual transformation starts for a successful future transformation. Webcasts, workshops, awareness workshops, mailers, and town halls all should drive this along with some smaller trainings to make people aware of how the work culture is upgraded with this.

Not done properly, it is a risk. The cognitive experience of any transformation is proportional not only to the technical expertise but also to employee experience that goes with it.

Attrition

High attrition numbers indicate that something is not good, although attrition will never be zero. But a balance should be struck, as attrition of even an employee assessed as mediocre is taking out some expertise, and that will require some effort to fill up that gap. Even so, no one can predict for sure whether it will be successful or not.

Attrition is also a risk if it happens more during the transformation's key phases. The cognitive solution is a wise man sitting and learning every possible rule of the game from everyone playing it. The more that seasoned resources are talking, the better.

The attrition plan must be developed in detail with the HR department beforehand to ensure that at least the key participants are not lost during or before the transformation.

Process-Related Risks

There are a number of supportive processes running in tandem to make the transformation successful. Any issue in that corner may also become a big risk sooner or later.

Let us discuss some of the main risks I have covered in a bit more detail.

Planning

This is by far the biggest risk discussed and will remain as such throughout the process. Forget all about "foolproof," because there cannot be a foolproof plan in the first place.

The cognitive transformation is a very different transformation as compared to all other projects done. This is a combination of technology and process transformation. The way it is achieved is also unique and so in some areas, as discussed earlier about the road blockers, could be extremely risky (e.g., the timeline and effort example discussed earlier with Figure 11-2). We see how the effect of missing one step at a time could have unplanned and huge impacts on efforts.

So, for process-related risks and all others for that matter, planning remains a big risk.

This book proposes a new framework called PEIB which is also focused in Chapter 9.

Budget

This is a big part of planning plan everywhere, from the individual level to the organizational. For an individual, it might be mostly because of lack of funds available in his bank account. But for an organization, it could also be because of nonalignment of thoughts between consulting advisory and leadership.

This is always a risk if it is not approved at all but more dangerous if it's planned to be provided in installments (perhaps based on gained foothold or value already coming out).

So, the risk of budget could be managed not only from a financial perspective but also by good planning and following a standard and logical framework like PEIB. Budget is mostly in instalments, and unless we have a strong framework for cognitive delivery, it is simply not possible to give a confident picture further to make it sustainable in terms of budget inflow.

Scope

This is a very evident category of procedural risks. The scope becomes a big risk if not done properly to outline what is needed, when it is needed, and in which form. There's no need to discuss this in detail, as it remains the same for all the projects done until now.

Schedule

This is related to two things: plans and operational efficiency of executing these plans.

We have already discussed plans in this chapter as the biggest risk of all. The schedule is a time-wrapped presentation of the same plan and marks a distinct stretch of time for every item in the plan.

So, we can say that this is the next level of planning; it takes it to the next level of detail by integrating the time factor.

Another aspect of the schedule is the execution aspect, in which we follow the schedule. If the schedule is not followed, then this is also a risk.

There could be a lot of challenges which could impact the timeline in the schedule. These cannot be controlled perfectly but should be controlled to the maximum extent possible.

The transformation schedule again needs to follow a standard framework like PEIB, which will provide more control over the execution with more confidence and the least deviation.

Market Dynamics

All of this transformation is being done for the benefit of the business. If there is a market decline in the middle of the process, it might become a risk for the transformation. So, to avoid this, the plan should be crafted in a way that the major initial engagement runs at the right time of the year, not toward the start or end, when there is more uncertainty.

Alignment

Here, "alignment" specifically refers to that between the internal and external coordinating bodies.

The alignment is a risk if not internal, and if it's not between the external and internal stakeholders, it's also a risk.

Internal alignment issues could come about because of a number of reasons; from the process perspective, it could be because a proper plan is not in place or because a good framework to manage it quantitatively and qualitatively is not there.

There could be internal-external alignment issues between vendor and organization stakeholders, and at every level this alignment issue could cause a risk. The alignment issues could be due to planning issues, absence of job clarity absence, or other ambiguities and points of confusion. These are the major issues, and moreover there can be any number of them.

These alignment issues are a big issue and should be mitigated by a strong process and definite framework. There should be constant monitoring with parameters defined to ensure tight integration, or else it's a risk.

Priorities

Planning could bring in the elements needed for a good transformation. But all of this cannot be done at once, and even in the case of sequential execution, the most optimal and viable sequence should be chalked out. The priorities should be defined.

When scope is defined, timelines are also wrapped around, but if prioritization is incorrect, the plan cannot be executed properly.

This could be dangerous to the cognitive transformation. We have already seen in this chapter one example of efforts spiraling higher when the proper order is not followed. This was just one example; there could be many.

So, while planning and scheduling the project (formalizing in PEIB), a priority step is also included to avoid this risk.

Multiple Regions

We are talking about enterprises going for a core digital transformation using the cognitive core. The spread of a single organization is aligned through a single effective digital core. This is irrespective of the size of the organization. The bigger the organization, the better the use case, because the smallest organizations might have people sitting in one region or even across one single hall or table and working together. Decisions are taken in close proximity and alignments could be done on a small paper napkin. But for larger enterprises, this employee experience and collaboration are created by the digital core. A virtual layer opens its shores around itself to all the parties, and they all connect through this single core. Sounds good, if done well. The risk is bigger in this case during implementation. The PEIB framework (or any similar framework that's in place) should be adjusted to include this aspect as well during the planning phase and finalization of the scope (formalizing). If this isn't done properly, the cognitive core could provide recommendations which are not relevant to some locations.

This should also be ensured by having the right mix of people participating from all relevant regions in layers as planned for execution.

Regulations

Whether we do business in one or multiple regions, the need for regulatory compliance is always there, governing various aspects like data secrecy. But when we talk about a single digital cognitive core of any organization operating across multiple regions, there are bound to be different regulations operating for similar processes in different regions.

This makes it more complex, and planning should be done carefully. Certain countries have very stringent laws around customer data, if that's being used. This might be a risk if overlooked.

Technology-Related Risks

Any technical transformation must list out the risks related to technology to ensure that mitigations could be planned to minimize the effects of such risks.

Cognitive transformation has both technical and process-related elements.

When we talk about the technology only, then it is also key. The technology focus and activities are also very niche.

This might cause some technology-related risks to occur. Also, the overall actions and capabilities to engage in the technical side of this transformation are very important for its success. This is dependent on the maturity of the internal IT organization of the transforming organization.

Let us discuss some of these technology-related risks further.

No Central IT

I do not consider IT to be the central IT for an organization until the tools, processes, and strategy for it are the same irrespective of span across regions.

If there is a separate IT organization present that only relates to the central IT organization while operating locally with its own specific rules of the game, this might become a risk for cognitive transformation.

It becomes costlier at times if we do not have an aligned IT core or hub already present. So, this should be standardized first before starting the transformation project.

Acquisition of IT Resources

The IT resources we are pointing to here are the hardware, software, and network hardware. These normally come from multiple vendors and are processed by multiple teams. If this is out of sync, the whole project might get delayed.

The risk is mostly only at the start of the engagement; over time, the impact becomes less.

The other aspect of this risk is capacity planning of hardware storage. This is critical, because if it happens in between, it is not only a question of acquisition again but also connecting it and making it functional together with the existing one or the one brought earlier.

Technical Failures

Technical success cannot always be guaranteed, and failure remains a risk for any IT-related transformation from start to end and even afterward. There are international standards to be followed to avoid such failures by ensuring good-quality components. There are best practices and good monitoring to avoid these potential failures.

But this still is a risk throughout.

Skill Unavailability

In any project, proper skill plays a huge role in ensuring good implementation or transformation.

Cognitive capabilities not only need good skill to be useful but also various experts in process, internal process, technology, and integrating many other technologies in the landscape.

Like any other project, skill availability remains a risk; even a person with the right skills moving out in the middle of the process is a risk.

Management-Related Risks

"Management of an organization" is a single phrase but not so unitary in practice. Within any organization, there are parts and pieces and hierarchical levels working together to make one management presence trying to guide the ship to sail in a single direction. But it's not uncommon to have different levels and organs of the same management presence working rather out of sync and creating issues stemming from less effective or out-of-context management, or even worse, mismanagement.

There are certain risks prominent in this category, which I will now discuss further.

Clarity and Willingness

The absence of clarity at any level could be a great risk. For such a huge strategic initiative, there should be clarity from top to bottom among the cooperating management line. Any ambiguity or confusion at one level might result in a manifold increase down the line.

Willingness at top means a go–no-go situation. But at levels down to the bottom, willingness is driven by passion or reward or penalty. The third one is the worst driver to achieve the expected actions.

There should be a clear consensus, understanding, and sharing of responsibilities to enhance the willingness to work together. Trust is also an important ingredient.

Any absence of these could be a risk, resulting in wrong or half-hearted solutions.

Governance Setup

All levels should cooperate and coordinate in a conducive, clear, and motivating environment. And for these transformation projects also, a proper governance setup should be brought into place. Each of them should keep watch over one part against the planned expectations and scopes. The whole organization cannot work on everything in parallel. Also, random people should not be able to jump into governing and driving various aspects. It must be done properly within a planned framework of responsibilities which are predefined.

A smaller representation of the hierarchy of people with a proper process defined at each level is called a governance setup, and this is essential for success; its absence, on the other hand, is a risk.

Involvement

Cognitive core transformations are much more collaborative than any other software project. It constantly needs management's presence. If this involvement is not there with a good understanding of the direction and motive, it could be a risk.

The various levels of management should involve themselves and continue until the end, taking calculated risks at every stage. This involvement is also required from top leadership down to the bottom to ensure that they are considering the value outcomes churning out at any specific point of time.

Since it is a strategic and newer technology (both), it needs more involvement at all levels.

Monitoring

A top priority of the plan should be the quality of the deliverables. That is where monitoring is important. It is done on KPIs and expected features, decided at the time of formalization of scope. These need to be monitored as well. These are a big risk if not monitored, because then it is very much like not having them in the first place.

Process

There are scenarios where processes are not optimized. This deficiency should be overcome as much as possible before starting such a strategic initiative.

The absence of crisp processes to manage these engagements is always a risk. Processes which are prone to malpractice or substandard ways of doing things might lead to the inclusion of wrong practices in the cognitive system itself and training it in the wrong direction.

Summary

In this chapter, I have given a detailed discussion of road blockers in the course of cognitive transformation. I also discussed the major risks and the reasons they exist.

The various road blockers are divided into four major categories:

- Method or Scope Related

- Planning Related

- Implementation Related

- Adoption Related

Each major category was also discussed, along with a list of its challenges.

The benefit of resource alignment was also discussed, with an example showing what happens if it's not in place; the resulting effort over time could spiral ever higher.

The road blockers could be due to the understanding of organizations about how they can utilize this cutting-edge transformation and how they actually do it once the scope is identified.

The planning elements should also be proper and quantifiable. The right resources and knowledge sources should also be aligned and on time.

In case the anchor points needed for a project like this are missing, there is a very high chance of deviation, and this should be managed.

At times, the overall adoption of the transformation is a challenge and road blocker.

The risks are another area where certain things should be identified beforehand. Some of the major headings of risk discussed here are as follows:

- People Related
- Process Related
- Technology Related
- Management Related

CHAPTER 12

Self-Evolving Cognitive Business

This chapter talks about businesses which are naturally cognitive driven. A business which is cognitively driven to the core to be responsive not only to needs for change almost in real time but also to business planning and monitoring driven by real-time data. Decisions in the cognitive computing environment are almost 100% data driven and always validated for biases.

Note   We discussed parallel evolving IT-BI systems (PEIB) and their properties in Chapter 9. In Chapter 10, we discussed the nuts and bolts of the PEIB to understand the implementation perspective of this framework. Chapter 11 helped us to understand the road blockers we might hit while we plan or execute cognitive transformation and the risks involved while doing it. This chapter now summarizes and consolidates all these learnings to describe a cognitive "self-evolving business," a dream which is possible now.

Before we proceed further in this chapter, taking a hint from the preceding note, let me quickly differentiate between Chapter 9 and this chapter.

The reason I am doing this because the central concepts described sound almost the same. But are they?

No; they are different. Chapter 9 discusses how the IT-BI system should evolve parallel to the needs of the business. There, I discussed the properties of such a transformation framework. In Chapters 10 and 11, I discussed the details of the framework and then hurdles in achieving it.

In this chapter, we are ready with all the understanding with which we can go from point A to point B.

Now, we should summarize in this chapter what the cognitive business looks like. Why was it needed? And how it is supposed to be?

With all the understanding in place, we will now directly talk about the self-evolving cognitive business.

© Rohit Kumar 2017
R. Kumar, *Machine Learning and Cognition in Enterprises*,
https://doi.org/10.1007/978-1-4842-3069-5_12

What we mean by self-evolving is explained in this chapter and summarized at the end. This helps us understand why this is a game changer.

We will divide this chapter discussion into three broad areas.

- What the problems are with the current setup in organizations

- How this compares to cognitive evolving systems

- What is to be expected and what not from cognitive setups

The first two points are covered together in the following section.

Conventional vs. Cognitive Self-Evolving Systems

We have discussed this from various angles in previous chapters. But it needs to be put into one single picture to see the overall situation; after that, we'll be able to talk about cognitive self-evolving systems. The question of what cognitive self-evolving is will be answered in the summary, but until that time let us just know it as a system which is progressively adapting business.

Until now, we haven't used the terms "adapting" or "evolving" for IT systems because these systems operate internally to business models as single entities once the cognitive digital core is merged with them and the PEIB framework starts to be utilized. So, now we can consider talking about both business and IT together as they work as one unit.

The current business has some highlights as their overall execution properties. Based on these highlights, we will discuss further how the current perspective differs from the cognitive digital core perspective. I will list them out first and then discuss them one by one. We will keep the discussion limited here, as much has already been discussed and the perspective of discussion is from business and is not IT versus BI gaps and relations.

The following are the highlights:

- Silos

- Mixing Results/Considerations

- Leadership Effectiveness

- Profilt & Loss Approach

- Expansion and Integration Issue

- Wastage and Overkill

- HR-Only Talent Management

Silos

Unfortunately, work still happens in silos even though we have high-end solutions like big data capabilities, predictive solutions, automated maintenance & production, connected devices, and mobile-based solutions. We have a world of high-end solutions already with high-speed computing capabilities available, but this problem still persists.

The credit or blame goes to how the solutions were developed and adopted for business. The solutions were developed per business problems or for business areas in general. They were not developed for the overall functionality of a specific organization. There are ERP solutions like SAP, which has industry-wise solutions with focus on a specific industry need and the capability to achieve customization of a higher order. But then this is for operational activities. The enterprise data which are connected through this do nothing but provide a good connection between KPIs that are independent of each other and possibly enable good reporting originating from them. They store and present facts from one repository. They have a replica of operations configured in each so-called module. But still they work in silos until someone goes and enters that door and peeks into the data.

A customer not happy with a delayed delivery or the way it is packaged sends data to distribution and customer relations but does not make the sales guy out in the market approach the same customer about the feedback sent some time back or posted say on Facebook.

A smart marketing solution like Hybris marketing tells how to manage marketing campaigns, but it does not have any view of changing weather conditions or sudden political or social roadblocks which require corresponding changes to the campaign, and once it is done it does not immediately initiate production planning modifications, almost in real time and without manual intervention.

It's like a reflex. Once a type of reflex is noted as a stimulus, the reactions are automatically executed by all related business organs.

The business value is the overall index of value of an organization with everything involving its length and breadth in the business. Due to this silo effect, it could not generate the full value out of it. There is no thread connecting these silos currently. We have high-end solutions working very effectively in the respective areas but they do not rhyme together and maximize the business values.

Business value is counted and maximized on a departmental basis. So, if I see some good product add-on for marketing, I go ahead and implement, increasing efficiency there. But that does not much help other departments like maintenance, procurement, or production. It has an effect on closely connected departments like sales and distribution to a limited extent.

The business of today is responsive to data or information, even up to near real time. But not much is used of this data other than some straightforward meaning coming out of it. So, if someone publishes a bad service comment on Facebook, only the customer relations department will see that hitting their dashboard. It's up to them now to resolve and share details with other departments which would use it if required further. For example, the product design team might have learned from a comment that "vibrations are not pleasant," but the customer relations team was able to help the customer by telling why a minimum level of vibrations is natural and putting the gadget on a rubber mat would have helped. Then, they decide not to share this with the design team, as they think this is normal and an essential property and with limited knowledge in product development they do not really see this as a product problem but a usage problem. Meanwhile, the design team was validating the new version at the same point in time and was looking for more areas to improve. They depend upon feedback which is a little old by the time it is sent to them, because this is additional overhead for the other team and again based on their understanding the bring it forward or not. This is a good example of business being responsive but not effectively using this data for every possible area they should have. This is because the connection is human and not automated.

The cognitive business would handle it differently. The departments are all connected and this is not only to share facts but also looking through them and comparing them from an n:n perspective. So, the two situations are illustrated in Figure 12-1.

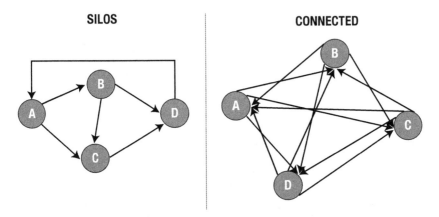

SILOS   **CONNECTED**

Figure 12-1. *Silos addressed in cognitive business*

The mostly unidirectional and open network of business departments in the current noncognitive business is causing a lot of opportunity areas to remain unexplored. However, the cognitive business reaps benefits because of the following.

- Every department gets guidance from every action of directly or indirectly connected departments to take decisions.

Take the previous example of machine vibration. This time, the cognitive system connects with this social media data and then does a sentiment or tone analysis. It would have immediately taken this learning, which is primarily targeted to the customer relation, to take an action. Also, based on the time it took for the issues to be resolved, it would have measured its effectiveness. The research team also would have received a recommendation by the system to see if something could be done about the vibrations, as just now one or more customers were talking about this problem. Also, some were talking about the competing product being smooth. The count of people calling out the product with the vibration is from a certain timeline and with a certain number or figure, while for the competing product the number of customers mentioning the vibration problem is higher but the number mentioning the smooth functionality is lower. This certainly gives weight that for more product acceptance and fighting the competition, the team should consider the design aspects of vibrations more.

This is also evidence based and automated, thus making the n:n entry of information shared between n number of departments.

- Business information and value generated when used to create value for other organizations increases the value perspective exponentially and not just the information share index

For example, the ERPs of today share information with each other as it is. But the cognitive computing here is additionally generating value and sharing this value to create value. See how:

Value 1: The value generated at the first stage was to efficiently help the customer support person by providing not only the negative sentiment but also how this has been handled for other customers safely and giving more edge to customer care to help. The value thus generated is good customer support assistance from this information.

Value 2: This value is then even sent to the HR department to share effectiveness of the representatives to close this issue.

Value 3: The same is immediately enriched with more evidence from a historical and competitive perspective and shared with the research and development team.

Value 4: The same information enriched with possible risk for this more-vibrating product is shared with management, together with evidence from predictions of the target marketing segment and other details like the number of comments per area, and then compared with the production unit involved and even down to the details of possible parts being supplied differently by different parts vendors.

Value 5: Maybe one part was responsible for more vibrations in the product as there is one component related to it and supplied by a different part manufacturing vendor for those areas getting more negative feedback over phone or social media.

This is shown further in Figure 12-2.

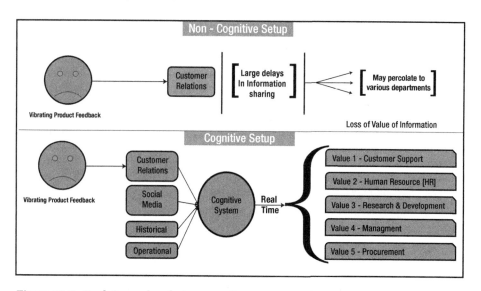

Figure 12-2. *Real-time value chain generation*

The cognitive computing-enabled businesses are thus not only capable of driving themselves from a situation by being responsive, the level which we have already achieved by now. Cognitive enabling can also help in aligning all resources and energies in changing courses of action everywhere to help an organization evolve into a better one with every such issue. The organization behaves as a living organism and learns to evolve to the next level of expertise with experience.

The business departments look connected but only for operational purposes. The decision making is in silos. The cognitive computing makes this just as well connected and evolves using this information and value propagation networked system.

Mixing Areas for Decision

This is in continuation from the previous and yet is slightly different. The departments are working in silos, irrespective of connected databases for common fact repositories, as explained in the last section. The departments, which have good response capabilities, also have channels of information among them mixed only through human gate-keeping. In the previous example of R&D getting data on customer feedback, it depends upon customer service to provide it after validating that it might be useful. There is manual gate-keeping between the two departments.

This point talks about the voluntary mixing of data from various departments (i.e., if someone wants to do a comparative analysis between multiple departments). This hits the human limitations like how much could be thought of at a time by the analyzing person or people and in-depth knowledge from every related department about dynamics, challenges, trends, and so on.

Over time, businesses have various needs to be satisfied to analyze data as a mixture from various departments, but that is limited to fixed analysis requirements. Taking out a completely new set of information which was not thought of earlier is a serendipity (i.e., discovered by accident and mostly not due to real effort). We have data scientists there to do some deep analysis, but it is not always very successful. This is limited by human cognitive computing speed and capabilities as mentioned before here. This does not connect n number of data from n number of organizations as shown in Figure 12-1 (right side) and look through them for a trend analysis, alert automatically in real time, and continue to do so.

A data analysis is possible for analyzing the relationship between slow delivery and delivery dispatch setup, vendor capability analysis, distribution effectiveness from plant to supplier, and such. But the moment an analyst has to do an analysis of a 1:n scenario where n is equal to all the other possible departments and subareas to discover whatever relation could be established, it is not possible, and this ties hands, irrespective of the data analysis capability available. The capability here is a sum of two factors:

- Effective tools to do analysis (writing queries on data or creating programs)

- Human factors like: Smartness, Intelligence and Experience of analyst

Tools with many functionalities together have unlimited capabilities, but the human capability of learning and using the learned knowledge's limited dimension limits them.

So, the following limit the decision or effort toward analysis:

- Possible to visualize limited data relations from n number of sources

- Learning capability to know the meaning of business processes from all business areas

- Limited capability to use all possible means learned or known

- Limited capability of time frame in which capability remains optimally productive; it degenerates in quality over longer continuous times of work

- Limited timeline can be given for analysis

- Experience variance of every individual in handling prior experiences with similar situations

- Physical and emotional environment (internal and external both)

This has been affecting the full potential utilization of business information, which is currently being generated in terabytes. As a result, business was using less than 2% of this information. The reason is the expectation that humans are to do what robots were supposed to, namely, parallel processing to a huge extent.

This task is taken over by the cognitive core digital transformation. We do not need data analysts to do that manually; instead, it's taken care of by the system itself.

Every query to the cognitive system with the ingrained enriched learning established will help run a deep analysis using everything possible present inside and even outside (Internet and IoT). The result is a very robust decision support at every departmental level for the cognitive business.

This is nothing but a business system which is very quickly evolving with the needs of every department over time. The business evolves overall and rapidly with the changes in its environment, and the orchestration required to replicate this among all the organs (departments) is synchronized automatically and in time.

Leadership Effectiveness

Leadership has many definitions. For our use, we define it as a set of people from top to middle to bottom who in a hierarchy take strategic, tactical, and/or operational decisions to effectively run the affairs of a business.

We have already discussed at length the benefit of the cognitive digital core in helping to uniformly run business.

The common problem discussed earlier was that when from top to bottom the strategy trickles down in the form of tactical insights for various departments and then as operational tasks to the bottom, it tends to lose context at times, which is bound to happen. There are controls established along with tools, processes, and audits to control this deviation, but these are also not very effective, and they consume time and effort.

Also, we had discussed earlier that the jigsaw puzzle of performance from bottom to top must be summarized; this is difficult and bound to get unclear and deviated. This might result into an overall picture very much deviated from the original plan.

So, this is kind of like a heat-losing flask. The heat is lost in between. The longer the chain, the more diverse the chain, and the more complex it is, the greater its chances to lose the desired warmth.

This is accepted that way and we have to live with this as uniform central control is not provisioned. It is managed only with the aid of controls and checks. The organization needs constant monitoring multiple times a year and month, or even weeks or days at the operational level, to ensure that goals are being approached as planned.

The cognitive businesses are immune to this and become more immune over time with more and more usage. This makes them a business evolving as planned, with two-way communication between layers turning into a flat communication model. The priorities of plans are available to everyone from the same distance, and results are returned to a single layer and not to multiple layers top to bottom or vice versa.

In Figure 12-3 we can see the difference clearly. On the left, there is an increase of entropy from top to bottom; setting up order from bottom to top is difficult and a lot of value is missed.

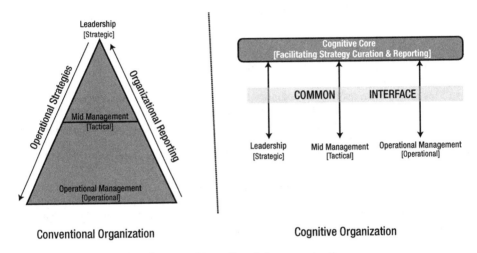

Conventional Organization   Cognitive Organization

Figure 12-3. *Conventional vs. cognitive self-evolving organization*

The hierarchy is flattened in cognitive core–driven organizations. All of them are at the same level interacting with the same core. The core in turn plays different roles relevant to that entity. So, if leadership needs to interact with the middle or operational level, the core interacts that way. Interacting here means getting relevant information. It is no longer directly people oriented; it happens via the cognitive core. There was no chance of leadership having access to data from the operational level in the conventional setup, considering its breadth. This is possible now with the cognitive setup.

This increases leadership effectiveness too. The pyramid of organization hierarchy is only a framework left as pyramid of role for driving the affairs of business. The physical setup and chain of designations disrupted for good.

This means the organization's cognitive core represents it and plays all the roles needed to interact with the other layers. The organization thus needs to evolve in one layer which encompasses all of them, the core. This helps it to evolve without any loss in transition, exponentially increasing its evolutionary effectiveness.

Expansion and Integration Issues

Expanding a business to multiple geographies or integrating with new acquisitions is always difficult, not only because of legal complexities and huge documentations to amalgamate the two companies but also beyond that. The new arm must be integrated with the old one and the two-way information and process alignment must happen. There is a great possibility that the new organization also might bring new knowledge and processes specific to the new business, which now needs to be absorbed by the already overextended big organization.

The new one should understand the old one's business culture, strategy, processes, and operational methods, and this is also valid for the other part as well. This knowledge should flow both ways.

This is the nightmare after the amalgamation has happened. The executives try hard for months to align things one by one. Suppose a company, Alpha, which is a huge IT service and product giant spanning continents, has hundreds of offices across the globe and a huge portfolio. It acquires another small niche software product company, Beta, which is a single-location small workforce.

Now Beta has been brought in because it has that specific cloud and supercomputing ability which would take Alpha toward a stronger position worldwide.

The new niche areas in Beta had been managed with a very different methodology, never used anywhere in Alpha. Also, as Beta is going to be an integral part of the big picture of Alpha, it has a very important role in its balance sheet performance in two years.

This means Alpha and Beta should adapt to each other quickly. The controls at both places should be put in place quickly. A conventional business would struggle on many fronts like process knowledge hand-holding after the initial orientation to Beta personnel by Alpha personnel, and adapting Alpha departments to Beta's new process for managing their product implementation, which is going to be used in many departments in Alpha. This must be done through manual publications, training, workshops, and knowledge repository build-up for both the marrying parties. This is a challenge which goes on for years, as seen in many cases. Communication becomes a major challenge at times after the merger and acquisition, and employees who already feel that the situation is trouble might get completely confused if they are not onboarded smoothly in the new organization. Employee retention thus becomes a big challenge. In our example, it is a merger of a small local player into a global process-driven organization. The difficulties go in both directions: the smaller organization is not used to such a process-driven culture, while the bigger partner will have difficulty adapting a huge number of processes to include the things required to accommodate the smaller one.

So, the overall stability of joint presence, the expected value of the merger, connecting the culture, and amalgamating processes are huge risks and make or break any merger or acquisition. The key is a good planning and good execution of tasks for a quick merger with the least and fastest-healing scarring.

The case of a cognitive self-evolving business is different. Before we talk about that, let us see what key things are to be done or in place.

- Focus on value perspective coming through the merger/acquisition

- Quick training of both sides to know what is required

- Joining the new body metrics to the existing one

- Ability to centrally monitor the new body with all old ones

- Better employee experience leading to less attrition

- Processes to make hybrid wherever required

These are a few things at first glance that would be mandatory after a merger/acquisition.

Failure to achieve these would have financial implications and hence spoil the value of merger. Very seasoned managers and executives are pressed into these activities. But still it has failed badly because it should happen at every level and a lot of issues could come up (e.g., as simple as the ground staff not being able to understand the benefit system after coming into the new system and worrying about their financials and growth prospective). The new home organization, though, has a very liberal and multitrack growth path, much better than their own original organization. But this was not the priority to be discussed in presentations and workshops, as operational initiation takes priority. This leads to dissatisfaction, and everything goes sour.

Now, however, the cognitive core system has quite a few shortcuts. The cognitive system is quickly extended with new knowledge already, keeping in mind the new incoming group. The organization-specific information is fed into it on top of this immediately after merger/acquisition. So, in our case, having seen the highest priority, the system has already enriched itself with core knowledge of cloud and analytics. At the merger, all the departmental data is fed. The operational systems and the HR systems are connected. All knowledge databases about products and features are also fed.

Now the merger happens: the cognitive system must be trained with a host of experts from both companies as well as external experts.

The system is the core thing which needs to be prepared, not individual departments. Meanwhile, orientation starts. And at the right time, the system is ready for use. No training required; a hint of how to use the cognitive system must be given or maybe a small training. Operational data already in the same environment are now within the scope of the core and handled and analyzed together. Any employees with questions could go and ask the cognitive assistants and they can answer 24/7 all that they need to know. The training has taken care of guiding process experts to make a hybrid process for operational systems, while the cognitive system automatically includes the new business details. This all is exactly as mentioned earlier for the PEIB process. The employee experience is not bad, with the help of the cognitive core. Once the onboarding of data and training happens using PEIB, the two organizations' businesses are merged, and joint monitoring and control is established with the helping hands of the cognitive assistant.

This made the evolution of the old company into the hybrid old+new very rapid; it was mostly done by putting efforts into cognitive digital core readiness. The rest is taken care of automatically.

Wastage and Overkill

This is very common in business. With time and increasing complexity, wasteful activities and processes add up. There are even certain departments which face overkill due to answering multiple departments with their own metrics.

This is always the scenario, however mature the organization may be in all aspects. There are some nooks and corners left which still use the unproductive way to do things. This is taken care of very well by the cognitive digital core organizations. The cognitive core not only helps in decisions sitting on top of ERP and all other internal and external sources, it also keeps an eye on the value perspective of processes, based on its internal knowledge of process and standards. It throws alerts and evidence-based facts regarding the same. It can point out the zero-value or low-value processes. For example, a manufacturing organization had one route to bring in raw material from the nearby mines they have been using since day 1. Now this is a tradition, and the drivers know what time they should drop the materials at the production unit and when to go for the next trip. They are following the supply properly and no issues ever come up on that front. Even the management is very careful about the raw supply run staying healthy and keeps rewarding the supervisors and truck coordinators for encouraging good schedule adherence. When the cognitive system came in and the new system was equipped with the GPS location-tracking facility, real-time map facility, and operational knowledge and algorithms for best-optimized network calculations, the system sent a recommendation to the manager to check the status of that. Things are good as always, but not in the optimized way. The truckers have been following a longer path all along, but now there exists a much shorter path. Also, during the rainy season or in case of traffic, the system could recommend a better route. So, this not only upgraded a new process to be more optimized but also increased profits by reducing fuel costs. Similarly, another factory line was suggested to follow a different order of processing to improve efficiency by a good figure. The maintenance department's data was also being used to see the best possible parts, seeing the historical efficiency and life expectancy of such replacements in the past. The machines could avoid the bit-changing stoppage as the cognitively based system was able to identify the material to be drilled, and based on the data received from the metallurgy department was able to decide the drill speed and bit. These are many of the ways the organization evolves by this living nature. It keeps rediscovering the ways needed to make it more and more optimized and lean.

HR Management

This is a very important department. Over time, the importance of HR is transforming from being merely a recruitment and employee management department into a much higher-order department.

With the compact work environment, work optimization, and the need for the right people at the right place, it has much more to do. There is also the need for better employee satisfaction for more optimized performance in the industries of today. The need to upskill and retain the right skills is also very important.

Tools like appraisal comments, complaint, feedback, and so on are not very effective, as they are prone to be tampered with or influenced.

HR needs to look into the employment history, social presence, CV analysis, psychometric analysis, and internal behavioral analysis through tests and mail analysis to put all employees into different clusters of talent as appropriate.

There should be data-driven and intelligent planning. Maximum efficiency in this is only possible through the new cognitive organizations. This is a very important aspect of evolving the work culture, satisfaction, retention, and capability built up in any organization.

What Then Is Self-Evolving Business?

A self-evolving business could be defined as an organization "which is not only sustaining successfully for the daily needs with most optimized lean processes and most controlled sanitized decisions at all levels, but keeps evolving or upgrading or modifying them (processes and decisions) due to 'demands challenging the organization' or 'challenging organization with new recommendations detected and determined by its own cognitive core.'"

Now if you look closely at what we have discussed before, we see more clearly what a self-evolving cognitive business is. The building block at core is the parallel evolving IT-BI system. This was set up using the PEIB framework guidelines and checklists. This now generates this kind of business.

The road blockers and risks are as mentioned in Chapter 11.

Before closing this section, let me quickly break the definition into some quick parts and explain; then we can move to the next section.

1. "...not only sustaining successfully for the daily needs with most optimized lean processes and most controlled sanitized decisions at all levels,

2. but keeps evolving or upgrading or modifying them (processes & decisions) due to 'demands challenging the organization'

3. or 'challenging organization with new recommendations detected and determined by its own cognitive core.'"

So, there are three parts of the definition. Let me quickly put some lines against each part so that the definition is crystal clear and the meaning is reflected without any confusion in understanding.

- "not only sustaining successfully for the daily needs with most optimized lean processes and most controlled sanitized decisions at all levels,

This means - These business organizations follow the most optimized way of executing processes at every level and keep optimizing it with time to take decisions that are most valid at the time of execution. The decision is also sanitized and controlled by evidence-based counter-recommendations if it is found to be hampering something in the long or short term.

- but keeps evolving or upgrading or modifying them (processes & decisions) due to 'demands challenging the organization'

This means - These business organizations don't just have responsive behavior to know immediately what the challenges and factors are, but they also immediately align the processes and decisions according to any external challenge or new route to be taken by the business. For example, a change is immediately made in the delivery route the moment a new bridge is available and open for use. The system determines the benefits and reroutes all shipments through this. The new route plan is recommended to the user with facts, figures, and evidence. On agreement, the route plan change is taken care of.

- or 'challenging organization with new recommendations detected and determined by its own cognitive core.'"

This means - These business organizations are as good at being responsive to factors in the internal environment. For example, when it sees any old plan or process being used and sees an alternative giving better value, it recommends a better solution and evolves the organization.

The self-evolving cognitive business organizations have the capability to quickly align themselves with internal and external needs as and when encountered and very efficiently adapt to those needs by upgrading all processes through recommendations and agreement. So, it evolves naturally and effortlessly itself, taking command of the central cognitive digital core. The people are left to ask questions of it, validating various recommendations based on evidences, and taking valuable decisions, which again could be executed by the digital cognitive core.

The next section describes some reality checks about the cognitive capabilities. The self-evolving cognitive systems are conceptualized around the cognitive capabilities. The cognitive capabilities have many assumptions which are built around them. I discuss some of them in the following.

Reality Check About Cognitive

What is expected from a cognitive capability? What kind of effect it is going to have on industry? What can we expect from this transformation?

Before I get into the details further, let me clarify here that there is no doubt about the benefits which could come out of the same. But again, this is a very new technology with a lot of challenges around it, like not many good cases in industry yet, good knowledge availability, good frameworks available (and so I proposed PEIB in this book), confusion around it, and so on. All of these have been already discussed in Chapter 11.

The cognitive systems have some core technical capabilities.

- It must be expert in core learning subjects, for which it has been trained enough, after being supplied with a mass of contents.

- It must be able to combine data from many sources with knowledge and analyze, predict, and recommend with evidence using a weighted response priority system.

- It should learn further and keep making new associations.

- Should be proficient in natural language processing and synthesizing. Also, it should be highly interactive.

So, it should be

- Expert in learning

- Adaptive and integrating

- Evolving

- Interactive

The core capabilities can make mappings and associations within loaded data just like humans do in association of memory. And then using a probabilistic model, it can look for the highest weightage path to decide the best possible answer or result. This is all done for billions of such records in a few seconds.

The context of input should be broken into nuts and bolts, evaluated with the back-end available knowledge, evaluated based on the training-generated meaning of the knowledge, and then presented based on the weighted response with the highest confidence index. All the evidence and reasoning are presented in the form of the data which was used to derive this confidence level.

There are some concerns and highlights about these solutions in the market. Let us now see some of them further.

Is Cognitive for Everyone?

The answer is both yes and no. Remember the discussion of the PEIB framework? When we were at the initialize phase, we were talking about a check condition to see if it is for the user.

We even said that for very small organizations and small businesses, it might not be usable. The size and complexity are one set of aspects which decide the use case. The readiness of the existing system landscape for the required IT infrastructure also decides it. For smaller organizations, some specific tools might be good, (e.g., chatbots on some applications), but converting all to cognitive might not make any sense. Where there is the possibility that all levels of managers from top to bottom could always sit under one roof and decide things together, it makes no sense to go through the cognitive transformation. But again, implementing it is never bad.

The other aspect is the type of business. The business use case decides if we really need a cognitive capability or not. If say a business needs a lot of permutations and combinations of products or possibilities of service available, and that depends on a lot of variables and inputs, good to go for cognitive. Otherwise slow-moving bigger corporations are good use cases. Always consider the bread and butter business areas (Chapter 10). If the core or bread and butter processes are not such, then it is optional for you.

Cognitive is great if trend analysis, real-time information, and data output make a lot of difference for your business: banking, finance, insurance, logistics, oil and natural gas exploration, and retail business all have these properties, while a firm making screws, however big it might be and whatever the turnover, would not necessarily be a use case.

There is no established cross-industry market trend analysis available, but the winners will be companies who see their core areas benefitting from it and go via frameworks like PEIB and implement it seamlessly.

Cognitive computing has entered in an era in industry when big data and analytics were being adopted with open arms. This was the phase when these technologies had just picked up after a long wait. The companies which have already entered to a bigger extent into this by this time also are good cases for this transformation. They have enough back-end and use case work already done.

As I mentioned earlier, there are legal implications as well. Proper control of the data across the organization should be made possible, segregating or masking data as per applicable data privacy policies.

Organizations should take considerable time to come up with a strategic future plan with a good evaluation for considering it.

Do not consider it just because there are some people already doing it, but at the same time ensure that you are not left behind or missing an opportunity because not so many people have started to adopt. It's time to do a deep evaluation (maybe using the PEIB framework or similar) with a context-free mind to see what the bare evaluation numbers say. If this looks good for the core business, then start with your first steps. Adopting now will have benefits tomorrow.

Is Cognitive Foolproof?

The answer is no. This is a machine with learning capability. It learns how you train, but again the fact is that it cannot be trained for everything. So, it might not know some things with certainty.

The core being probabilistic, it does have a certain level of failure possibility. So, keep in mind that it is not foolproof. It makes life easier but cannot replace the human brain in business. It could give terrific insights and low-weighted responses both depending upon the enrichment and availability of data under the hood.

Cognitive cannot be foolproof, but neither are humans. But the failure rate of cognitive is less than that of humans. Humans also have emotional quotients, which means they can make emotional decisions. This cannot be done by cognitive machines. So, where it is beneficial, it might not be that much with cognitive systems. Emotions do have value in human life, like strong commitments made in a friendship. But for cognitive computing, in which all is practical and weighted analysis, it might seem unresponsive or less effective in emotional realms.

So, the cognitive systems could fail too. But one good thing is that they do not make same mistakes again. This is not a guarantee with us. This makes the cognitive system more and more effective over time.

Are All Vendors/Products Good?

This is a tricky question. Understand some bare facts. Cognitive computing became a commercial fact only a few years back when IBM brought Watson to market. There are many other companies now selling products that are called "cognitive" but really aren't. I mentioned some technical properties at the start of this chapter. If these are not fulfilled, it is not a cognitive system.

Again, I do not claim I have knowledge of every product available on the market. So, what is the best way to decide? The following are some things you should keep in mind.

- The solution should be a real cognitive solution and not just some machine learning miracle. It is not only showing learning and improving responses, it should be thinking and recommending with weighted confidence.

- There should be good industry- or subject-enriched data already being promised and not a blank system with nothing. This will make implementation easier too.

- The system should be able to be stepped up in capability with increased data volume.

- Look for buying options, as the rental system may be risky. The data and enrichment lie outside your organization and there is a risk that tomorrow, when you change vendors for similar service, you must rebuild things, as one vendor's solution might not support another vendor's solution.

- The knowledge enrichment or training is crucial. Look for a vendor with extensive industry experience and support from experts to train the system and help your team.

- Look for solutions which are extendible to many areas of business and not working for only one or two areas of the business, and if you evaluate the same for you.

So, be very careful in selecting the right partner for your success. A choice of good partner makes it much more likely to be a successful project.

Self-Cognitive Capability?

Will I be able to make my own cognitive capability from scratch? Do not reinvent the wheel. I have seen some customers talking about this, but it makes no sense. The cognitive system is a combination of many technologies: it is not only machine learning or predictive analysis. The developers producing this have spent a lot of time and money to do so. If you have an option then to consider all of them and decide on the one for you, why not do so?

However, your own capability should be there to manage this. Unless you do not have plans to develop your own capabilities in this direction, it is not a good idea to depend on vendor capabilities. Keep training and grooming your in-house team to manage and support the implementation.

Is Cognitive Taking Jobs Away?

Again, yes and no. There are jobs which might go but again cognitive will also open avenues for some to shift to a new field.

The overall impact would be more toward the jobs which are already routine activity oriented (e.g., an employee resource manager). These people do nothing but compare resumes based on technology/skillset, location, preferences, seniority, and so on to match with openings within an organization. This job can be done better by cognitive systems. They can additionally do analysis of resumes, check social profiles, correlate all previous assignment data, and so on to try to match applicants with jobs.

It could also take away some repetitive jobs like testing. But in the main, it should not have a huge impact. Cognitive entered immediately after big data and analytics. But the dilemma of this era was that 98-99% of data which was brought in and accumulated in these systems was never used. The analytics was being done on but a few percent of data. So, immediately after this when a given cognitive system is evolved, it has to first make sure the data in ERP and various other systems are using this data first to ensure the big data and analytics investments are streamlined and 98-99% of this data sitting in big Hadoop boxes is being used to make decisions. So, at the moment cognitive is there to assist more and taking away the need for people to do jobs better suited for computers. The people are left to do more decision-based and business activities and freed from data and report preparations.

Summary

In this chapter, I have discussed the self-evolving cognitive business. With all the learning by now on PEIB and roadblocks, we know how to implement a core IT system which is cognitive in nature.

Earlier chapters described in detail the core IT infrastructure and transformation path, road blockers, and risks, while this one described the resultant self-evolving cognitive business.

I gave the definition here as follows: "not only sustaining successfully for the daily needs with most optimized lean processes and most controlled sanitized decisions at all levels, but keeps evolving or upgrading or modifying them (processes and decisions) due to 'demands challenging the organization' or 'challenging organization with new recommendations detected and determined by its own cognitive core.'"

The various highlights for business are described in between. The following list helps explain conventional vs. cognitive self-evolving business:

- Silos

- Mixing Results/Considerations

- Leadership Effectiveness

- P&L Approach

- Expansion and Integration Issue

- Wastage and Overkill

- HR-Only Talent Management

Then, in the last section we did a reality check on cognitive solutions. Here I discussed about the basic technical nature of the cognitive systems.

I tried to answer some questions that are commonly asked about cognitive. We even talked about the impact of cognitive in taking away jobs. But I do not see this as a major challenge currently.

CHAPTER 13

■ ■ ■

Path Ahead

In this concluding chapter, we will discuss the path ahead for organizations, IT service providers, and IT consultants.

■ **Note** Up to this point, we have discussed all the necessities from business intelligence basics up to the transformation roadmap and road blockers for a cognitive digital transformation. In light of all these things, I will now discuss the path ahead for organizations, IT service and product providers, and IT consultants working at the ground level. These are the three parties for this kind of transformation. What they should keep in mind to have a successful transformation strategy is discussed here.

As mentioned, we have been discussing all the necessary knowledge about the cognitive core digital transformation. We discussed the self-evolving cognitive organization in Chapter 12. This chapter offered a comparison between a conventional and a cognitive organization.

We will talk here once again about what organizations should take care of when initiating a path toward cognitive transformation. But we will also discuss the path ahead for IT service providers and IT consultants. The cognitive core transformation needs all three parties to work effectively to achieve optimal results. This chapter will explain what these partners should consider key to moving from where they stand now to becoming a cognitive organization, an IT service/product provider, or an IT consultant.

Path Ahead: Implementing Organizations

This section talks about the path ahead for a conventional organization to start moving toward cognitive core transformation.

The transformation requires all available knowledge of how to go for it, what road blockers and risks to expect, and the expected nature of this kind of organization. We have discussed all of these from Chapter 10 to Chapter 12.

© Rohit Kumar 2017
R. Kumar, *Machine Learning and Cognition in Enterprises*,
https://doi.org/10.1007/978-1-4842-3069-5_13

One important question remains: what is the generic path ahead for an organization to move in this direction? The direction and transformation roadmaps in Chapter 10 are very technical in that they have details for initiating into the transformation. We have discussed PEIB there, a system to let organizations do this using various checklists.

Although a lot of dimensions have already been covered from the organization perspective, still for the sake of a concluding discussion that also includes the other two parties (i.e., IT service providers and IT consultants), I will mention very briefly some important points for organizations implementing it again here.

I will mention these under the following headings, very short and concise.

- Strategic Value

- Transform People and Culture

- Top-Down

- Time Taking

- Customization and Usage

- Right Partner and Solution

- The Three Keys

- Decentralization

- Momentum

- Security

The path ahead is certainly cognitive, but these points are keys to be considered while doing this.

Strategic Value

We have discussed this many times earlier in this book. These transformations are strategic: consider questions like "why," "how," and "what" when thinking, but consider "why" the most.

If "why" is not understood and satisfied, it cannot be a good strategic move. The organization should be completely re-envisioned in terms of the new form it should take in the context of "why."

"Why" tells us about the need of change and limits the need around the reality. The following are some example questions:

- Why do we need a cognitive digital core?

- Why it is applicable to my organization?

- Why does the processes need to be transformed?

- Why will this be good for my customer experience?

- Why will this help me to have a better operational efficiency?

Then comes "what." So, questions like

- What kind of organization I want to transform into?

- What is applicable for us?

- What processes need to be transformed first?

- What transformations would suffice for a better customer experience?

- What will make it a more data-driven organization which offers a better employee experience?

Then at the end comes "how." So, some questions like

- How should I proceed?

- How much money and time resources I should invest?

- How should I go about selecting right solutions?

These are some of the basic thinking precursors given as examples; there will be many.

In Chapter 10, we talked about the bread and butter processes that should be taken first when deciding where to start. In our example there, we took production and maintenance as the first ones to be picked. This is a very important aspect. The PEIB framework should be used to decide this properly. Every single organization might have a different starting bread and butter point, based on the way it does business and its current standing in the market. The starting points and sequence should be decided strategically. Some of the departments could transform in parallel too.

The following are thus the key thoughts for this section:

- Always keep this marked as strategic transformation

- Always decide first why; you would need then answer other questions

- Always have a clear strategy for moving ahead over the timeline

Transform People and Culture

This was mentioned in brief in Chapter 11 as well. We talked about this when we were talking about the road blockers and risks.

The transformation is not a single person's or a bunch of people's initiative. It does not happen in just any form. The transformation needs to be aligned internally as well to make clear grounds for its acceptance, for collaboration, and thus for success.

Proper and timely information, directives, and knowledge sharing are key. The need for and understanding of how to deliver beyond biological cognitive limitations and biases, and so on, is to be inculcated from top to bottom. The understanding for data-driven culture should be established.

Top Down

The cognitive transformation is always bottom up and it promotes a flat decentralized work environment.

But the program must be managed from the top down. The reason is simple: this is a strategic initiative and the vision of strategy is made at the top and can be monitored and coordinated only from the top. Of course, any other project, even the conventional ones, are also managed from the top. But the level of engagement should be different here. In conventional projects, the budget and results are decided and monitored from the top, but activities are managed mostly at the department level. In this case, the management of the ongoing activities should also be monitored and managed to an extent by top management. Only keeping an eye on the results and budget won't help. The direction of development and implemented results should also be clearly analyzed to see if they align to sum up with the overall strategy, as the end product would be an organization-level system.

Time Taking

The end product for a cognitive business transformation is a multispecialized recommendation system, able to have extremely effective recommendations made for each decision and utilizing all information from throughout the organization.

But this does not happen quickly. The cognitive core has to come up brick by brick and will take a long time to be able to start working at its intended level.

This also means there are very good chances of deviation as well. So, instead of waiting for a longer time and putting the risk higher, it is good to have stops decided upon. This is described in the PEIB priority checklist as well.

The priority checklist as mentioned in Chapter 9 will also help by having stops in between to see progress, and also the validation KPIs/functionalities listed earlier would keep the overall transformation on track with clear validation checks.

Customization and Usage

The cognitive core is a highly customized solution. It comes with basic enriched knowledge needed, which is more what is common for that segment or kind of business. But then the transformation involves training it for your specific business, which means customization. The more it gets detailed knowledge specific for the organization and the more it is enriched with answers for your way of business, the better the cognitive core becomes.

The cognitive systems have learning capabilities which result in their thinking capabilities. This happens more and more over time and over usage by every possible user type. So, it has to be extended to as many user types as possible, which means the system is getting trained in all possible aspects more and more. This is why this is also mentioned in Chapter 11, the chapter for road blockers and risks. A limited usage won't help.

Right Partner and Solution

The selection of a right vendor partner and a right solution is key. From the use case and technology perspective, this is a new paradigm. Also, doing it independently by buying a software solution is not the way it should be done. It needs a very deep collaboration with a vendor partner not only to put in place the technical bare bones, UI, and so on, but also to tailor the plan to provide consultations and solutions with its powerful capabilities.

The right vendor should not be someone with the best flyers and demonstrations only. Some of the characteristics to look for in a vendor are as follows:

- Able to provide industry-specific transformation roadmap

- Deep business consulting to transform the organization, as a way of thinking and doing business might need to be re-envisioned; the specialized vendor team should help with that

- Partnering from envisioning stage and not only installing and doing technical stuff

- Able to customize the UI as per need with necessary authorizations

- Better if running on its own hardware solutions rather than engaging a third party for this. This will keep the focus on transformation; hardware capabilities, configuration need, and supply at right times should not distract; platform is a key strategy in cognitive digital transformation

- Flexible enough to give pilot demos to show complex areas

- Able to help develop capabilities to run things internally

The selection of the right vendor is a very necessary thing, as getting all the necessary ingredients including good human resources is difficult. Also, very few industry stories and clear use cases are available. The more experienced the vendor, the better.

As for the solution, it should be of the right type to fulfill the needs of the organization. The properties of a good product are discussed further in this chapter in the "Product Quality" section.

Three Keys

There are three focus areas for every organization which should drive the cognitive business transformation. It could start from any selected bread and butter sequence as decided in the strategy.

The three main areas of focus are as follows:

- Customer Experience: At the end of the day, business is done to provide products or services to as many people as possible. Also, the reached audience (i.e., the existing customer) should not be lost to competition, and sales per customer should be sustained and wherever possible increased (e.g., cross-selling).

This means a good customer experience. The utility energy companies of now do not look only for how to expand into new areas for more customers. They have smart metering and cognitive solutions to utilize multiple power sources for supplying them. They have such solutions to pass on price benefits to customers on a daily basis by counting in factors like what combination of source and fuel type to use on a particular day (e.g., microgrid of solar, wind, or hydroelectric). They have mobile app solutions to let consumers view their power bills almost in real time. They know a large number of customers would like to use services from an energy provider which not only maintains a constant supply but also helps them to save money.

Another example could be a solution for Internet sources like social media to keep an eye on customer sentiments and feedback.

So, customer experience should be the foremost focus always.

- Process Optimization: As I have mentioned earlier also in this book, "It's time to look inside for changes and optimization rather than just looking out for better possibilities or opportunities."

Cognitive business is about this. So, process optimization should be a focus when making choices for a cognitive business transformation. Keeping an eye on change needed while re-envisioning the organization is necessary. A good vendor partner is also very helpful here to think in the right direction with its experience. There might be a solidified thought process about how to run a process, but the expert from the vendor's specialized team could also help in dropping something like that and doing it in a different way.

Naturally, the processes are optimized in a cognitively transformed organization, but it has to be planned also for additional benefits.

- Employee Experience: A very important benefit of cognitive business is the possibility to increase the level of employee collaboration and effectiveness. The system should be used as much for its own benefit as well. So, the employee experience should also be enhanced using the cognitive capabilities. This does not reduce the number of people needed, but makes all of them more usefully focus on execution rather than preparing for that.

This takes out the preparatory activities and directly engages them in what they are hired for. The data pointer is taken care of by cognitive solutions.

Decentralization

The cognitive business makes knowledge and interactions decentralized. This protects against dilution and confusion. There is a single core which interacts with all and which has knowledge of all. We have discussed this earlier in this book.

But the organization should ready itself for such a change; there should be an awareness and acceptance of the same.

This in simple terms makes organizations more and more effective by overriding the pyramid for trickling down vision and strategy and also summing up results from bottom to top for monitoring the resultant overall strategy execution.

Momentum

The cognitive transformation keeps improving with time. The momentum of enrichment should go on. Since the operational systems are different from this setup and are used for better decision making mostly, there is very much a chance for people to overlook this.

Knowledge should also continue to be added to the new area as it comes into the purview of the business of that organization. So, if the organization was making diesel and gasoline cars and now they plan to start making hybrid cars in the future, the cognitive core should start to be trained in that direction as well.

Another example could be as follows: say an organization was working in America only and wanted to shift a manufacturing base to India as well; all necessary stuff like regulatory, geographical, financials, and so on should start to be entered into the cognitive core.

So, by good usage, good knowledge content addition, and good training, the momentum of the transformation should be sustained.

Overall from an organizational perspective, there should be a good strategy to initiate and run the transformation and keep the evolutionary momentum going.

The path ahead especially for big enterprises is cognitively driven business as a whole, and not just for certain business areas.

Cognitive is the game changer in industry 4.0.

Security

The cognitive era will see far different security risks, both internal and external. The systems would thus need a high-grade cognitive-enabled security. The security should be a thinking and watching one, looking into global alerts and patterns of activities to help create a secure environment.

There is a very great possibility of a security risk initiated through a cognitive system made for such a purpose. The cyber presence throughout the world, including government agencies, makes cybersecurity a very important aspect of security more generally. It could also be used to derail economies; indeed, there is a very good chance that any country could also get into a destructive mode to do so at a large and organized scale. To fight this, preparedness toward high-grade cognitive-based security should also be planned. This could be created parallel and would thus know better about the bricks and pieces of the system, rules, usage, and authorizations.

Path Ahead: IT Service and Product Companies

I have observed that many good players in the market are not in a good position for getting into cognitive engagements.

Not all could jump into product development toward cognitive solutions. There are other good opportunities like being a partner in selling a product or a specialist in implementing a certain product. Even some solution development in niche areas which could be provided as SaaS or IaaS could be an option; for instance, targeting a segment of customers who are at lower revenue levels and need some small cognitive value add. There are lot of startups in this area; for example, Flatiron Health providing oncology solutions like OncoAnalytics, Narrative Science providing a business narrative solution called Quill, and Enlitic providing healthcare diagnostic services.

There are several players already in the market. The cognitive computing market is predicted by Grand View Research Inc. to be about $50 billion (http://www.prnewswire.com/news-releases/cognitive-computing-market-size-to-reach-usd-4936-billion-by-2025-grand-view-research-inc-609468895.html).

So, there is and will be much for every IT service and product provider to serve for their customers or prospective customers.

Some promising companies in this area are

- **IBM**: IBM Watson is a cognitive system that provides a huge range of capabilities in various domains to partner between human and machine for a better collaboration and more effective decision making.

- **Google DeepMind**: This cognitive solution is applied in two areas. First, it is helping Google optimize its own process. It has helped Google to reduce its data center cooling expenses by 40% (as published by Google on its DeepMind website). Second, DeepMind Health is helping the UK's National Health Service to provide citizens with the best medical service by assisting medical staff in times of emergency and making critical recommendations.

- **Cisco Cognitive Threat Analytics**: Detects and responds to threats in computer environments and networks by using cognitive capabilities.

- **Microsoft Cognitive Services**: Has various APIs to provide cognitive abilities (i.e., vision, speech, language, knowledge, and search).

- **Intel Saffron**: A cognitive solution for executives to detect and control risks, workforce issues, skill gaps, and any duplication issues in any project.

- **CogniMem Technologies, Inc.**: Offers many cognitive-related solutions like CogniMem cognitive computing chips for pattern recognition, intelligence for sensing, and intelligence for data mining.

- **Clinakos**: Has cloud-based solutions as SaaS in the healthcare domain.

- **Coseer**: Has many industry and business area–based cognitive solutions.

- **Resilient Cognitive Solutions**: Has many cognitive decision support systems for military, transportation, healthcare, energy, financial, emergency response, and so on.

- **Hewlett Packard Enterprise**: Has data analytics to convert data into visionary directives at the enterprise level.

I have listed further some key points to be considered by IT service and product companies to engage in better strategies to move toward cognitive transformation.

Strategy Build

There are various opportunities in the cognitive domain for IT companies. The first and most obvious is in the direction of product development. But as I mentioned earlier also, not every company can just jump on the bandwagon to make a new product. A small SaaS-type product serving a specific area may be possible, but a full-fledged product would take a lot of invested effort and time.

It is always advisable to look into the product domain, but there are other opportunities as well, like the following:

- **Partnership in selling products**: Sell existing products to previous and new customers

- **Deployment partner**: Become deployment partners for multiple products

- **Business domain consulting partners**: Provide business domain and process consulting and even to help enrich loaded knowledge content

- **Knowledge resource aggregator partner**: Help provide knowledge content for various cognitive applications as standard bundles

- **Product development partner**: Become a development partner in developing or further enhancing any existing product

- **App development partner**: Become a development partner for theme app development for various use cases for an existing cognitive platform

These areas are also very promising for IT companies to pitch into the cognitive transformation business.

This could be enabled only via a good, realistic strategy. Just the fact that everyone is doing a certain thing should not be the scale of comparison. The capability should be aligned with the enterprise's own capabilities, both financial and technical.

The long-term goal should be getting into developing a robust practice around this. But starting with these options is not bad. This helps in starting with just a little investment and risk as compared to going big in developing a full-fledged product.

A good strategy should be in place to create a central center of excellence (COE) around the cognitive practice. This should cut horizontally across all the industry- and technology-based practices to have access to all customer projects. Apart from developing competency around this area, it should also promote a think tank group to get engaged in research on every existing customer project to see the relevant case fit for proposing the planned area of cognitive engagement. It should also allow the development of proof of concept (POC) and other knowledge content around this.

In the case of product development, an R&D organization already exists, but one could also be created foreseeing the future strategy of product development, maybe to start at a lesser scale.

This strategy will help to minimize risk and help to start a venture into this domain with the majority of existing capabilities. This would give good confidence to move ahead. It is easier to get into the business and learn by getting your hands dirty then it is to stand at bay and assume. This is the safest way to proceed.

So, first and foremost, a strategy is needed in the right direction with short- and long-term goals. This will require assessment both of the existing inventory of capabilities/resources that could be used right away and of which new resources will be needed.

Product Quality

In a case where a product is being presented to the customers, there are certain attributes which should be considered very important from a customer point of view:

- **Industry/Process Oriented**: A customer would be more willing to invest in a product which would show some kind of prebuilt capability in a particular industry or process, although the prebuilt capability does not actually drive the product 100%. The custom capability for the specific customer will drive it, which accounts for a good training of the system. But preconfigured basic content means that the time and effort to bring the system to action would be less and there would be an extremely high degree of enriched data already in the system for the specific industry/process (e.g., industry, oil and natural gas, financial accounting).

  So, it is always good to have products oriented this way rather than providing open-ended software to be established in a certain industry/process. The latter would entail higher risk as well on top of the effort and cost.

- **Modular**: The customer would like to have several combinations of industry and process abilities pre-enriched to be used as building blocks for their organization. In that case, a modular approach will always be appreciated. This would allow the customer to decide more flexibly and economically what they actually need and not what they have to somehow buy. The bill of materials should reflect exactly what is needed. The software should also be developed in a way that it supports modularization and integration as needed.

- **Scenarios**: There should be POCs or test scenarios already built up in the system to demonstrate its capabilities to the customer. Seeing is believing: the moment the capabilities are transparently visible to the customer, the acceptability goes up. Also, preplanning the demonstrations helps in making good presentations to the prospective customers in this area easily, instead of getting one done only when needed. The upper hand in this case is that the cognitive systems already come with pre-enriched data and that makes demonstrations possible.

- **Consulting and Roadmap**: If the individual modules come with good roadmap directive documentation and are aligned with necessary consulting abilities, they are accepted more. This gives a distinct capability of quantifiable points for expectations and project plans. For IT companies, it also becomes easier then to provide the solution with properly marked resources and plans.

- **Hardware**: A hardware platform bundled with the solution is always a benefit. There are reasons for that. The concept of having a solution programmed close to a certain hardware configuration makes it more efficient. This is very important in cognitive solutions, as data and computation needs are huge. Also, the solution comes preloaded with enriched data; if the hardware is separate, it might be necessary to load the enriched data onto the new hardware, costing time and money and increasing the risk factors of mistakes, hardware supply delays, and configuration issues. It is always good to provide it as one package or in the cloud.

- **User Interface and Apps**: A good possibility of easy development of user interfaces as needed and of apps which could use the platform is considered an added advantage and functionality by customers. This goes beyond the customization capabilities and even enables the users to create new apps when needed using the same platform. Also, the user interface should be extremely user friendly.

- **Integration**: The cognitive core should be able to connect with all possible data sources existing in the customer's landscape and so should have integration capability for connecting with all, using all possible protocols. It should be able to bring in any kind of structured or unstructured data for maximum usability and benefits.

- **Security**: Good security features and secrecy management should be robust for better acceptance.

- **Processor**: The cognitive chips work as human neurons. They have extremely high computational capabilities with extremely low power consumption needs. Cognitive systems running using such processor chips would be always preferable to ones working on John von Neumann architecture, which is the architecture for conventional chips. This could be a big differentiator.

These are a few very important aspects of product quality which would be a winning edge for the cognitive solutions/products.

Incubation and Inculcation

The next stage after putting the strategy and product in place is a short incubation period to align all first-level capabilities (knowledge resources, rules of the game, organization structure definitions, existing human resource engagement, hiring, sales content development, orientations, etc.).

Then starts the inculcation phase. Organizations implementing this should consider it to be strategic; the same counts for the IT companies as well. Knowledge about cognitive computing, the targeted engagement, and so on should be started to be inculcated among the workforce. The engagement here also runs from top to bottom. The stronger the inculcation and abilities are at the top, the more chances of better and stronger results. The awareness at the top is extremely important, and this should not just be on a superficial level but go layers down into the bare bones of the solution. A thorough and good training and orientation should be run.

There should be various levels of training and certification to engage the new thought process and awareness further down at every level.

This should be also planned together with organization-level leadership messages and hackathons to further screen the organization for potential talent and ideas.

Now at this stage the organization is ready for the first engagement, with all required resources on board. Sales and marketing teams also might need to be refreshed on this expected engagement.

Market Outreach

This is now the stage for market outreach, which should have two distinct go-to market areas.

- Existing customers

- New customers

Various forums and outreach modes could be utilized now.

Market outreach to existing customers is very important. Longstanding customers, and those with the relevant (planned engagements) kinds of business, should be targeted first. This should be a win-win. More focus should go toward generating some numbers in this area as customer base and experience gain than should go toward generating revenue. The deep understanding of their business and the long-term relationship should be utilized to pinpoint suggested solutions, with good POCs and demonstrations if possible. This approach should help them also get into the comfort zone of this being done by a provider with a deep understanding and experience of their systems and business. Cognitive systems are highly customized solutions; this gives a plus point of having a vendor partner who already knows a lot. The IT company also gains expertise and customer numbers in this new area.

For the new customer, the outreach should be carefully chosen. It should not feel as if it is a pitch for a product or service. It should be placed as a strategic alliance for transformation. We already know the level of engagement required and expected from vendor partners, and from the very start IT companies should rely more on relevant use case demonstrations and transformation consulting capability with domain expertise here. There should be a plan properly packaged for that specific customer and with a sequence of engagement to capture low-hanging fruit first for the customer and with a clear picture of the transformation roadmap with benefits and risks clearly defined. No two customers could be considered alike, so the same "red, green, or yellow" presentation for an industry would not work completely. The base capabilities could be the same, but that does not drive the cognitive solution for a customer; what drives it is the customization benefits for them. The solution should be aligned with the customer's goals. So, it will be good to do thorough homework about these before proposing a solution.

Good case studies of already completed implementations/transformations should be showcased for capability confidence in the market.

It is very important to have people with the right knowledge and capability to be put on the customer forefront. The needed people are those who not only can speak this language efficiently to gain the customer's confidence, but also have equally good understanding of their own product's capabilities and offerings.

Center of Excellence (COE)

This is a very important internal organization. This should work not only in aligning all types of resources toward enabling the engagement. This should also be doing some specialized creations like

- Use case libraries

- Cookbooks

- Effort estimation tools

- Frameworks for transformation (like PEIB)

- Lessons learned

- Training contents

- Awareness contents

I have discussed COE to some extent already in the "Strategy Build" section.

Project Management COE

In IT companies, this organization takes care of developing guidelines, trainings, and certifications for project managers.

This should also run special courses to enable the project managers to better handle specific projects and customers.

The in-depth technical, functional, product, services, pricing, and risks should be explained in depth in such trainings.

Any new lesson learned in this direction should also be brought in here. Also, the forum should engage and encourage the members to have an open discussion to discuss any road blockers and issues with a wider audience. This will improve management capability sharing.

Cognitive engagement being relatively new, there might be some level of hesitation and confusion among the project managers. There should be subject matter experts (SME) and leadership connections organized at various times to increase effectiveness.

Success stories should be shared in detail to increase capability.

Collaboration

A good level of collaboration between the industry towers and COE should be there, keeping the COE at the center. This will help the easy maturation of the organization in this area.

A single node connecting all would not only get details from all but could also easily help all of them with knowledge trickling from multiple towers.

Skill Development and Maturity

This is also a key value area. Skill development should have a great deal of dedication and focus. With an array of skills from technical to functional, a right combination should be planned using the appropriate skill development programs.

The maturity of the skills should be reverted back to the company by again creating and storing contents by these consultants.

Cognitive solutions are 70-80% good consulting and knowledge creation. So, a good number of people with relevant sets of knowledge should be developed.

These are the key factors or points that should be considered by IT companies for a go-to-market strategy for pocketing more and more cognitive transformation business. The good thing is, from big bang product IT companies to small cognitive startups, there is not much industry exposure in the real sense. There are limited areas of expertise or limited full-fledged expertise. So, all of them have a good chance in the market. Besides, the current market figures are very small and the major part of this is still to come.

These points should be kept in mind by the IT companies as they look at the path ahead.

Let us talk about the path ahead for IT consultants now.

Path Ahead: IT Consultants

There is lot of chaos and worry in the market when we look toward cognitive computing as a job-eater and a technology that's very complex to get into. So, many predictions are flying around the market about potential job losses due to digital transformation and automation.

Whether it will eat jobs or not is debatable. Ginni from IBM says it will create new opportunities as it brings in new cognitive technology area and data-related jobs and additionally some new jobs which never existed. On the other hand, some industry experts have been providing various figures about the potential risks to the simpler and more repetitive jobs. They also mention that there is substantial risk about the jobs done as repetitive tasks by human resources, and 24/7 support also engages a lot of people. Replacing these to a large extent with cognitive solutions would at least imply a lesser workforce. Also, the bots would take away jobs involving a lot of telecalling and also office assistants. The robots and other cognitive solutions are more robust and cheaper as compared to the human workforce. In America, there is a prediction of 6% job loss due to robots by 2021 (https://www.theguardian.com/technology/2016/sep/13/artificial-intelligence-robots-threat-jobs-forrester-report).

Forrester says in more detail that the robots will create 9% more new jobs and kill 16% by 2025, and so the net loss of jobs would be 7% (https://www.forrester.com/Robo ts+AI+Will+Replace+7+Of+US+Jobs+By+2025/-/E-PRE9246).

My take on this is different. Take an example from history. There have always been replacements with the advent of technology. Machines replaced people to do muscular jobs during the early days of the industrial revolution and further until now. But then we needed people to run those machines. Similarly, we can say that the corresponding workers in the current situation might be replaced by cognitive computing in production, since they will be not required. I agree to some extent that we will need fewer people, but machines cannot replace people 100%, no matter how smart they are. The cognitive computing machines could think "almost" like humans with much "higher" correlating associative details from billions of pages of knowledge and data in a fraction of a second. But they still cannot think like humans. Cognitive computing is here to help people what they do best. They are there to support people and not replace people.

Yes, some jobs may go, due to redundant or low-level activities or both. But then, a greater number of jobs will be created in new areas to support and run these cognitive systems.

There are certain low-level jobs in IT where not much goes on in terms of consulting or complex programming (e.g., system monitor or data loading monitor); these might need fewer people due to automation. But again, due to the new dimension of jobs, these losses might be compensated (e.g., an ERP consultant could easily reskill to learn cognitive skills). These people are good in one or more domains of knowledge, along with technology consulting, and they could be good material to be transformed into cognitive resources. Another example could be security consultants; they should be easier to transform into personnel using cognitive monitoring. But jobs like a tester running a repetitive test program to check the product coding might not be needed once we have enough confidence in the capability of cognitive to replace them. Even a programmer might not be required for regular programming tasks as cognitive computing should be able to replace him.

Moreover, a lot of cognitive computing capabilities are still in their infancy and counting them into job loss exaggerates the numbers (e.g., the popular fear of automated self-driving cars eating up driver jobs). It's not clear how many more years it will take to get a stable version on a production scale. Again, legal norms and practices will be set up to enable widespread use. It does not look like it will be knocking down employment numbers in the near future, and by the time it will start to pick up previously human-required tasks, there will be additionally new kinds of jobs already in place to support the loss in driver jobs, and so on. So yes, future jobs will be more specialized and that too means that future workers will be expected to be at different levels of expertise. The lowest level currently might vanish and a new lower level will be defined, which will be higher than the current low.

So, let us wait and watch exactly what happens once this era settles down and goes to full swing. Meanwhile, one fact is there about the new skills. The new skills have to be considered by newcomers to the IT industry and the ones already in the field. I will further discuss the path ahead suggested to both of these types.

Existing Workforce

This comprises the people already inside and not yet into the cognitive side. There are many groups and options which could be mentioned here. These people have a benefit of being the first level to see the technology in its infancy and have the opportunity to become first batch of experts now. Most organizations have already started to transform the workforce by training them in relevant areas. I have divided the current workforce into two major regrooming groups as follows:

- Reskilled

  - Coding/Scripting

  - Product [Technical] + Industry

  - Industry + Product [Functional]

  - Management

  - Content Management

  - Security Consultants

  - Administration

  - Change Path

I will discuss each of these groups one by one. These groups are based on the type of regrooming that could be done to create a cognitive workforce. There are subgroups based on the current kind of jobs.

Reskilled

This group of people consists of people who are trained or reskilled by their employers, as is frequently happening now. Many big and small IT companies are doing this.

The various subcategories defined are based on the combination of the existing pool of people and related job areas in the cognitive computing area.

- Coding/Scripting: This is the bare code- and script-writing job to create or update a cognitive product. The relevant current job is programming. The various programmers, even if they're from different language backgrounds, could get into this area. As frequently mentioned, programming is a concept; the specific language is something which comes after. A set of grammar and syntax makes a language. So, it becomes comparatively easier for people who have a programming background to get into this area.

- Product [Technical] + Industry: This is technical knowledge of product configuration and installation. A person in this subcategory uses the various technical functionalities and cognitive computing concepts to become an expert in a product with or without industry domain experience. This is good for people with major technical backgrounds and functional knowledge as additional skills. Their current orientation and experience make them good candidates for this kind of capability. Industry-specific training could be targeted toward their experienced industries or domain knowledge, if any, or by choice.

- Industry + Product [Functional]: This is primarily for people with domain expertise. A core domain- or industry-based training in one or more industries and know-how of product and cognitive computing are in scope. They are the people helping consulting to map departments and processes into the cognitive system.

- Management: This is the project and program management crowd. They're trained with specific needs, process, frameworks (like PEIB), and risks related to cognitive transformation. These specialized managers manage it better.

- Content Management: The knowledge and content management experts in IT companies could look into this area. This area is also good for others in clerical jobs.

- Security Consultants: Security consultants can venture out into cognitive security, data privacy management of content, and authorization and access management.

- Administration: This area is for database administrators.

Change Path

This is a completely reskilled resource. The resource either at his own expense or organization plan gets completely reskilled by some focus program in-house or outside.

The benefit of the reskilled and change path resources is that they are experienced. This experience, in spite of being in other areas, is still valuable, as experience had already made them seasoned corporate consultants and that makes them more useful.

New Workforce

The new workforce can be trained in more concrete ways than the existing workforce. This is an entirely new workforce, and training is easier in a way because of the absence of prior learning. The existing workforce faces the biggest challenge of unlearning.

This workforce is also of two types.

- Pretrained Campus Hire
- Non-pretrained Campus Hire

Pretrained Campus Hire

This is the workforce coming out of learning institutes or colleges and trained via academic courses relevant for cognitive computing, like artificial intelligence, machine learning, pattern analysis, natural language processing, data mining, robotics, statistics, behavioral sciences, and so on.

They could be of high quality coming with some good full-fledged degree program, with or without industry expertise. Some universities even have collaborative programs on cognitive computing and products together with industry knowledge. Cognitive transformation is 70-80% business domain and process enrichment and training, so it makes sense for this to have a business flavor.

There might be some hires coming from low-level centers trained or certified into some smaller areas of work.

But this is a good way to selectively pick up the cream from the market, which would be immediately productive. But being new, they still have to be instructed in corporate work discipline and ways.

Non-pretrained Campus Hire

This workforce is fresh too. But its members haven't been directly trained in cognitive courses or the like. This is a set of bright students picked up from colleges and trained as per need in the organizations.

The path ahead for IT consultants, both existing and to be, is to get into the cognitive learning areas as soon as possible. This not only would make them ready for new kinds of needs but also give a sense of confidence for being with the times.

This is just the start; it would be easier for the existing employees to enter as well. But this opportunity should not be missed, as these people are fortunate to be in the workforce now.

Thanks and Goodbye!

This concludes this book. We have by now discussed the following.

- Basics of business intelligence

- Basics of AI, ML, and NLP

- Basics of predictive analytics

- Details about cognitive computing concepts

- Transformation roadmap using the new framework PEIB

- Road blockers and risks in achieving this

- Path ahead for organizations implementing, IT companies, and IT consultants

This now brings the discussions to an end. I hope this book will help my readers to have a deep understanding about the cognitive transformation and how to achieve that. This should now enable them through the PEIB framework introduced in this book to think in a more systematic way about how to adopt the cognitive transformation with quantifiable metrics to avoid any deviations.

Thanks for going through the thoughts expressed in this book!

Index

© Rohit Kumar 2017
R. Kumar, *Machine Learning and Cognition in Enterprises*,
https://doi.org/10.1007/978-1-4842-3069-5

U

V

W, X, Y, Z

Get the eBook for only $5!

Why limit yourself?

With most of our titles available in both PDF and ePUB format, you can access your content wherever and however you wish—on your PC, phone, tablet, or reader.

Since you've purchased this print book, we are happy to offer you the eBook for just $5.

To learn more, go to http://www.apress.com/companion or contact support@apress.com.

Apress®

Printed in the United States
By Bookmasters